Critical Essays on
Language Use and Psychology

Daniel C. O'Connell

Critical Essays on
Language Use and Psychology

Foreword by
Ragnar Rommetveit

Springer-Verlag
New York Berlin Heidelberg
London Paris Tokyo

Daniel C. O'Connell
Department of Psychology
Loyola University of Chicago
Chicago, Illinois 60626, USA
and
Department of Psychology
Georgetown University
Washington, D.C. 20057, USA

Library of Congress Cataloging-in-Publication Data
O'Connell, Daniel C.
   Critical essays on language use and psychology.
   Bibliography: p.
   Includes indexes.
   1. Psycholinguistics.   2. Psycholinguistics —
Philosophy.   I. Title.
BF455.026   1988   401'.9   88-2039

Camera-ready text prepared by the author using WordPerfect™ 4.1.
Printed and bound by Edwards Brothers, Inc., Ann Arbor, Michigan.
Printed in the United States of America.

9 8 7 6 5 4 3 2 1

ISBN 0-387-96703-6 Springer-Verlag New York Berlin Heidelberg
ISBN 3-540-96703-6 Springer-Verlag Berlin Heidelberg New York

*This book is dedicated
with gratitude to my family.*

Foreword

Ragnar Rommetveit

University of Oslo

Let me start this introduction to Professor O'Connell's
Critical essays on language use and psychology with some
reflections on psychologists and crabs. It so happens that the
first professor of psychology in Norway had the middle name
Krabbe ("Crab"). His full name was Harald Krabbe Schjelderup.
Hence, the crab became our symbol for the psychologist. For many
years a "crab feast" was held every autumn in Oslo in order to
celebrate the material union of crabs and psychologists and
ponder (symbolically and metaphorically) their shared fate.

A comparison between the predicament of the crab and that of
the modern psychologist may indeed be illuminating, once we make
certain assumptions about their unique epistemic missions and
systematically explore the severe constraints on their heroic
search for knowledge. The crab is ordained to unravel the
mysteries of the ocean, yet doomed to crawl sidewise on the
bottom. His catch, alas, is most of the time mollusks and
cadavers of sea creatures, and he cannot help envying the fish
swimming freely above him.

The psychologist's mission is to unravel the mysteries of
the human soul. His obligation to seek insight into essential
and socially significant human problems is rooted in thousands of
years of humanistic, philosophical and religious thought, whereas
his notions of what constitutes proper scientific knowledge
appear to be strongly influenced by admiration and unreflective
imitation of his successful big brother, the (simplified and

idealized) natural scientist. The modern, theoretically pretentious and methodological conscientious psychologist's actual attempts at assessing the depths of mind and the essentials of the human condition make him for that reason appear a slightly tragi-comical figure in the eyes of the poet and the sage: He is eagerly watching the rat in the maze and measuring human intelligence, yet most of the time catching merely meticulously quantified trivialities.

Current academic psychology may be described as a ramification into a wide range of conceptually and methodologically separated sub-disciplines of something that a hundred years ago constituted a global, multi-faceted and vaguely defined topic for significant philosophical discourse. The field's identity has to be defined in terms of existing training programs and obligations to institutionalized professional psychological services rather than any underlying theoretical-methodological unity. The significance of psychological knowledge is to a considerable extent assessed in terms of its instrumental relevance to societies in pursuit of economical and technological progress. As Professor O'Connell puts it: "Modern psychology has been defended as a way of understanding and improving the human condition. Somehow the second part of this purpose has come loose from the first part in recent years" (p.242).

Lack of theoretical unity is reflected in competition among alternative paradigms for psychological research, i.e., in lack of consensus with respect to the constraints inherent in human self-understanding and the nature of psychology as a science.

Knowledge of a truly cumulative nature is scarce. Imitation of natural science paradigms and adoption of computer terminology, however, are reflected in deceptively deterministic accounts of human behavior. And popularized versions of such accounts make for a peculiar kind of human self-understanding that, in caricature, resembles an enlightened state of paralysis: The psychologically well-informed layman feels relieved from assuming responsibility and offering reasons for her or his conduct because the latter presumably can be "explained" as a necessary consequence of antecedent conditions <u>without any reference to her or his subjective agency</u>.

Popularization of mainstream psychology, it may be argued, thus tends to encourage human fatalism rather than self-control, freedom and dignity. This is in Professor O'Connell's opinion a consequence of philosophical agnostic innocence, unreflective imitation of natural scientific modes of explanation, and programmatic evasion of issues having to do with man's subjectivity, prerequisites for intersubjectivity, and embeddedness in culture. He is addressing us as fellow human beings, as <u>co-responsible for knowing</u>, and inviting us to seriously reconsider the constraints and possibilities inherent in psychology as an intellectually honest and respectable academic discipline. His book is "not written by a scientist, but by a human being" (p.222).

Professor O'Connell's brilliant polemic against current fads and fashions within psycholinguistics and mainstream cognitive psychology is thus not at all based on intellectual arrogance, but on profound insight into the rich traditions of thought out of which modern man's wondering about himself and the universe has emerged and on a sense of humility and awe toward the riddles of the human condition we hardly ever encounter in hectic and competitive academic debate. What remains true under conditions of complete silence, when there is nobody around to be impressed by what you say and no pressure upon you to play the game of the clever academician, may indeed bear little resemblance to the fashionable "truths" of modern psychology. Only the former kind of truths, however, can under optimal conditions be transformed into human wisdom.

In his excursions into the riddles of the human condition, Shakespeare, the fish, was free to exploit the whole range of semantic potentials of everyday language. By dissecting written language into nonsense syllables, Ebbinghaus, the crab, made psychology acceptable to scholars suffering from a phobia of human subjectivity. In order to develop a truly scientific psychology, it has been argued, we must cut all ties of dependency upon an understanding of our subjectively and immanently meaningful world _from within_ -- other than our reliance upon the mysterious and presumably infallible intuition of the native speaker-listener. "Postmodern man" is, in addition, a victim of the _divide et impera_ of explosive scientific progress: The post-information-explosion academic scene is replete with information in terms of unrelated fragments of scientific-technological expertise.

To engage in psychological research in order to seek human wisdom is accordingly considered by a majority of psychologists today to be a symptom of extreme naivete and/or megalomania. It is indeed a futile venture -- once we endorse the (often unreflectively taken for granted) philosophy of science and epistemological assumptions of mainstream cognitive psychology. But Professor O'Connell contests that philosophy of science and those presuppositions. He knows the game of the clever academician from the inside and has seen through it without becoming a cynic. He feels sad when students seeking wisdom are offered stones instead of bread and happy when encountering psycholinguistic research born out of naive human wonderment rather than academic opportunism. His thorough familiarity with the archival literature within the psychology of language and his own impressive empirical contributions to the field make him, in addition, an outstanding critic of the fragile empirical foundation of mainstream psycholinguistic models of language use. Like the small boy in H. C. Andersen's tale, Professor O'Connell has had the courage to claim that the emperor is actually naked in situations in which the academic establishment has nearly unanimously praised his fictitious clothes.

Engaging in empirical psychological research in a state of sincere and naive human wondering and with the ultimate goal of attaining human wisdom requires humility, patience, tolerance of ambiguity, and even talents to cope with existential dilemmas. This is perhaps particularly cogently revealed in studies of ordinary language use: We are, as participants in language, a "form of life" in some significant sense imprisoned within human meaning, and yet, as researchers, capable of reflecting upon and investigating our very embeddedness. To acknowledge such

constraints and possibilities by no means relieves Professor
O'Connell of the obligation to engage in stringent, rational
argumentation and carefully planned empirical research in his
persistent search for alternatives to mainstream paradigms. But
it allows him to speak to us from his heart about matters of
profound significance to us as scholars and morally responsible
human beings.

Preface

Frau Pliquett ushered me into a small office on the top floor of the Psychological Institute, all the while explaining with obvious pride that this was previously Professor Wolfgang Köhler's office. Apparently he had used it during his occasional visits to West Berlin while he was a member of the board of trustees of the Free University of Berlin. Professor Hans Hörmann had cherished Köhler's friendship and valued his counsel during the sixties until his death in 1967.

And now, a year later, I was beginning a Humboldt Fellowship in the same office, as the guest (<u>Gastprofessor</u>, as the sign on the door read) of Hans Hörmann.

The details may seem too personal, surely irrelevant to the preface of a book. But it was there that these pages find their origin. It would surely sound more elegant to say that I went to Berlin with a definite research program in mind. Actually, I had hoped to translate Hörmann's (1967) <u>Psychologie der Sprache</u> during my stay, but the contract had already been negotiated with someone else. To make matters worse, an old Jesuit brother at Neue Kantstraße #1 had told the deliveryman (with the books I had sent to myself) that there was no Pater O'Connell at that address. For eight long weeks, I was left with the one book I had hand carried, a newly published <u>Psycholinguistics: Experiments in spontaneous speech</u> by Frieda Goldman-Eisler (1968).

Over the weeks, I became increasingly taken with the notion of time as an analytic key to the study of language performance. Until that time, I had been involved mostly with verbal operant conditioning, verbal learning of nonsense strings, and some

visual perception. During doctoral studies at the University of
Illinois (Champaign-Urbana), I had engaged psycholinguistics
under the tutelage of Professor Charles E. Osgood, but somehow an
avenue of research had evaded me. An additional two years of
exposure to the Harvard Center for Cognitive Studies with all its
heady enthusiasm had also failed to penetrate the darkness.
Quite bluntly stated, my intuitions found both the neobehavioristic and the transformational bases of psycholinguistics
thoroughly unacceptable. In those days, I genuinely feared that
the latter was simply beyond my ken, even if it did seem to
violate my common sense. Today I have become less modest in my
disagreements.

     While the neobehaviorists were playing with nonsense
strings, CVC trigrams, and individual words, and the transformationalists were preoccupied with isolated sentences and demonstrational materials, Goldman-Eisler was at least engaging spoken
discourse and the actual communicative use of language. And back
came the simple questions about higher processes with which I had
eagerly begun graduate studies.

     It has always appeared intuitively clear to me that language
use must reflect, more than any other observable behavior, human
higher processes. Goldman-Eisler provided the clue to a methodology: the temporal organization of spoken discourse. And so I
became, during the course of the 1968-69 academic year, a
measurer of ontime and offtime; of pause duration, phrase length,
speech rate, articulation rate, hesitation; in short, of all the
temporal aspects of speech I could isolate.

     Twenty years later, the questions remain. But I think I

have learned enough to know that the experts do not know as much as they say they know; to be confirmed in my lack of reverential awe for theories of speech production that rely on speculations about abstract, trumped up, demo experiments; and to invest genuine reverential awe in a transcendence of the human spirit that defies neat packaging or any of the delimitation that the package metaphor implies.

I am also a debtor. If there is any wisdom in this book at all, it is from my mother, Letitia Rutherford (nee) McGinnis. My father died when I was only four years of age, and my mother bravely carried on to raise five children, in what I can only describe as a paradoxical mixture of poverty and joy. Any love of life and of encounter is from my siblings. My teachers and students alike have taught me well, despite my stubborn resistance and my plodding mind. And, be it said loudly, the Society of Jesus, of which I have been a member for more than forty years, has nurtured my intellectual life with great generosity and care. The research itself has been a team project from the very beginning up to the present, and the colleague who has shared the most has been Dr. Sabine Kowal, who, along with Professor Hans Hörmann, co-authored the very first article and is still co-authoring research papers with me (see O'Connell, Kowal, & Hörmann, 1969; Kowal & O'Connell, 1987b).

Finally, the book is deliberately agonistic. By the time I had received my doctorate (1963), I had already published three articles critical of three former presidents of the American Psychological Association: Gordon Allport (O'Connell, 1958), O. Hobart Mowrer (O'Connell, 1961), and Charles E. Osgood (O'Con-

nell, 1962). I have found American psychology extraordinarily
uncritical, ahistorical, unphilosophical, and frankly, out of
contact with its primary subject matter, the human condition.
And so, my voice is not intended to sound moderate, but radical.

My more specific preoccupation is with so-called psycholinguistics, a field I consider to have been a disaster from its
modern beginnings in America in the mid twentieth century. The
disaster resides not in every researcher and certainly not in
every research project, but in the assumptions, methods, and
despotic dogmatism of mainstream psycholinguistics. The obvious
culprit lurking in the background is the modern transformational
(and post-transformational) linguistics. Nonetheless, I have
neither the expertise nor the wish to launch a critique of modern
linguistics. What the book does address -- loud and clear, I
hope -- is the de facto incompetence of modern linguistics to
engage psychology.

The American Psychological Association (1985) has gone on
record for the opposite position. Noam Chomsky shared the APA
1984 Award for Distinguished Contributions to Psychology with
John H. Flavell and Floyd Ratliff. Chomsky's citation read as
follows:

> "For enlarging our definition of scientific psychology. His
> critical and creative genius inspired linguists with a new
> conception of grammar and of linguistic theory. Not only
> has he demonstrated that an understanding of grammar must
> be central to any serious understanding of the human mind,
> but, by both method and example, he has shown psychologists
> how such understanding can be achieved and developed." (p.

286).

This is exactly what he and they have utterly failed to do: An understanding of grammar most certainly need not be central to any serious understanding of the human mind! Or, as Hörmann (1981) has put it, generative linguistics "has nothing (or practically nothing) to tell us about the actual processes of meaning and understanding" (p. viii).

But psycholinguistics has gradually oozed into cognitive psychology and is now rather firmly ensconced there. And this too is folly, but for different reasons, one of which is that cognitive psychology (despite lots of triumphalistic hype) has no idea who she or he might be.

Whatever legitimate and heuristic psychology of language use is to emerge will be ineluctably social and dynamic, simply because language use is always communicative and purposeful. And the purpose is not at all addressed by terminology such as transfer of information. Quite the contrary, "The speaker acts so as to modify the momentary consciousness and hence also the current behavior, experiences, thoughts, etc. of the hearer" (Hörmann, 1981, p. 305).

The book, then, is intended as heresy against mainstream psychology and psycholinguistics. I have been a critic all my life; now some other folks will have an opportunity for some fun -- but not unless they read the book.

Most of the research to be cited in the following pages as evidence has been carried out by my students and/or myself. The book is not intended as a review of the literature, either in general psycholinguistics or in the temporal organization of speech. An incisive and critical review of the latter has been completed recently by Sabine Kowal (1987) in connection with her <u>Habilitation</u> research on the public speaking of politicians.

The Alexander von Humboldt Foundation has generously supported the beginnings of this work in 1968-69, has offered occasional support in the meantime, and now once again has given me the opportunity to write the following book through a 1987 fellowship, this time at the Technical University of Berlin with Sabine Kowal.

The Aquinata Hospitals, Mater Dolorosa Parish, Monika Stift, and Pfarrer Michael Schlede have over many years sheltered the shelterless during my visits to West Berlin. Thanks to Michael Lugtenburg's and David Kramer's help, word processing has gone smoothly.

Daniel C. O'Connell, S.J.

West Berlin

May 1, 1987

Contents

Part One

Introduction

In this single chapter, I wish to explicate my _modus procedendi_. What I wish to do -- criticize, establish the need for tearing down the tenement and relocating -- does need justification, lest it appear to be no more than picky and mean spirited. It probably will appear to many to be so anyway, despite my _apologia pro vita mea_. That will sadden me, but so be it.

Note that my apology is only a plea for my academic and scientific stance, not for my personal life. In the latter regard, I am like all of us, a foolish little child who stands in wonderment before the awesome, mysterious universe. I am content with that simplicity before the Lord of the universe.

Chapter 1

The Making of a Cynic

I like to think of Roger Ebert and Gene Siskel, the American film critics, whose television program, <u>Siskel & Ebert & the Movies</u>, has been such a delight. Whenever the little dog makes his cameo appearance, someone is in trouble; they are reviewing a <u>dog</u>.

Cynics are dogs by etymology and connotation. People do not have much taste for the captious critic or for the prophet of doom. The latter I am not, nor do I fit the definition of cynic as someone who knows the cost of everything and the value of nothing. Many would, however, think of me as the captious critic and would grant me a half-star rating were I a film.

The habit of argumentation and criticism is learned. In my own case, my widowed mother was the first teacher. Each evening at supper, the family would be led into a discussion of current or perennial issues. Pros and cons were thrown into the arena, sides were taken, arguments were presented. No one ever seemed to be the winner or the loser, and above all no one got hurt. It was our family entertainment.

Then at the ripe old age of 13, I was sent off to the Jesuits at St. Louis University High School, where I promptly joined the freshman debating team. My freshman partner and I are still arguing more than 45 years later. We did not win a lot of debates, but we enjoyed them tremendously.

Take an already argumentative, idealistic young man, mix well with several years of ascetical reflection and a commitment to the life of a religious order, add seven years of philosophical and theological studies (not to speak of a couple of years of highschool teaching) before sending him off to graduate and postdoctoral studies, and you have an excellent recipe for a critical approach to just about any academic discipline.

There were several well intentioned efforts to change the course of my critical development while I was at the University of Illinois. They all reflect an implicit, pragmatic philosophy of science or at least convictions about a lifestyle compatible with the pursuit of science. Let me relate them here anecdotally.

The first can be characterized as "murder will out." Throughout my career, whatever critical studies I have undertaken sprang from an initial intuitive reaction: "I don't buy that; I don't believe that's what happened; something's wrong with the experiment." When Don Dulany and I (Dulany & O'Connell, 1963; O'Connell, 1965) first became interested in finding out what was really going on in Verplanck's (1962) "Unaware of where's awareness: Some verbal operants -- notates, monents and notants," I mentioned to Professor William Kappauf what we had in mind. His reaction was essentially that such counter projects aren't worth the trouble; that intelligent scientists would all recognize Verplanck's errors; that other research projects must therefore be given priority.

In the event, Verplanck disrupted Dulany's convention presentation by misquoting me, chided Dulany in private for allowing "a Jesuit to collect data for him," and effectively brought it about that our research was thoroughly passed over in subsequent discussions and in the archival literature until almost 20 years later when Ericsson and Simon (1980, 1984) bluntly stated regarding the Verplanck research:

> Dulany and O'Connell (1963) showed these results derived from two artifacts. . . . Hence, the experiments provide no evidence whatsoever that the rules verbalized were inconsistent with the behaviors. (1984, p. 138)

The moral of the story is, I think, quite clear. Yes, murder will out, but not without a helping hand. Simply to trust in the inevitability that human intelligence will be in the ascendancy is thoroughly unwarranted. Systematic errors in the archival literature, on which further conclusions will inevitably be based, cannot be allowed to go unchallenged.

What usually happens in lieu of critical confrontation is not the gradual surfacing of empirical truth at all, but instead the eventual burial of the issue altogether. In fact, this is one of the dynamics responsible for the gradual fading away of many once burning issues in psychology. In modern American psychology, issues become popular fads. When we lose interest in the fad, it fades away. This is the antithesis of confrontation and is the source of much confusion and consternation in our discipline, particularly for idealistic young people who demand that important questions be engaged, if not for the jaded oldtimers.

The second intervention on my behalf was on the part of Don Dulany himself -- the "don't ruin your career" principle. I had given a manuscript to Dulany with the request that he advise me about trying to have it published. His concern was quite gratifying, but his advice was essentially: Don't try to get it published unless you want to ruin your career! The critique of Osgood's semantic differential as a measurement of meaning was finally published in an Italian journal of the philosophy of science (Methodos; O'Connell, 1962), a safe hiding place from the vast majority of American psychologists, who are in any event disdainful of non-American (and in particular non-English-language) psychological publications.

The purpose of this second anecdote is certainly not to criticize a friend. I was truly grateful for Dulany's concern. My own career, however, has been and is atypical; there are many young psychologists who could not do what I did, who are con-strained to toe the line. In many cases, the pressure is relatively innocuous; we are all constrained, for example, to compose manuscripts to please editors. But in some cases, it constitutes an intolerable tyranny. It would be a tragic error not to acknowledge that scholarly communication is sometimes favored or hindered by much less appropriate factors than scholarly quality (e.g., charm, nepotism, seduction, politics, reciprocal back scratching). In other words, it is quite realistic to expect situations in which honesty and the integrity of one's scholarship will demand that one take the risk of being professionally damaged.

The third intervention was on the part of Professor Morton Weir. It was his first year on the faculty at the University of Illinois. After a colloquium at which I had energetically argued some basic epistemology, he commented to me: "What does it matter? You just get everyone angry at you." It was, again, a friendly intervention and hardly enuntiated as a philosophical principle. Nonetheless, it did and does reflect an American pragmatism that is quite impatient with any and all discussion of the philosophical underpinnings of modern psychology. If my diagnosis is correct, it is one of the persisting causes of poor communication with non-American psychologists. Moreover, it reflects a nagging pathology in American psychology that prevents us from engaging comprehensive and underlying questions because of our operationalistic and neobehavioristic heritage. Or as William Verplanck insisted in our unhappy confrontation: "Data always speak for themselves." No, they don't!

My three anecdotes can perhaps be summarized as three underlying principles of American psychology: (1) Don't bludgeon the obvious; (2) Protect your career; (3) Don't challenge the status quo. All three cover over very dangerous tendencies in the intellectual life.

(1) The obvious means in the concrete: what is clear to me. It does not take many hours of teaching for the beginning teacher

6

to become aware that it is indeed a most pernicious assumption. The good teacher must turn each lesson in many different directions; must exemplify, metaphorize, rhetoricize, and above all, repeat: <u>Repetitio est mater scientiae</u>. It is a tragic paradox that American psychologists seem incapable of recognizing some things that truly <u>are</u> obvious -- such as human freedom and dignity.

The presidential address of George Miller (1965) at the APA convention is an excellent example of the need for repetition of the obvious. Miller asked me to read a draft of the speech, certainly not because of any expertise I had, but because I was on the scene. I read it and liked what I read, but told him he had to say the whole thing several more times in different ways because otherwise no one would understand what he wanted to communicate. Go back and read the address, and you will find that he did exactly what I had suggested. For many reasons, all of them having to do with our own biases, assumptions, functional fixedness, enmeshment in various systems and societies, the <u>obvious</u> needs to be exploded before it can be metamorphosed into understanding.

(2) The <u>career</u> has become the real finality of American psychology. In terms of priorities, value systems, choices, and decisions, the career has become the be all and end all for many leading scholars and for many too who will never become leaders in their field. The career is what has to be protected above all. For this reason, I have come to admire most of all those

scholars who have mastered in their oral and written pedagogy that awe inspiring phrase: "I'm sorry, I don't know!" I have personally experienced this wisdom in Gordon Allport, Roger Brown, Jerome Bruner, George Miller, and many others, and have also found it seriously lacking in many.

A little story about Jerome Bruner can serve to exemplify the phenomenon. One day in the midst of one of his Harvard seminars, someone confronted him with the fact that what he was talking about as if it were a great new breakthrough had been in the archival literature for years. Bruner flashed a broad smile and said simply: "Well, why hasn't someone told me?" He is one of those who know that protectionism is no less dangerous in scholarship than it is in world trade.

If the solution were not equally as dangerous as the protectionism itself, I would prescribe the probe technique suggested to students by Charles Osgood to find out what a theorist "really thinks about his theory": Wait until he has had several Manhattans; then ask. Unfortunately, the theorist who can combine sobriety with light heartedness about his or her own theory is a rare commodity. Protectionistic carefulness for one's own theory or for one's career is not a matter of prudence, but of foolish selfishness.

(3) What is so nice about the status quo? I am convinced that egotism and cosy complacency are not the only sources of support for keeping things as they are. The triumphalistic hype and obvious social pride that distort and undermine the very

8

purpose of virtually all our introductory textbooks in psychology
spring from a thorough misunderstanding of the purposes and
processes of science.

Scientific generalizations and theories are best thought of
as stepping stones that are to be left behind in our enthusiastic
running toward intellectual freedom. The very purpose of
theories in science is to provide an intellectual springboard to
be left behind as we move on. Hence, an acute awareness of how
little we know is much healthier than a sense of the importance
of what we already know. The reality is that we know precious
little about the human condition. The status quo is only an ugly
frog that can be transformed into a prince.

And so, I have learned from sad experience to be cynical.
But the anecdotes alone cannot adequately state my grounds for
cynicism. Let me try to further express some of these grounds.

Over the years, I have become convinced that most of the
articles published in our professional journals are not read by
the vast majority of psychologists, even within their own
narrowly defined fields of competence. The most compelling
evidence comes from the few who should <u>best</u> understand the
archival literature -- those who cite it in scholarly research
themselves or hand it on to others in textbooks. The prevalence
of misquoting, misunderstanding, misinterpreting, and accepting
from secondary sources instead of taking the time to study the
primary sources carefully is simply too great to support any
other hypothesis. Many examples of this sort of aberration will

be provided in subsequent chapters.

All of the above could still be the product of my own personal peevishness. A case needs to be made that modern American psychology -- and for better or worse, American psychology still maintains its world hegemony -- is in trouble. Decadent is actually the word I would like to use -- rotten to the core. Strong words, indeed, and irresponsible if due to peevishness alone.

Let me begin with the following summary of the state of psychology:

> It is a sign of the immature state in which psychology finds itself that one can scarcely utter a single sentence about mental phenomena which would not be disputed by many.
>
> (Brentano, 1874/1960, p. 42)

Perhaps things have not changed a great deal, but immaturity in 1874 is still not the same as decadence in the late twentieth century. We have had a long time in between to regress or advance.

Obviously, the thesis of decadence cannot be proven. I can only ask the reader to consider the situation in view of some reflections. One past president of the APA, Jerome S. Bruner, has recently claimed that "psychology is more splintered, less unified, more beset by contradictions than it was when I started" (cited in O'Connell, 1984a, p. 20). The retiring president of the Deutsche Gesellschaft für Psychologie, Franz E. Weinert (1987), has characterized the situation as follows:

10

Anyone who has investigated the state of our discipline over a long period of time will be satisfied just about as often as disturbed or even enraged. (p. 2; my trans.)

In the same report, he included news reports about the 1959 convention of the organization: "What's presented is stuff we already knew or dumb kid stuff" (p. 2; my trans.).

I will mention only one introductory textbook (Hilgard, Atkinson, & Atkinson, 1979); however, its many years of popularity and its many editions make it a legitimate representative choice. Even after seven editions, a triumphalism that is nothing more than pious wishful thinking is proclaimed: "As society has become more complex, psychology has assumed an increasingly important role in solving human problems" (p. 3). The following comments on motivation are simply ahistorical nonsense:

> The term "motivation" was not used until the beginning of the twentieth century. If people are viewed as rational beings whose intellects are free to choose goals and decide on courses of action, then a concept of motivation is unnecessary; reason determines what a person does. This conception of the human being, called rationalism, was the predominant view of philosophers and theologians for hundreds of years. A person was free to choose, and choices were good or bad, depending on one's intelligence and education. It was assumed that the good choice, if known, would automatically be selected. Within this viewpoint, a

11

person is very much responsible for his or her own behavior. (p. 281 f.)

There are so many things inaccurate in the passage, it is difficult to know where to begin. Motivation is most certainly not a twentieth century concept. And putting the philosophers and theologians together in one great rationalistic pot, where free choice equals automatic selection based on intelligence and education, is not only philosophically naive, it is thoroughly inaccurate historically. However, the assumption that the concepts of free choice and of motivation are mutually exclusive is the authors' basic error. Howard and Conway (1986) could well have had the preconceptions of the above passage in mind when they wrote recently: "Certain preconceptions regarding the proper form of scientific explanations have made empirical demonstrations of volitional influences on human behavior improbable" (p. 1241).

The APA (1986, p. 1) itself has contributed to the introductory morass with a ludicrously naive definition of psychology, presumably simplified for the sake of highschool students: "Psychology is the science and profession concerned with the behavior of humans and animals." Chapter and verse straight from John B. Watson!

If, as Rychlak (1978) has claimed, "most psychologists today are embarrassingly unschooled in the fine points of theory," it is because, in their perduring operationalism, neobehaviorism, and pragmatism, they are genuinely convinced that theory has no

12

relevance for psychology. Even this might be excusable if our practical professionalism actually lived up to its claims. But this too is quite questionable. If, as Berman and Norton (1985) claim, "trained and untrained therapists achieve comparable levels of improvement" (p. 405), then one must at least wonder whether the claims of the profession are legitimate. Seymour Sarason (1981) has been one of the most outspoken critics of psychology in recent years. He has characterized modern psychology as ahistorical, asocial, undervaluing of understanding and overvaluing of measurement, and unable to grasp how behavior in standardized situations is related to behavior in naturally occurring situations. His conclusion is no less radical than my own: "Customary and traditional psychology has to be transcended and replaced" (p. 183). Kilpatrick (1983, 1985) has painted an even more pessimistic picture of modern psychology as seductive and destructive.

At the very least, then, there is reason to step back from modern psychology and ask a few questions. In that vein, I would like to close this first chapter with a passage from Robert Coles (1986). It reflects his own crisis with science during his medical school years. In his consternation, he sought out Reinhold Niebuhr:

> During his lectures Niebuhr constantly asked us to step
> back from the influential assertions of this century --
> to shun the secular certainties so many of us find appeal-
> ing. He gave us, instead, a wry and detached look at our

history -- while all the time refusing to let such a point of view turn into sour cynicism, or an excuse for social and political inaction. Above all he stressed our sinful side -- the pride, the egoism that constantly attends us -- while at the same time reminding us that such self-centeredness ought not be granted sway over us, as in that philosophical surrender that goes under the name of skepticism or a wary resignation in the face of this life's negatives. (p. 18)

Yes, <u>Wissenschaft</u> has always built its own egoism, and the science of psychology is no exception. The <u>Wissenschaftler</u> is in turn the only one who can dismantle his or her own egoism. To do so one must somehow step back from the science of psychology a few steps and even shun a few "secular certainties".

Part Two

Basic Approaches

There are two approaches to a psychology of language use
that have been tried and found wanting and a third approach that
is perfectly feasible. The trouble is that the first two have--
through historical circumstance, error, and club politics--
become the acceptable mainstream settings for a psychology of
language use, particularly in the United States.

The two culprits are psycholinguistics and cognitive
psychology. The third approach is still a nameless waif,
associated with the names of a number of largely isolated
scholars, including K. Bühler, Derwing, Hörmann, Linell, and
Rommetveit. I wish to associate this approach particularly with
the Organon theory of Bühler.

Essentially, the Organon approach emphasizes language as a
social tool and rejects both the autonomous status of language
(psycholinguistics) and the informational approach (cognitive
psychology) to language, and emphasizes instead the use of
language as a social, communicative, purposeful, conscious,
creative tool.

The three chapters in this section consider in turn psycholinguistics (Chapter 2), cognitive psychology (Chapter 3), and
Bühler's Organon theory (Chapter 4).

Chapter 2

Psycholinguistics: A troubled Marriage

We tend often to forget the prenuptial background of a troubled marriage. Such is certainly the case in the present instance. The ahistorical and aphilosophical orientation of American psychology makes for rather myopic landscapes.

Not only was research concerned with language use quite notable in the early years of modern psychology, it was well integrated with general psychology. Cattell, James, the Sterns, Stumpf, and Wundt were all part of this picture, as Blumenthal (1970) chronicled in his historical overview. A separate psychology of language use, however, was not necessary. It would have introduced useless conceptual impedimenta and would have led to harmful isolationism.

But there were many others too whose names -- to our loss-- have long since been forgotten; e.g. (just to sample some of the earlier years), Wallin (1901), Snell (1918), and McCarthy (1954). The research of these prepsycholinguistic scholars does not fit neatly under the "association metaphor" that George Miller (1974) claimed to have characterized the period of language related research up to 1950. Nor would the research of Karl Bühler (1934) fit that description. Although he is finally beginning to be recognized once again for his profound insights into the psychology of language use, Bühler was very much forgotten along with the many others for more than a half century.

Nor does this early tradition of research on the psychology of language use fit neatly under the psychology of learning as Miller (1974) would have it. What did happen, however, roughly between 1920 and 1950 was that behaviorism held sway in America. The net effect on research concerned with language use was a pervasive sterility. O. Hobart Mowrer's (1954) presidential address to the APA is a stereotypic sample of such research at a high level of neobehavioristic sophistication. The neobehaviorists were finally beginning at mid century to try to cope with the extraordinary complexity of language use. Skinner's (1957) Verbal behavior, which was so thoroughly attacked in Chomsky's (1959) book review, is another classic example of the neobehavioristic approach to language use.

Then, all too quickly, the revolution (or the whirlwind courtship, to return to our metaphor) came. Rubenstein and Aborn (1960) reported that the first use of the word psycholinguistics occurred in the late forties. By 1954, the Indiana University conference was over and Psycholinguistics (Osgood & Sebeok, 1954; 1965) had become a reality. The marriage vows, such as they were, had been exchanged.

But what were these marriage vows? What were the mutual expectations from the new union? From the two elements of the word, it should be sufficiently clear that some sort of inter- or cross-disciplinary venture involving psychology and linguistics was intended. It should be noted, however, that in 1954 generative, transformational, or Chomskyan linguistics did not even

17

exist. The general tenor of the book edited by Osgood and Sebeok emphasized mediational neobehaviorism and information theory, and was otherwise fairly eclectic. From the side of the psychologists, the hope was certainly that the linguist would bring to research on the psychology of language use a new sophistication regarding language itself.

But let's turn things about for a moment and ask what the linguist could have hoped to gain from this marriage. Sophistication of some sort? About what? If not about human use of language (behavior, performance, awareness, understanding), then about what? The incontestable facts of the case are that the psychologists did want to _learn_ about language; what the linguists wanted to do and proceeded to do was to _teach_ the psychologists about language -- and, in fact, about language use. Not only is this a chauvinistic disruption of our marriage metaphor, it constituted from the very beginning an unhealthy relationship between the two components of the new interdisciplinary domain.

All the road signs were set up for a one-way street. Linguists had nothing to gain but power; psychologists had nothing to give. They had made themselves dependent on the monthly paycheck from linguistics in the form of the hypotheses available only from linguistic theories. This was the basic error. To put it bluntly, it is irrational for any discipline to limit itself to hypotheses based on theories from another discipline. The reason is very simple: It is impossible for the receiving discipline to challenge a theory based on empirical evidence and methods other than its own. Hence, the development of a genuinely interdisciplinary science with a definite object of study and a clear scientific finality was out of the question from the very beginning.

I am well aware that my thesis is radical: Psycholinguistics was an irrational enterprise from its inception! But if we proceed with that thesis in mind, many otherwise inscrutable or seemingly contradictory developments will fall into place.

In the two years (1963-64 & 1965-66) that I was a National Science Foundation postdoctoral fellow at the Harvard Center for Cognitive Studies, the scenario to be expected (given the above thesis) played itself out week after week at the Thursday brown bag lunch/colloquium sessions.

The generic generative or transformational hypothesis, as developed by George Miller and his students in dependence on Chomsky's (1957) Syntactic structures, went something like this: The generative structures of language are paralleled by psychological processes. Or, as Hans Hörmann expressed it:

> At a certain period of its development psycholinguistics
> considered it to be its task to prove, by means of research
> into performance (only this can be examined by empirical
> research), the "psychological reality" of processes and
> concepts which had been postulated by linguistic competence
> theory. (1986, p. 63)

Notice that the theory was outside the competence (apologies for the pun) of the psychologists; it was accepted ex aliunde.

19

The response to a typical demonstration of such parallelism was quintessentially chauvinistic, in keeping with our marriage metaphor, on the part of the linguists in attendance -- "So what?" Why does a woman stay with a chauvinistic man? One might imagine that some light would have dawned on the psychologists who were the victims of such chauvinism. Of course, performance did not touch, much less confirm, a competence theory; it was logically impossible.

To my own knowledge, there was only one person who immediately backed away from the entire Harvard-M.I.T. concept of psycholinguistics and accordingly made no effort even to have his Harvard doctoral dissertation on some of the performance hypotheses published: Lee McMahon (1963). Several years later, he indicated to me that he thought further efforts to pursue the generic hypothesis were silly. It was only much later that archival evidence of the silliness began to appear. To this day, McMahon stands as an anomalous figure in the history of modern psycholinguistics.

Still more light can be thrown on the long-drawn-out controversies of the sixties regarding competence and performance. What Hörmann (1986) has referred to as "the errorless ideal speaker/listener" (p. 63) was called competence by Chomsky (1965):

> Linguistic theory is concerned primarily with an ideal
> speaker/listener, in a completely homogeneous speech
> community, who knows his language perfectly and is unaffect-

ed by such grammatically irrelevant conditions as memory limitations, distractions, shifts of attention and interest, and errors (random or characteristic) in applying his knowledge of the language in actual performance. (p. 3)

There is no bridge possible between such a competence and performance. But for many years now, psycholinguists have been intent on making Chomsky's never-never land apply somehow to real language use. Clark and Clark (1977) are the ones who have most clearly expressed the concept of the ideal delivery:

For there to be a speech "error" there must be a "correct" way of executing a sentence, and this will be called the ideal delivery. When people know what they want to say and say it fluently, they are giving an ideal delivery. Actors saying their lines, except when making deliberate errors, come close to the ideal delivery, and so do practiced readers and orators. For theories of speech production the ideal delivery is of central importance. They all assume that people strive for the ideal delivery, and every deviation points to something that has gone wrong in planning or execution. (p. 261)

There are a number of things to be noted in this description. There is but one correct way of delivering any sentence. Furthermore, this performance model is dictated by the formal characteristics of the given sentence, its linguistic structure, not by any communicative, social, contextual, or circumstantial factors. Finally, although the linguistic community has very carefully eschewed the stance of prescription or anything even suggesting or having the appearance of being normative, this ideal delivery is openly prescriptive. In actuality, the concept has nothing to do with language <u>use</u> and is not at all necessary, nor of central importance, for a theory of speech production. On the contrary, the concept has seriously interfered with and prevented the legitimate development of such theories. <u>There is no one best way to speak any sentence</u>. Rommetveit (1979) has put his finger on the basic problem very succinctly:

> How can linguistic competence be defined without any reference to communication settings: And if no such specification is included, how can psychologists ever hope to be able to relate such a competence to performance? (p. 30)

The thesis of psycholinguistic irrationality is also appropriate in view of the history of the concept of generation. In this instance, the poor teachers in American schools where the fad of transformational grammar was experimentally introduced were the victims. Students and teachers alike came away with their understanding of the English language thoroughly messed up. Of course, generation is a purely logical and mathematical concept that has nothing to do with human language use, but the confusion and harm were already accomplished at the hands of teachers who had not the slightest idea what generation was all about, much less transformation. A citation from Hörmann (1986) indicates why Chomsky cannot have his cake and eat it:

> His concept of generating was not meant psychologically; he

22

does not maintain that his model describes the temporal relationships of the conception or the understanding of a sentence. The clearer this becomes for the psychologists, the more the importance of Chomsky's model for psycholinguistics is weakened -- a process which has of course taken years. (p. 69)

The concept of deep structure provides a similar test case for the thesis of psycholinguistic irrationality. The need for a deep structure analysis can be established only if sentences are considered _in vacuo_ or _in abstracto_. Rommetveit (1979) has rejected the need for such a concept of deep structure outright:

> By accepting such an _ad hoc_ deep structure as a tentative description of what the sentence in some more profound sense _is_, we are actually endorsing _a false picture theory of language use_. (p. 26)

Rommetveit was convinced, moreover, that the acceptance of the concept of deep structure on the part of both George Miller and David McNeill was due:

> to _their definition of surface structure as devoid of semantics_, and _what is achieved_ is nothing more than _a retrieval of semantics in terms of awkward notions from categorial grammar_. (p. 28)

An anecdote from the mid sixties may throw some light on the vast distances that existed between psychological and linguistic orientations at that time. I recall a conversation with Tom Bever (on a stairwell between the eleventh and twelfth floors of

Harvard's William James Hall) in 1966. I was insisting that sentences are simply not disambiguated the way transformationalists say they are. Bever simply could not fathom what on earth I was talking about; of course they are. I thought immediately of that conversation when, 20 years later, I read Per Linell's (1982) monograph on The written language bias in linguistics. It was only then that my own intuition was clarified. Sentences are ambiguated by being isolated into written form. Linell listed a number of the familiar "ambiguous" sentences, e.g.: Flying planes can be dangerous; He has plans to leave; What disturbed John was being disregarded by everyone; The police were ordered to stop drinking after midnight. Then the following commentary was added:

> The orthodox generative literature maintains that these
> sentences have several readings, and these readings with
> their distinct meanings are disambiguated in speech. Note
> the written language perspective underlying this reasoning;
> the linguistic objects, i.e. the sentences are treated as
> being ambiguous as such, but distinct readings may be
> signalled in speech. But if speech is primary. . . it would
> seem natural to talk about ambiguation in writing, rather
> than disambiguation in speech. (p. 73)

The claim that linguistics is an autonomous science is also part of the early history of psycholinguistics. But the claim is complicated by Chomsky's (1968, p. 84) argument that linguistics is a subdiscipline of cognitive psychology. Again, Chomsky

24

cannot have his cake and eat it; there are intrinsic contradictions between an autonomous version of linguistics on the one hand and dependence on cognitive psychology on the other. Linell (1982) has argued that Chomsky's "actual theories and methodological recommendations" (footnote, p. 38) are completely opposed to such a marriage of linguistics and cognitive psychology:

> The intense and rather devastating critique that has appeared in the 1970's demonstrates the failure of Chomskyan autonomous linguistics as regards its claim for psychological validity (e.g., Derwing, 1973; Linell, 1979a; Botha, 1979). (footnote, p. 38)

As I have already mentioned in the Preface of this book, the APA (1985, p. 286) was taken in by Chomsky's benevolence toward cognitive psychology. Hans Hörmann was not! This was one of Hörmann's most important insights. And it is to the credit of Robert Innis that he has realized the importance of Hörmann's position on this matter. The passage from Innis's Introduction to Hans Hörmann's (1986) posthumous textbook is very much worth citing even though it is difficultly and densely worded:

> Perhaps the chief opponent of the arguments and selections of data that Hörmann adduces in this book is the rationalistic, monadological orientation that ascribes primary importance to the admittedly massive cognitional achievement of language and contends that, ultimately, not only does language as an independent system of signifiers exist independently of the language user but also the

study of its formal structure in itself supplies us with
the guiding principles, chief questions, and heuristic clues
for a specifically psychological study of language. It is
precisely this thesis that Hörmann claims has stifled and
misled research in psycholinguistics since the great attack
by Noam Chomsky on Skinner's behaviorist language theory.
(p. 4 f.)

In other words, the abstract calculus, the autonomous linguistics, cannot serve as the basis for a psychology of language use.

It is ironic that even "the great attack by Noam Chomsky on
Skinner's behaviorist language theory" shows the two scholars to
have been much closer to one another, particularly in their
reliance upon abstractions, than either wanted to admit. Linell
(1979b) has analyzed these similarities and concluded that "both
give mechanistic and paramechanistic paradigms, which are rather
bad adaptations of natural-science type theories to social
phenomena" (p. 198).

Derwing (1979) has insisted that many of these ideas are
traceable back to Bloomfield's Language and have been directly
incorporated into the work of Chomsky and his followers:

Linguistics has been characterized (one might even say
plagued) by the following two unique features: (1) the
acceptance of the language product (i.e., language forms,
or the "output" of language processes) as the primary, if
not exclusive, object of investigations, taken in isolation from its context of use; and (2) the adoption of a

26

similarly "autonomous" view of the language "system" (as
revealed, say, by analysis of the language product) as a
"thing unto itself," which existed "out there" somewhere,
isolated from real speakers. (p. 165 f.)

Derwing's conclusion was that Chomsky's psychologizing was purely
terminological, allowing Chomskyan "imaginations to run completely wild" (p. 168), free of all "psychological constraints"
(p. 168). If Derwing's comments seem harsh, his conviction that
the only link between Chomsky's ideal speaker-hearer and real
speakers and hearers is established by "a totally unpardonable
sleight-of-hand" (p. 173) is even more forthright.

Perhaps my own discussion begins to sound like overkill too;
but the issue is too important -- and has been too long swept
under the rug -- to be dismissed lightly. Chomsky desperately
needed a link to jump a pure descriptivism to the firm ground of
explanation, but it was simply not to be found. Frankly, I find
Derwing's bluntness not only refreshing, but necessary: "Talk
about either 'psychological reality' or 'explanatory power' of
modern grammatical theories is just that -- talk" (p. 178).
Finally, Derwing's comments regarding language as a tool anticipate what we will have to say about Bühler's Organon theory in
Chapter 4:

The linguist's fundamental error was that he started at the
wrong place, and everything else went naturally downhill
from there. He started by examining the tool, rather than
by asking questions about the use to which that tool was

put. (p. 182 f.)

Steiner's (1975) critique of Chomskyan linguistics was made
primarily from the standpoint of a litterateur, but he too has
questioned whether the study of language is or ever can be a
science in its own right, autonomously. More pointedly, he
questioned seriously:

> Whether any context-free system, however 'deep' its loca-
> tion, however formal its modus operandi, will contribute
> much to our understanding of natural speech and hearing.
> (p. 107)

Along with Chomsky, modern linguistics moved temporarily
away from the field observations and other empirical techniques
of ethnology and anthropology toward a non-empirical approach
characterized instead by the intuitions of the linguistic expert.
The logic of this intuition is evident in the sometimes inordinate penchant of linguists for prefixing an asterisk to unacceptable sentences. The logic goes something like this: "I cannot
find a legitimate reading for this sentence, and in the only
reading(s) I can find for it, it violates a rule." The logic is
essentially the same as that of the experimenter who thinks an
experimental subject is limited to options A and B. Our understanding of neither readings nor of the available options of
experimental subjects is exhaustive. Both intuitions are
extremely dangerous as scientific procedures.

As a matter of fact, the vast majority of sentences thus
cast outside the pale are nonetheless capable of perfectly

legitimate readings. Note that our use of the term _readings_ in this context confirms Linell's (1982) point regarding The written language bias in linguistics. Paucity of readings is closely related to the deliberate impoverishment of context on the part of linguists -- limitation in many cases to a sentential string of words alone. I used the phrase "capable of" deliberately at the beginning of this paragraph in order to emphasize the fact that no sentence has a single determinate meaning in isolation (in abstracto, in vacuo, in se). I will say more about this later when I come to the Organon theory of Bühler and to Hörmann's further development of it. For the moment, I wish only to insist that the effort to construct a complete linguistic domain out of isolated sentences alone, bereft of all performance components, is in itself absurd. It reveals the consequences of non-empirical, abstract, intuitive linguistics at its worst, and it has led to an abundance of confusion and error. Innis (Hörmann, 1986) has pinpointed the theoretical problem as "the assumption that to explain the functioning of language one had to have recourse exclusively to language immanent factors and elements" (p. 5). It cannot be said too emphatically that language immanent components simply do not suffice to explain the functioning (use) of language!

A very different approach to the dependence of language on human use -- but still an approach quite in keeping with what I have been proposing here -- can be found in Ong (1982):

Thought is nested in speech, not in texts, all of which have their meanings through reference of the visible symbol to the world of sound. What the reader is seeing on this page are not real words but coded symbols whereby a properly informed human being can evoke in his or her consciousness real words, in actual or imagined sound. It is impossible for script to be more than marks on a surface unless it is used by a conscious human being as a cue to sounded words, real or imagined, directly or indirectly. (p. 75)

Let me conclude this brief discussion of the inadequacy of language immanent components to explain language use with a simple example. I think it would be fair to say that a classical transformational grammarian would happily asterisk the following: "YOU IS DEAD BUT YES IS ALIVE AND WELL." This sentence is neither from a corpus in dialect, nor is it grammatically incorrect, nor is it artificially concocted for the reader's edification. It is, however, translated from the German, but only as a convenience for the reader; nothing is changed thereby. Suffice it to say that Sabine Kowal's car (which did indeed die during the dreadful 1986-87 Berlin winter) had been personalized into Du, and our word processor (whose continued vitality we were deeply grateful for) into Ja. The sentence needs justification only because of the exaggerations and abstractions of some grammarians. The discernment of structure in this example (e.g., use of second or third person) is de facto dependent on the user's intention in a concrete setting.

One more aspect of the generative approach to linguistics

must be mentioned: the treatment of sentences. The sentence constituted the basic unit of analysis. Furthermore, this analysis was a literal one. Quintilian's "_Paene omne dictum metaphora est_" should have been a warning that the fundamentalistic theories of meaning had to be fundamentally wrong. But as recently as Norrick's (1981) volume on semantics, only literal meaning has been deemed worthy of linguistic theorizing. Even when acknowledged to exist, figurative "readings" were to be considered derivative from the literal sentential meaning (but see Gibbs, 1979). It should also be noted that even the identification of sentences is extremely problematic in the case of spontaneous speech, as O'Connell (1977) has pointed out in the archival research.

It is true that linguistic theorizing is subject to rapid change; some of the positions described above are currently being repudiated by linguists. But no one is able to keep up with the very latest linguistic theorizing. It should surprise no one if many psychologists have given up hope of finding anything worthwhile for a psychology of language use in modern linguistic theory. Like the cries for help of the young shepherd in _Aesop's fables_ who enjoyed crying wolf, the linguists' claims to provide something of merit for psychologists may well now fall on deaf ears. This is surely the moral to be derived from Hörmann's (1981) comment that generative linguistics "has nothing (or practically nothing) to tell us about the actual processes of meaning and understanding" (p. viii), and his similar view of the semantic theory of Katz and Fodor (1963): "The history of science provides few cases where the authors of a theory. . . have shown that much determination in seeking to preserve the elegance of their theory at the expense of its goals" (p. 107). Schank and Birnbaum (1984) have recently stated that "even the strongest partisans of generative linguistics" are now convinced that "there is no evidence that people make use, in comprehension or generation, of the kinds of rule devised by generative linguists to describe linguistic phenomena" (p. 221). Or, as Ong (1982) has succinctly put it:

> Computer language rules ('grammar') are stated first and thereafter used. The 'rules' of grammar in natural human languages are used first and can be abstracted from usage and stated explicitly in words only with difficulty and never completely. (p. 7)

An additional problem associated with dependence on linguistics on the part of psycholinguistics is that an appeal to an independent philosophy of science has become difficult. Much of the philosophy of science concerned with language has in recent years emanated from the club itself. In particular, representatives of the M.I.T. school have established themselves as philosophical commentators on their own linguistic positions. To say the very least, this is not what either linguistics or psycholinguistics has needed. On the other hand, it is hardly surprising that most philosophers of science are loath to engage the constantly shifting sands of linguistic theory, terminology,

32

and evidence.

Let us return to the psycholinguistic revolution itself to ask why it came to pass in the first place. Why were psychologists so ready and eager to be seduced and abandoned? Part of the answer must be sought in those sterile years of behaviorism and operationalism in the first half of the twentieth century. Undoubtedly these years had left some psychologists ready for a change in the direction of mentalism. But a new mentalism was not to be found in mid twentieth century America except in the renewed interest in language. The convergence of research funds, bright new researchers, a promising new (untried) approach to language, and the prospect of a new interdisciplinary approach were all factors. Karl Bühler's (1934) insights were sadly not yet accessible. He had been condemned to oblivion because of his defense of Jews during the Nazi regime in Austria; and the postwar European psychology had not recovered sufficiently to have any notable influence on the course of events in America. The clarity of Bühler, Hörmann, Rommetveit, and others might have precluded much confusion in the psychology of language use at mid century in America.

Until this point, I have given no definition of psycholinguistics. A nontheoretical preliminary definition would simply describe it as the psychology of language use, which in turn should rightfully include all uses of languages: speaking, listening, writing, reading, thinking, learning, and more. Obvious as such a definition might seem, it is not quite what the archival literature reveals. To begin with a quite recent description, Dell (1986) has given the following:

> Psycholinguistics is concerned with three basic and interrelated aspects of language -- acquisition or how language is learned; comprehension, or how sentences are understood; and production, or how sentences are spoken. (p. 283)

Note that both comprehension and production are limited to the level of sentences. Perhaps the most important clue, however, is the very last word of this citation; spoken sentences are actually the only ones envisioned as objects of study. Without acknowledging it, Dell was actually paraphrasing the brief definition given by Clark and Clark (1977):

> One of the principles that gives the field coherence is that psycholinguistics is fundamentally the study of three mental processes -- the study of listening, speaking, and of the acquisition of these two skills by children. (p. vii)

Clark and Clark's text has been a very influential one. Reading and writing are completely excluded from the domain of psycholin-guistics by their definition.

The emphasis on sentences has led to a serious neglect of text or discourse levels of analysis until rather recently. In fact, Hörmann (1986) has insisted that the grammarians have no business going beyond the level of the sentence anyway:

> The largest linguistic unit is the sentence. . . . Texts

are not right or wrong, but rather more or less acceptable.
(See de Beaugrande, 1980.) The sentence is, so to speak,
the playing field of grammar.

But paradoxically, despite all the emphasis on speaking, the
sentences that have found their way into the analyses of psycholinguists have been for the most part written ones, isolated
ones, and demonstrational ones at that (i.e., sentences that
ordinary people would not be heard speaking).

One way linguistics has sought to expand on the legitimate
domains of phonology, syntax, and semantics has been through the
addition of the domain of pragmatics. Whether this addition is
anything more than an ad hoc Band-Aid is quite questionable.
Hörmann's (1986) vote has been a definite negative:

> The reason why the step from linguistics to the psychology
> of language is such a difficult and large one lies in the
> character of this (additive) assistance: can we really
> divide the scientific description of a system used for a
> specific purpose into the description of the system and the
> description of its use? Can we divide up the impression
> that a painting makes on us for description's sake into the
> impression that the colors make and the impression that the
> figures make? We can without a doubt. But what have we
> actually described? (p. 77)

The "(additive) assistance" is, of course, pragmatics. Hörmann's
point is simply that pragmatics is needed by linguistics only
because linguistics has insisted on separating language into the

"description of the system" and " the description of its use".
What is important for scientific understanding is precisely the
"system used" or the system in use.   The very existence of the
separate domain of pragmatics is a consequence of the theoretical
impasse created by the theorists themselves through their
contrived separation of the system from its use.   The cure, then,
does not address the underlying pathology.   That pathology has
been described quite specifically by Derwing and Baker (1978):
"Language is not learned in isolation and it is not used in
isolation -- why should it be described in isolation?" (p. 206).
Instead of an additive domain of pragmatics what is needed is
that:

> Linguists must become accustomed to thinking psychologi-
> cally.   Psychologists of language must break the habit of
> allowing "pure" (i.e., nonpsychological) linguistics to give
> them their concepts, constructs, and theories. (Hörmann,
> 1986, p. 78)

My first published opposition to psycholinguistics made use
of the very same marriage metaphor that has served as background
for this chapter.   At the first German conference on psycholinguistics, my paper was entitled The honeymoon is over (Graumann,
1969).   At that time, Carl Graumann pleaded that we give the
psycholinguistic marriage a chance in the day-to-day of married
life.   Almost 20 years later, I would make the following modest
proposal: A lot of everyday married existence has ensued without
much evidence that the relationship is a healthy one.   The vows

were wrongly engaged and the relationship has been stormy and counterproductive. At the very minimum, the family name must go. The change back from the name psycholinguistics to the maiden name (the psychology of language use) acknowledges that the marriage has been exceedingly troubled. Others have suggested that the poor lady distance herself from her past by compromise and assume the name "linguistic psychology" (Derwing, 1979, p. 184) or "human linguistics" (Yngve, 1985; see also Yngve, 1986).

The likelihood that such a suggestion will be adopted across the board is minuscule indeed. But if it serves rhetorically to call to our attention the fact that the psychology of language use has not enjoyed a felicitous relationship to linguistics over the past several decades, the proposal shall have served its purpose. I, for one, prefer to speak of the psychology of language use in any event. My reasons should be clear by now. The bride has been treated rather shabbily; it's high time she be allowed to and encouraged to return to her family to regain her sense of autonomy and self-respect -- and above all to become, once again, part of the family of psychology.

Chapter 3

Psycholinguistics and Cognitive Ooze

Returning to the nuclear family unit after three decades in a troubled marriage is easier said than done. What name is she to use? Does she bring household furnishings and offspring along with her? Times have changed -- and the family unit along with them.

And so, the most likely domain for psycholinguistics to ooze into has turned out to be cognitive psychology. This could be thought of as a tragic decision; but, like so many familiar tragedies, it is tragic precisely because it was not a decision. It happened gradually, partly because of the learning background of many of the psycholinguists themselves, partly because of the various institutional settings (cognitive research centers) that were "the logical place" for studies of language, and partly because of the preoccupation of cognitive psychologists with language phenomena. This preoccupation has been quite salient in the areas of artificial intelligence, computer simulation and methodology, and problem solving; all these areas are closely related to and dependent upon language use. It was accordingly quite easy for psycholinguistics to be accepted into cognitive psychology without further ado -- and clearly without any demand for a change in name.

The ooze metaphor is intended to suggest not only gradualism but another aspect of the new location as well: unclarity. There has been considerable hype in recent years about cognitive

38

psychology, almost a triumphalism, as if psychology were on the verge of astounding breakthroughs in science. It is my own conviction that there is no substance corresponding to or underlying this hype. I say this with a modicum of terror, because I am currently the director of a doctoral program in cognitive psychology (at Loyola University of Chicago). Nonetheless, it should be said: There is no more conceptual commonality or cohesion within cognitive psychology than within any of the other conceptual fads that have already come and gone in modern psychology because they have been tried and found wanting.

The present chapter presents two simple theses: (1) The psychology of language use does not belong within cognitive psychology, but landed there as a victim of circumstances; (2) In any event, cognitive psychology itself is currently not a coherent, clearly defined domain of the science of psychology. The first of these two theses will be developed more thoroughly in Chapter 4, where I will also give a rationale for social psychology as a more reasonable home base for the psychology of language use. But the first thesis must nonetheless be enunciated here in order to warrant our preoccupation with cognitive psychology.

What is cognitive psychology, then? First of all, I must say that it was a great deal more coherent in the beginning, when T. V. Moore (1939) published his Cognitive psychology. His approach was straightforward. A cognitive psychology had to be defined by its subject matter. The Latin cognoscere -- to know,

39

to ascertain, to come to know, to learn -- defined the subject matter quite well. Hence, all aspects of learning and knowing, logic and problem solving, memory and forgetting, were at home there. Ulric Neisser (1967), more than 30 years later, defined cognitive psychology according to subject matter too: the cognitive to the exclusion of the dynamic, the social, and all else. And although he didn't acknowledge Moore's pioneering work, he was in this respect in accord with him.

Later, however, Neisser (1975) complicated matters considerably by distinguishing cognitive psychology from behaviorism by method, while retaining the distinction from dynamic psychology by subject matter. By then, his definition of the cognitive field of research was expressed as follows:

"Cognition," in today's terminology refers to the total of processes and activities by which people (and other organisms) acquire and use information. (p. 159)

By 1975, information had become the buzz word. It was not the subject matter that was changed, or even the methodology, so much as the conceptualization itself. Neisser certainly had no intention of analyzing data, from that moment on, solely in terms of the bits and bytes of information in his data base. He was, in fact, for the most part simply rechristening with the term information whatever was to be investigated. Whether or not the concept of information was appropriate for everything in the cognitive domain was not even posed as a further question by Neisser.

It is all the more surprising that by the very next year, in a book later to be heralded as "a philosophical book" by Hans Aebli (Neisser, 1979, p. 7), Neisser (1976) was already changing "today's terminology" to incorporate, of all things, conscious-ness:

> In writing Cognitive psychology a decade ago, I deliberately avoided theorizing about consciousness. It seemed to me that psychology was not ready to tackle the issue, and that any attempt to do so would lead only to philosophically naive and fumbling speculation. Unfortunately, these fears have been realized; many current models of cognition treat consciousness as if it were just a particular stage of processing in a mechanical flow of information. (p. xiii)

Unfortunately, Neisser did not take the concept of con-sciousness any further in his 1976 book. What was clear in the book, however, was that Neisser thought of the psychology of language use as a part of cognitive psychology; his Chapter 8 had language perception and production as its topic.

But the book was philosophical only in the minimum sense that Neisser thought he had found some methodological and conceptual answers to some perennial problems. He did indeed address the importance of time for the integration of perceptual processes (but largely by way of a promise in his Introduction) and attempted to explain the origin of introspection ontogeneti-cally. It is, however, rather ludicrous to refer to the book as philosophical. What Neisser actually did was simply to shift his

41

scientific approach once again without justifying the shift. Pious words in an Introduction about the dangers of an informational approach (e.g., lack of ecological validity; cf. Neisser, 1985) are hardly the positive grounds for a new approach.

Perhaps Battista (1978) came closest to the 1976 version of Neisser in terms of the incorporation of consciousness into cognitive psychology:

> Cognition is the most common form of adult consciousness. Cognition is the state of consciousness involved in conceptualization or reflection upon experience and is thus more complex than sensory, perceptual, emotional, or affective consciousness. (p. 61)

But Battista too has done little more than assert that human cognition is conscious; both true and important, but not instructive.

The vast majority of contemporary cognitive psychologists are still formulating a definition of cognitive psychology in terms of information processes or of computational processes in turn derived from informational conceptualizations. In his textbooks, Anderson (1980, 1985) has defined cognitive psychology purely in terms of information processing, to the neglect of even the representational component. Shallice (1978) has even argued that "'consciousness' in phenomenological language becomes isomorphic to 'selector input to the dominant action-system' in information terms" (p. 133), but such a readiness to combine cognitive and conscious conceptualizations is hardly widespread.

Mandler (1985), on the other hand, has defined cognitive psychology not in terms of information processes, but purely in terms of "process," considered as a metatheoretical concept. He has explicitly disavowed the centrality of information processing, artificial intelligence, and the computer model of human cognition for purposes of defining cognitive psychology. Neumann (1985) too has found little hope of scientific respectability in dependency on information technology and engineering, but has called instead for the "pursuit of psychological solutions to psychological problems" (p. 23; my trans.).

Until quite recently, linear flowcharts and branching tree diagrams have been fairly characteristic of cognitive psychology and have contributed to both a digitalized, compartmentalized, static concept of language use and to what Rommetveit (1979) has referred to as "a false picture theory of language use" (p. 26). Walter Ong (1969) has traced this "hypervisualism," as he has named it, all the way back to Peter Ramus in the sixteenth century and to his influence on the modes of western thought.

An example of the penchant for such linear flowcharting at its worst can be found in Anderson (1980). He applied it to the concept of attention, which was represented as a rectangle from three sides of which output arrows extended perpendicularly. There was no input whatsoever (which seems to make attention into some sort of deity), yet somehow attention was supposed to run the whole show. Mercifully, the diagram has been deleted from the revised edition (Anderson, 1985).

In fairness, it should be said that flowcharts seem to be on the wane, and more complex concepts such as parallel processing and interactive processing are replacing them (e.g., Neisser, 1976, p. 103; Rumelhart, McClelland, & the PDP Research Group, 1986; Scheerer, 1985, p. 31; Stemberger, 1985, p. 143).

Anderson's concept of attention also reflected a tendency on the part of cognitive psychologists to hypostatize concepts, endowing them with personal agency. We used to refer to such formulations disapprovingly as homunculi, but they have obviously gained considerably in stature in recent decades. Levelt's (1983a) terminology reflects a similar tendency to ascribe agency to hypothetical concepts:

> The parser can, moreover, derive information other than
> the intended message, such as linguistic aspects of the
> speech string: whether particular phonemes of words are
> spoken, whether particular referents are mentioned, the
> parser can detect syntactic and prosodic features, voice
> qualities, etc. In short, a large variety of aspects of
> parsed information is accessible to attention. (p. 49)

Note that this parser is like a jack-of-all-trades; it derives information, detects features, makes information accessible to attention. Levelt's reference to "the intended message of the speaker" might perhaps be thought to reflect adequately the agency of the speaker. The same benevolent interpretation is not possible, however, in the case of the listener; the role of the parser is not linked to a responsible human agency. Both

Anderson's and Levelt's usage remain excellent examples of what Sampson (1981) has called "cognitivism" for its inordinate emphasis on "the structure and processes within the individual's mind that are said to play a major role in behavior" (p. 730).

Meanwhile, the tendency of cognitive psychologists to bill computer programs as psychological explanation continues. Hunt and Lansman (1986) have recently proposed a model of attention and problem solving that answers what they thought of as the major criticism to be lodged against mathematical models: "For being elaborate models of highly specialized laboratory paradigms" (p. 446). But their conviction that it would suffice for the model to be "at once broad and precise" missed the real problem. The model was only "realized as a computer program and used to simulate a variety of phenomena" (p. 446); it tells us nothing about human attention and problem solving.

Pribram (1985) has proposed holographic explanation as a new approach to cognitive psychology; but there is no evidence that such an approach is suitable or heuristic either for cognition in general or for a psychology of language use. Pribram's effort to extricate himself from the current theoretical impasse by means of holograms is redolent of the effort by Miller, Galanter, and Pribram (1960) more than a quarter century ago to heal behaviorism by making it subjective -- without really engaging the subjective at any level beyond the descriptive. In the German edition of Miller, Galanter, and Pribram (1973), Hans Aebli referred to the book as critical in the "cognitive revolution"

(p. 7; see also Baars, 1987; Gardner, 1985). If critical be taken to mean in some minimal sense that the book reflected the malaise in neobehaviorism, so be it. Other than that, it was an empty tour de force. Apart from an occasional reference to their TOTE acronym (Test-Operate-Test-Exit), the influence of the book has been negligible. It most certainly addressed neither the old problems of neobehaviorism nor the new problems of cognitive psychology in anything like a satisfactory fashion.

The various examples and versions of cognitive psychology given above should suffice at least to give the reader pause regarding the wisdom of subsuming the psychology of language use under the umbrella discipline of cognitive science. Fodor (1981) has proclaimed cognitive science to be "philosophy rediscovered-- and, I think, vindicated" (p. 26). There is, however, no evidence that cognitive science is really anything more than "a system of processes for the manipulation of information" (Hunt, 1982, p. 33). If this suffices to resuscitate philosophy, then philosophy would be better left unrediscovered. I would hope that philosophy could aspire to more than that in the modern world.

Basic to the information conceptualization of language use is the conviction that "people use language to convey information" (Norman & Rumelhart, 1975, p. 4). It sounds like a perfectly adequate description of language use until one begins to ask questions. Does information transfer really describe language use, or is communication by means of language both more

46

than and other than mere transfer of information? My own conviction is that the information transfer model is completely inadequate. Hörmann (1981) has put this conviction both succinctly and eloquently:

> Thus the utterance in itself does not convey any information to the hearer: it only guides the hearer in creating the information for himself. (p. 308)

My own reaction to this statement was first formulated for my review of Hörmann's (1981) To mean -- to understand:

> The intentionality of the hearer therefore incorporates a conscious finality antecedent to analysis of any utterance; that finality guides him through the utterance to what the speaker means. Behold, the transparency of language.
>
> (O'Connell, 1982b, p. 410)

In other words, when we listen to someone speaking, we are looking for understanding -- of his or her meaning. We see right through the words to what is intended. That does not insure in all instances a correct or comprehensive grasp of what is intended. It simply reflects the fact that the object of our understanding is not just representations, but intended meanings!

In that same review of Hörmann's book, I mentioned:

> Some of the most dedicated cognitive scientists have suspected the inadequacy of the computer model of language-related behavior but have failed to adjust their stance.
>
> (p. 410)

George Miller (1974), for example, suggested the likelihood "that how people understand sentences has nothing to do with how computers compile programs" (p. 408). Philip Johnson-Laird (1981) has commented that "there may be certain aspects of human mentality that cannot be captured in any theory that can be modelled by a computer program" (p. 143), but he then "identifies the contents of consciousness with the parameters that govern the computations of the serial processor" (McNeill, 1987, p. 264; see Johnson-Laird, 1983). Ades (1981) has gone so far as to say with respect to the model: "It is time for a purge" (p. 15). Osgood (1963) had rejected the adequacy of the computer analogy a quarter of a century ago (cited in Jakobovits & Miron, 1967, p. 110)!

A quite different relationship between cognitive psychology and the psychology of language use has been suggested in a brief pronunciamento of Bever, Carroll, and Miller (1984):

We think that each of the disciplines represented -- psychology, linguistics, and computer science -- has a contribution to make towards an integrated solution. We expect

> from psychology a richer theory of learning as it applies to formal knowledge;

> from linguistics a better understanding of the nature of language;

> from computer science the development of physical models that can deal in part with the kinds of knowledge that human beings exhibit.

48

The form this integrated solution is to take, however, seems entirely unclear at the moment. Periodically in behavioral science a movement emerges that presupposes an integrated solution to be implicit in the correct combination of contemporary disciplines. The current instantiation of that position is "cognitive science," a superset of the disciplines represented in this book. One program for this enterprise is clear: cognition should be pursued in the image of linguistics. Unlike traditional psychologists, many adherents to this position are nativist, mentalist, and relationalist, although none of these positions is necessary for them. (p. 11 f.)

Suffice it to say that the expectation from psychology of only a better "theory of learning" is a throwback at least to the fifties. Psychology has a great deal to contribute to an understanding of the social process of communication; but in the abstract approach to language reflected in this citation from Bever et al., social and communicative elements are completely neglected. Under the guise of the new "cognitive science," an entirely outmoded approach to language use is presented. What linguists actually know about cognition must be judged from their record, and that I have tried to portray as accurately as possible in Chapter 2. The record is certainly not such as to justify our being sanguine about pursuing cognition "in the image of linguistics". The reason for the poor record is very simple: The linguists have been for years concerned with "the nature of language," rather than with the nature of language _use_. Cognition is an aspect (one of many) of language _use_. The irony is that Bever et al. intended "cognitive science" to be understood as a movement "in behavioral science". To date, the linguistics from which they wished to learn of language _use_ has been stereotypically non-behavioral.

Although a detailed consideration of their argumentation would carry us far beyond the scope of this book, the insistence on the part of Dreyfus and Dreyfus (1986) that artificial intelligence research has been completely unable to engage human intuition surely cannot be neglected. To say the least, they would hardly agree with Fodor (1981) that current cognitive science is "philosophy rediscovered" (p. 26).

In sum, there are several very straightforward reasons why language use simply cannot be properly investigated and understood within the available cognitive paradigms, and why language use doesn't belong under the umbrella discipline of cognitive psychology neither from a logical nor from an empirical point of view: Language use is ineluctably communicative and therefore social. It subserves as a tool (or _Organon_ or means) a conscious, deliberate, transcendent agency of human persons. All of that needs to be talked about further in Chapter 4.

50

Chapter 4

Tools of the Trade

My chapter title is, I'm afraid, a rather unsubtle reference
to the key concept on which I wish to build this chapter, and
therewith a positive approach to a psychology of language use.
Language is, first, last, and always, the tool (or _Organon_ or
means) with which trading (exchange, communication) is accomplished. Trading refers also to the broader scope of commerce,
the economy, society. All these levels are within the scope of
language use and reflect saliently the implicit contractual
element of language use. It is, first and foremost, negligence
of these social aspects of human language that has led linguists
and psycholinguists astray. I would like to make both the
urgency and the insight expressed by Derwing (1979) in this
regard my own:

> We must put an end to the reification of _language_ as a
> "thing apart" and begin to see the situation from the
> perspective of the language _user_. For language is only
> a means to an end -- and that end is achieved by putting
> linguistic devices at the service of all the other cogni-
> tive mechanisms which constitute the general mental make-up
> of man. (p. 184)

I wish to dwell at considerable length on some of the
scientific consequences of this "reification of language" before
proceeding to Bühler's _Organon_ theory, Hörmann's use of it, and
some further constructive approaches to a psychology of language

51

use.

Richard Wiese and I (O'Connell & Wiese, 1987) have discussed elsewhere what we have referred to as "orphaned aspects" of language use. The orphaning concept is deliberately meant to suggest serious negligence and profound blindness to crucial aspects of linguistic reality. The thesis is grounded in our conviction that linguistic reality cannot be properly investigated and understood apart from language use. To consider these orphaned aspects, one must step back from mainstream psycholinguistics and cognitive psychology and begin to ask questions-- "step back from the influential assertions of this century -- to shun the secular certainties so many of us find appealing" (Coles, 1986, p. 18).

Let's start with the simple question: What do humans communicate? It seems to be a naive question, and perhaps partly for that reason, it has traditionally been answered naively! It seems to be the almost universal conviction of linguists and psycholinguists alike that words simply _carry_ information from speaker to hearer. This is what Reddy (1979) has named the _conduit_ metaphor:

> (1) language functions like a conduit, transferring thoughts bodily from one person to another; (2) in writing and speaking, people insert their thoughts and feelings in the words; (3) words accomplish the transfer by containing the thoughts or feelings and conveying them to others; and (4) in listening or reading, people extract the thoughts

and feelings once again from the words. (p. 290)

Linell (1982) has complemented Reddy's description with the translation or recoding theory, "another metaphor for basically the same perspective on linguistic communication" (p. 145), as follows:

> The theory just sketched is obviously inspired by Shannon and Weaver's classical model of technical information transfer. It recurs in almost every introductory textbook on linguistics or speech communication (e.g., Denes & Pinson, 1963). I have given it couched in basically physical terms, but essentially the same type of translation-theoretical approach permeates generative psycholinguistics, where, instead, scholars prefer to talk about abstract mental representations corresponding to the constructs of linguistic competence theory. Thus, the message is there automatically processed through a series of purportedly "linguistically significant" representations. (p. 145 f.)

The upshot of all this is an extraordinarily important implication: "It is thus assumed that the meaning of what is said can be gained simply by applying a linguistically correct analysis to these linguistic products" (p. 146).

Linell has given several reasons why this model fails to account for human communication:

> First, the situational interpretations relevant to speaker and listener are never equal to the linguistic meaning

associated with the utterance itself; . . . Secondly, there
is no complete linguistic meaning nor any fully developed
intended interpretation in the mind of the speaker before
the utterance has been compiled and its outer form has been
determined; . . . Thirdly, there are no uniquely correct
situational interpretations; . . . (p. 149)

Linell's three reasons have spelled out the intrinsic limitations
of the "linguistically correct analysis." In other words,
meaning cannot be arrived at from such analysis alone; meaning is
not pre-existent to the utterance; understanding does not exhaust
intended meaning.

Theo Herrmann (1985) has traced the same problem addressed
by both Reddy and Linell back to the isolation of the speaker-
hearer system in traditional psycholinguistics. This has made
the focus of the scientific problem "the human being as language
processor," instead of "the human being who also understands
language and also speaks" (p. 41; my trans). The point to be
made is that speaking and listening are exercised occasionally,
from time to time, as part of the general human psychological
processes of dealing with reality. Speaking and listening can be
investigated and understood only within that larger system.
Herrmann credited both Bloomfield (1933) and Vygotsky (1934/1962)
for these insights regarding the occasional nature of speaking
and listening as well as for their implications for the psychology of language use.

Ong (1982) has also described the conduit metaphor and

emphatically rejected it:

> Thinking of a 'medium' of communication or of 'media' of
> communication suggests that communication is a pipeline
> transfer of units of material called 'information' from one
> place to another. My mind is a box. I take a unit of
> 'information' out of it, encode the unit (that is, fit it
> to the size and shape of the pipe it will go through), and
> put it into one end of the pipe (the medium, something in
> the middle between two other things). From the one end of
> the pipe the 'information' proceeds to the other end, where
> someone decodes it (restores its proper size and shape) and
> puts it in his or her own box-like container called a mind.
> This model obviously has something to do with human communi-
> cation, but, on close inspection, very little, and it dis-
> torts the act of communication beyond recognition. Hence
> McLuhan's wry book title: The Medium is the Massage (not
> quite the 'message'). (p. 176)

If we wish, then, to further pursue the question as to what
humans communicate, we can hardly rely on the answers dictated by
the "reification paradigm" itself, nor can we rely on the
conduit, translation, recoding, or medium versions of human
communication.

Language is not set apart autonomously from the rest of
human psychology. Instead we must ask of every instance of
speaking and listening: What is the occasion for the language
use? How do the speaker(s) and listener(s) relate to one

another? What does each know about the situation and about the other(s)? What does the speaker intend to accomplish? What are the cultural and societal conventions within which speaker and listener are operating? And what is the listener interested in seeing accomplished in this setting?

Once such questions have been seriously engaged, it becomes clear that the larger setting, with all its implicit understandings and affective, motivational, circumstantial, social, contractual elements, enters into the determination of both meaning and understanding. And the silliness and futility of "assigning 'propositional content' to mere semantic potentialities" (Rommetveit, 1974, p. 87) becomes apparent. The words alone (together with any other purely linguistic units, for that matter) simply do not tell us what is being made known (being intended and understood) at a given moment in time. This is why Rommetveit has spoken of _message structure_. The message structure and intended meaning do not arise solely from the linguistic structure of the speaker's words and sentences, but from an implicit contract in a setting of partially shared intersubjectivity. The speaker does not transmit a prepackaged message to the listener; the listener comes already prepared to understand, and this readiness influences what he or she does understand. Hörmann (1981) has characterized the listener's understanding as "the outcome of his incessant striving to make the world and all events around him intelligible" (p. 308). This in turn is completely compatible with Herrmann's integration of speaking and

56

listening with the rest of human psychology and with Rommetveit's (1979) concept of anticipatory comprehension, "Vorverständigung" (p. 24), or listener readiness to understand. Rommetveit's term has been adopted from the hermeneutic-dialectic philosophers.

Another concept that is central to all this is Hörmann's concept of "sense constancy" or "Sinnkonstanz." Let me return to my book review of Hörmann (1981) for a description of this concept:

> This constancy of meaning is indeed analogous to the perceptual principles of organization and integration of size, shape, and color. The latter too make perceptual objects out of sensory elements, make the world intelligible. The intentionality of the hearer therefore incorporates a conscious finality antecedent to analysis of any utterance; that finality guides him through the utterance to what the speaker means. Behold, the transparency of language.
> (O'Connell, 1982b, p. 410)

The concepts of intentionality, consciousness, and finality are unavoidable in such a view of meaning and understanding (Hörmann) or of message structure (Rommetveit): "The utterance in itself does not convey any information to the hearer; it only guides the hearer in creating the information for himself" (Hörmann, 1981, p. 308).

The radical departure of this formulation from the formulations of traditional psycholinguistics must be spelled out in bold relief. A human agent purposefully intends to communicate a message to a listener, to change the other's consciousness somehow; and a human agent listens purposefully and consciously in readiness to understand. Short of this, the linguistic units remain sterile ciphers in the air or on the page.

And so, it was not accidental that intentionality, consciousness, and finality were among O'Connell and Wiese's (1987) orphaned concepts along with the communicative, contractual, creative, social, and cultural aspects of language use. We had subsumed the affective, attitudinal, emotional, and volitional aspects -- in general, the dynamic aspects -- under the communicative. But it is important that the dynamic aspects also not be overlooked or neglected. In this respect too, a uniquely cognitive subject matter is completely inadequate to reflect comprehensively the relevant aspects of a psychology of language use. Far from coping with the dynamic aspects of language use, both the abstract linguistic approach and the purely cognitive approach have deliberately excluded them. It should be clear by now that they cannot be eliminated from consideration, if we are even to begin to learn how to answer the question with regard to any genuinely communicative situation (i.e., any language use): What is really being communicated?

Let me give a pleasant little example that incorporates many of these elements in two spoken syllables. It is an example that I have used in many classes as a demonstration question and in many communicative settings as a genuine question. In the former case, it is almost never understood; in the latter case, it is almost always understood. It can be transcribed simply as "GEE CHET?" with a rising interrogative intonation. When understood, it is completely transparent; the listener does not need to reflect and analyze. When not understood, analysis doesn't help; it must simply be translated for the listener into "Did you eat yet?" before any light dawns. And even then, students are reluctant to admit that the shorter version is actually used-- and actually understood. The communicative setting is clearly the critical difference! And this setting clearly includes the appropriateness of the question on the part of the speaker and its relevance for the listener.

Simply stated, linguistic structure cannot be adequately ascertained without knowledge of the setting. <u>Words and sentences do not have meaning in isolation</u>. That is to say that their meaning in isolation is indeterminate, precisely in the sense intended by both Rommetveit and Hörmann. The semantic potentialities of words and sentences (and other linguistic units such as phrases and clauses) remain open. It is in this sense, then, that linguistic structure can be said to be dependent upon the total language use situation for the activation of its potentialities.

We began with the concept of language as a tool. Potentialities are but one aspect of tool usage. The comprehensive treatment of language as a tool is Karl Bühler's contribution to the modern psychology of language use. It is no less than astounding that his work has been almost entirely neglected for over 50 years. After leaving Austria for the United States, he produced no further comprehensive work. One can only speculate whether or not his Die Krise der Psychologie (1927) and Sprach-theorie (1934) might have had their rightful influence, had he not emigrated, and had World War II not all but destroyed German-language psychology. It still remains a mystery that postwar psychology in both Europe and America did not rediscover his genius until quite recently.

A number of current works give promise of genuinely reviving interest in Bühler's contributions, e.g., Graumann and Herrmann (1984), Innis (1982), Jarvella and Klein (1981), and Knobloch (1984). But more than any other scholar, it has been Hans Hörmann (1967, 1976, 1977, & 1981; and their English versions, 1971, 1981, 1979, & 1986, respectively) who has done the most to bring Bühler to the attention of current psychologists. Innis (Hörmann, 1986) has said that Bühler was "the greatest source of inspiration for Hörmann" (p. 15), especially in the Sprachthe-orie, "an incomparable synthesis of linguistic, semiotic, psychological, and philosophical materials and insights" (p. 15).

But let us begin with his earlier (1927) work first. His goal, even then, was quite clear: "I did not start out to reform psychology, but to find the axioms of the psychology of language" (p. 29; my trans.). Psychology must begin with the following as subject matter: "Experiences, the integrated behaviors of living organisms, and their relationships to the products of human endeavor" (p. 29; my trans.) Bühler's keen awareness of social

60

processes was evident in his principle that "the origin of semantics is to be sought not in the individual, but in the _community_" (p. 38; my trans.); and similarly that control (_Steuerung_) is to be defined as "the reciprocal, goal directed influence of members of a community (of lower organisms or of humans) on one another" (p. 65; my trans.). It is not at all difficult to discern in some of these seminal quotations the sources of Hörmann's emphases on the social, goal directed, conscious aspects of the speaker-listener setting.

Bühler's emphasis on the social aspects of language use was of central importance. He gave as a crucial reason why Wundt's structuralism floundered, that his theory did not "take the necessary step from individual to community at the decisive point" (p. 34; my trans.). It is perhaps even more important that Wundt was _not_ criticized for appealing to consciousness, finality, or experience, but for not transcending a faulty introspective methodology. In fact, in a charming passage, Bühler also accused the behaviorists outright of using "experiential psychology" on the sly "to select what is _meaningful_ in the behavior of both animals and humans" (p. 46; my trans.). His play on the word "_sinnvollen_" (his quotation marks) and the phrase _mit den Sinnen_ should be noted, but it goes beyond our purposes here (and my skills of translation) to nuance the translation or dwell on it further.

Levelt (1981a) has pointed out that it was Bühler (1908) who carried out "the first major study with verbal reports as

61

experimental data" (p. 190 f.), and that Ericsson and Simon (1980) overlooked this historical fact. It would appear to me equally negligent that Ericsson and Simon (1985, p. 385) in their definitive book on Protocol analysis allowed a total of seven typographical errors in their two Bühler bibliographical entries (cf. Carroll, 1986, p. 414, for a record seven errors in one Bühler entry). One might be tempted to wonder whether anyone is actually looking at Bühler's works.

All this has been largely propaedeutic to a consideration of Bühler's Organon theory. I am reminded of a movie from a few years back entitled The gods must be crazy. The theme is set when a Coca-Cola bottle appears "miraculously" from the gods (tossed from a passing aircraft) in the midst of an aboriginal African tribe. The uses to which the gift is put are delightfully portrayed -- everything from rolling pin to musical instrument to weapon to millstone.

There is a simple lesson to be learned by psychologists of language use from this little fable. When all is said and done, a tool is defined by its use. It is not limited by any sort of necessity to one use. We might revert to a brief consideration of functional fixedness in this regard. The inability to adjust to creative possibilities of tools has always been thought of as a mark of narrow-minded inflexibility and of a lack of adaptability and spontaneity; and the ability to do so a mark of intelligent flexibility, convergent thinking, and cleverness.

Language is a tool, defined as to its use by the people who

use it. Those who would assign propositional content "to mere semantic potentialities" (Rommetveit, 1974, p. 87), who would have the autonomous structures of a language system dictate meaning, who would make figurative meaning necessarily derivative from literal meaning, are simply suffering from a chronic case of functional fixedness. They have forgotten what humans do with tools.

Note that the argument does not rely on a denial of linguistic structure any more than our fable depends on a denial of the roundness and hardness of a Coke bottle. Language is _not_ only language in use. The importance of insistence on this point can be exemplified in Gauger's (1980) misrepresentation of Hörmann's position in this regard: "Language is nothing other than its use" (p. 422). This does not represent Hörmann's true position at all. It is quite another thing to say, as Hörmann has consistently maintained, that language can be adequately understood only through an empirical study of language use.

I have resisted the temptation to incorporate here Bühler's famous illustration of the _Organon_ model. It can be found (most recently) in Hörmann (1986, p. 79). For our purposes, Hörmann's summary suffices. The "phenomenon" in question in the following citation is "the concrete linguistic event":

> Three different aspects are called up from this phenomenon
> to make it a sign in different ways: the phenomenon is a
> _symbol_ in its relationship to objects and events which it
> represents; it is a _symptom_ in its dependence on the sender,

whose inner situation it expresses; it is a _signal_ by power of its appeal to the receiver, whose behavior it directs.

Representation, expression, and appeal are, according to Bühler, the three characteristic accomplishments of language -- today we would say, somewhat more carefully, the three characteristic functions of the sign. (p. 82)

One of the most important aspects of this _Organon_ model is that the three functions of the sign are incorporated into a single model. Accordingly, the model is intrinsically social, interactive, and communicative and thereby precludes the abstraction of the sign from the communicative setting of language use. This is precisely why it serves so well as the basis for a radical departure from traditional psycholinguistics.

In the remainder of this chapter, I wish to discuss several additional aspects of language use. They are quite compatible with Bühler's model, but go quite beyond his treatment of language use. Two of the aspects, _productivity_ of language use and _transparency_ of language use, are salient in Hörmann's thinking; two other aspects, the _social_ and the _communicative_, are salient in Rommetveit's thinking.

Productivity. Language use is obviously productive or creative in the sense used by Chafe (1977): _What_ the speaker wants to talk about does not completely determine how he talks about it. But this sense is entirely minimalistic. Over and above this sense of productivity, there arise from any individual instance of language use new consciousness, new finality, new

64

insights. The little question "What do you make out of that?" reflects this emergence quite succinctly. Even the inability "to make anything out of it" -- misunderstanding of an intended meaning or message or the failure to understand -- yields new awareness: frustration, embarrassment, anger, panic, disappointment. But in "an intersubjectively established social reality" (Rommetveit, 1974, p. 25), <u>the post-message situation can never be the same as the pre-message situation</u>. The situation itself is always changed by the message. Hörmann (1986) went beyond the Aristotelian notion "that language represents the world" to assert:

> that many things in our world are actually first made with and through language and therefore that the view of a true representation, in language, of a (language-independent) reality is questionable. Here a new function of language is touched on: that of constituting objects. It was emphasized by Humboldt (1963) (and after him by many others): "Language is the producing organ of thought," not the reproducing. (p. 83)

From the listener's or reader's point of view also, this productive aspect of language use is very important. Linell (1982) has expressed it boldly and clearly:

> There are no uniquely correct situational interpretations; both speaker and listener may, e.g. vary in their depths of intention and understanding. . . Any interpretation is in principle inherently negotiable and extendable, i.e. there

are no fixed meanings being transferred in communication.
(p. 149)

Or to return to Hörmann's (1981) wording once again, the listener is successful "in creating information for himself" (p. 308), not passively receptive of prepackaged meaning.

Is the listener's creativity, therefore, _ex nihilo_, out of the blue? No, not at all. Productivity, indeed, creativity, are both prerogatives of the human spirit. Human beings are capable of grasping a situation, of understanding. The evidence is made use of actively, but the synthesis belongs to the listener. Although I dislike the word input because of its reductionistic and mechanistic (i.e., informational) implications, there is no problem in admitting that the input is made use of. The point to be made is that the listener is not limited to the momentary input, but goes "beyond the information given," to use Bruner's (1957) words. This is the point at which traditional psycholinguistic and cognitive colleagues part company with Hörmann. But Hörmann's position is realistic: Every speaker and every listener bring a whole world with them and reshape it as they communicate with one another.

Transparency. To reshape the world, one must be in contact with it from moment to moment, continuously. This contact is maintained in Hörmann's system through "sense constancy" or, even more correctly, by analogy to the other perceptual constancies, through "meaning constancy". This is a far more subtle and genuine concept of input -- or rather of contact -- than the

66

purely informational one. The contact itself is not arbitrary, but based on the continuity of the perceptual with the sensory. Or, as Henle (1983) has put it, "Epistemologically -- that is, from the standpoint of knowing as such -- there is no intermediate process" (p. 53). Nor is the transparency some sort of illusion. Language use actually does bridge from consciousness to consciousness transparently. The listener is not concerned with the tools the speaker uses, but is largely <u>unaware</u> of the specific tools used. For example, when Sabine Kowal asks me a question, I typically do not know five seconds later whether she asked the question in English or in German. It is unimportant to the concrete language use at that moment. What I am aware of is what I make of the question. Meaning and understanding are thus transparent. In its simplest terms, this means that "one sees what is intended so to speak right through the words and sentences" (Hörmann, 1976, p. 58; my trans.). We see through the language tools as through a window. And "because language is transparent, we cannot localize where meaning is or whence it springs" (p. 406; my trans.). The very last sentence in his <u>Meinen und Verstehen</u> sums up transparency once again: "Sounds and words and sentences become transparent; they disappear and what is intended appears in consciousness" (p. 506; my trans.).

This consciousness is the psychological side of the coin. On the other side are Henle's (1983) metaphysics and epistemology of "philosophical realism" (p. 80). The objects of propositional attitudes are <u>not</u> the symbols or representations themselves, but

67

the intended meaning, Fodor (1981, p. 24; cf. Fodor, 1987) to the contrary notwithstanding.

Knobloch (1984) has discussed transparency at considerable length and has pointed out that the linguist loses transparency in isolating language itself (the tool) as the object of study. The linguist thus makes the transparent opaque precisely in order to make the tool into the object of a science. Hence, the linguist does not look through the window but at it. All this constitutes no problem at all, until the linguist begins to accept this analysis itself as a theory of language use and of the language user.

The Social and the Communicative. Rommetveit's preoccupation with the social and the communicative aspects of language use is quite compatible with and complementary to Hörmann's approach. It has, however, always astounded me that Hörmann and Rommetveit, both of whom I have admired professionally and personally, have made no use of one another's work. Perhaps it is actually better this way. Their complementarity serves analogously as a double blind development of "profound aversion for the generativists (as Hörmann refers to them) or the Harvard-M.I.T. school (Rommetveit's favorite term)" (O'Connell, 1982b, p. 412).

Rommetveit (1974) has called for "a radical change of approach" (p. 83), an emphasis on social and communicative aspects of language use, as follows:

What is needed at the present stage is thus neither additional formal devices nor more subdisciplines, but a more comprehensive and thorough analysis of basic premises for intersubjectivity and contractual aspects of verbal communication. (p. 125)

In concluding his After Babel, Steiner (1975) has contrasted two extreme states: on the one hand, perfect communication, in which "all human tongues will have re-entered the translucent immediacy of the primal, lost speech shared by God and Adam" (p. 474); and on the other hand, nulla communicatio, in which: "Words will rebel against man. They will shake off the servitude of meaning. They will 'become only themselves, and as dead stones in our mouths'" (p. 474). Rommetveit (1974) has selected the former state, perfect communication, to clarify the reasons for communicating:

> Ellipsis, we may claim, appears to be the prototype of
> verbal communication under ideal conditions of complete
> complementarity in an intersubjectively established,
> temporarily shared social world. (p. 29)

Keilson (1984) too has referred to the "Unio mystica" that is "almost silence" (p. 917), and Henry Miller has suggested that "speaking begins only at the point where communication is endangered" (1970, p. 61; my trans.). In other words, one speaks because one does not understand. Complementarity this side of the grave is always partial. On the other hand, were there no complementarity, there would also be no inclination to communicate. Language is totally social. It arises only where there

69

are both need and possibility of communication between persons. How this is to be carried out involves not only the structure of some given language, but also a complex set of implicit contractual relationships. This is the setting of Wittgenstein's (1958) language game -- "an intersubjectively established, temporarily shared social world" (Rommetveit, 1974, p. 29).

In short, to recapitulate the foregoing chapter, I would contend that the psychology of language use is alive and well in (parts of) Europe. The materials are almost entirely available in English; they just are not part of the psycholinguistic and cognitive zeitgeist and weltanschauung. Both Hörmann and Rommetveit have called for a radical change, not just some minor terminological adjustments or methodological token changes. Most of the psycholinguists of the world have not been ready up until now for such a revolution in their own thinking.

And where does the psychology of language use belong, if not under the protection of either psycholinguistics or of cognitive psychology? The fact that both dynamic and social aspects of language use have been seriously neglected would seem to make social psychology the best candidate for harboring the homeless discipline. After comparing Bühler to both Wundt and Mead, Graumann (1984) closed his chapter on "Wundt -- Mead -- Bühler" (and the entire book as well) with the following plea to subsume the psychology of language use within social psychology:

> Every science of signs must articulate and axiomatize the
> domain of social living, where alone signs exist and are of

consequence; and this is even more the case with a science that has as its subject matter -- just as social psychology itself -- social living. (p. 247; my trans.).

Beaugrande (1987) has echoed the same conviction rather pointedly:

The human sciences cannot be a neutral, disinterested embodiment of "scientific objectivity" in the same sense as the natural sciences. A human science that disavows its own social context is not disinterested; in effect, it just affirms the prevailing interests of science. Such tactics can promote isolationism and fragmentation. As long as the relationship of a given theory to the realities of society is not explicitly and carefully discussed, the fundamental assumptions incorporated into the theory tend to remain invisible and immune from attack. The theory can then be presented and treated as the only possible one -- as an essential presupposition for all research and experimentation that therefore cannot challenge the theory as a whole but only rearrange its details. Finally, the theory supplants the reality as the object and goal of scientific inquiry. Thus, a science that ignores or obscures its own context is in danger of becoming circular, stagnant, or irrelevant. (p. 1)

In a footnote to the above, Beaugrande further applied his comments to formal grammars in American linguistics and pointed out that the grammatical models were not demonstrably "particu-

71

larly insightful," but were simply "more tractable than real language" (p. 1). In other words, the linguistic models violated the transparency of language use much as Knobloch (1984) described.

In view of the urgent need for resocialization of the psychology of language use, it is perhaps, in retrospect, not anomalous at all that Osgood and Sebeok's (1954) Psycholinguistics: A survey of theory and research problems first saw the light of day as a Supplement to the Journal of Abnormal and Social Psychology.

Part Three

Sources of Cynicism

I have already claimed in Chapter 1 that even those who should be expected best of all to understand the archival literature in their area of expertise, namely those who write the textbooks and/or continue to do research in the same area, cannot be counted on to cite the research accurately and use it correctly. To demonstrate this aspect of psychology's decadence across the board would be far beyond the scope of this book. Part Three is dedicated to a narrow-band treatment of the topic, i.e., in the area of temporal organization of speech production.

Three chapters are devoted to three categories of psycholinguistic literature dedicated to this topic: (1) chapters on speech production in introductory textbooks; (2) some articles of major importance; (3) some passages that reflect important misunderstandings, artifacts, or misuse of data.

I do not wish to argue that the psychology of language use (specifically in the matter of temporal organization of speech production) is worse off than other research areas of psychology in these respects. I present the evidence simply as one example and as one facet of a decadence that I consider to exist across the board in psychology -- in research, publication, and teaching.

Chapter 5

Chapter and Verse

The present chapter is itself about chapters -- chapters and
sections of textbooks on the psychology of language use. My more
specific interest is the treatment in those chapters of the
empirical questions concerned with the temporal organization of
speech production. This more specific topic, the temporal
organization of speech production, has become the preoccupation
underlying most of the research my colleagues and I have carried
out over the past two decades. Hence, it provides a convenient
litmus test for such textbooks. Some textbooks completely
disregard all questions of temporal organization; some go further
and disregard all questions of production itself.

There is, however, a close connection between production and
temporal organization. All language production, whether in the
modality of speech or of writing or of ASL or any other, takes
place in real time. By and large, psycholinguistics has profoundly neglected this fact. Rommetveit (1974) has made this
neglect quite clear:

A characteristic feature of current approaches to acts of

verbal communication. . . is a tendency to spatialize and

detemporalize events. This is not only true of structural

linguistics, but also of general programmes for research in

psycholinguistics whose proponents claim agnostic inno-

cence and/or detached independence as far as any kind of

philosophical heritage is concerned (Miller & McNeill, 1969). (p. 5)

This Platonic heritage has shown itself also in the "reification of aspects of events" (p. 5). By these Rommetveit intended such as "internal and external structures of sentences" (Bever, 1970, p. 312), "deep sentence structures" (Rommetveit, 1972), and "underlying conceptual realities" (Fillmore, 1972, p. 9). And as Rommetveit concluded: "<u>What people actually say</u> is hence often relegated from the Platonic universe of <u>what can be said by 'the idealized speaker-hearer'</u>" (1974, p. 5).

Once spatialized in theoretical conceptualizations, whether in left-to-right terms or flow charts or other spatial models, speech production has no longer any temporal dimensionality. It can be handled readily in abstractions and with written demonstrational materials.

Before proceeding further, let me exemplify with two excerpts from two textbook chapters, how the neglect of temporal factors can very subtly subvert empirical logic. The first is from the chapter on sentence production in Fodor, Bever, and Garrett (1974):

> Perhaps the best sources of information from which to infer sentence-production processes are cases in which the functioning of the production system is less than optimal. Spontaneous speech is characteristically nonfluent and replete with traces of the speaker's changing decisions about what to say and how to say it. (p. 419)

The second is from the chapter on producing language in Harris and Coltheart (1986):

> Spontaneous speech and written language have many important differences. The most striking difference is that whereas formal written language consists of clearly segmented sentences which are normally completely grammatical, spoken language is not clearly divided into sentences, and typically contains many errors. (p. 212 f.)

The same fundamental error, however, was made in both passages. The reason why so much fancy footwork is necessary in spoken discourse is that it is precisely an interactive, communicative, social enterprise. It goes on in time, and the _tempus utile_, the usable time, is always limited by the social context and indeed by the very purposes for which speech is used. "Formal written language," on the other hand, is not time bound in any sense of the word. The reason is that formal written language is not a human behavior at all; it is, in the Bühlerian sense, the product of human enterprise. In other words, the passages above are comparing apples and oranges: speaking and the written. Were we instead to play fair and compare speaking and writing, we would find that writing too has its mistakes, editing, improvements, deletions, additions, etc. But even these can be sometimes bypassed in both writing and speaking, if we have the _time_ to sit in the shade for three hours of ruminating before we put pen to paper or fingers to word processor or words upon our lips.

In fact, however, the same comparison is made in much of the literature of the psychology of language use. That does not make it any less absurd. And once again, the precise absurdity is occasioned by the utter neglect of the fact that the temporal organization of speaking is of basic importance to any study of speech production -- or, for that matter, of writing.

As we shall see, once some consideration began to be afforded to temporal organization of speaking, the next danger was to conceptualize anything that made speaking differ from "formal written language" as error or disfluency. This too is both erroneous and the product of the same Written language bias in linguistics (Linell, 1982). Dell's (1986) recent formulation was more moderate and realistic, even though at the same time shortsighted:

Why is the language-production system error-prone? The main reason, I feel, is that the system must be productive. That is, it must allow for the production of novel combinations of items. (p. 319)

Notice that Dell did not speak of speaking, but of "the language-production system" itself. Again, modality is not what determines whether time is to be a factor. Note too, once again, that "production" itself is still not the problem; and in this respect, Dell was failing to get at the root of the problem. Production with an unlimited amount of time such as can be dedicated to preplanning or editing would either eliminate errors entirely or at least so diminish them as to render them no longer characteristic of language-production systems. _Time_ is the essential component that has been traditionally and consistently eliminated from research on the psychology of language use. The time in question, by the way, is not the sort of temporal measures that have been traditionally used -- reaction times, latencies, onset times, etc. -- but real time used for ongoing communicative purposes by means of language.

We can well proceed now to the various textbooks and their chapters on speech production. There are three _loci classici_ that can be used as one of the criteria for assessing these chapters. They are Boomer (1965), Goldman-Eisler (1968), and Maclay and Osgood (1959). This is an oversimplification of sorts; a number of Goldman-Eisler's articles were published well before 1968, for example. But whether or not a textbook writer (after 1968) referred to one or more of these sources gives us a fairly good criterion for suspecting emphasis or neglect of temporal organization in the textbook. Another criterion is whether or not the text even has a chapter or section on speech (sentence, language) production.

I find it of interest to note that there are a number of textbooks that fail on both criteria; i.e., they referred to none of the three sources and had no section on speech production. These include Deese (1970), List (1972, 1981), Miller (1981), and Slobin (1971, 1974, 1979).

By way of contrast, one of the earliest introductory textbooks written after the psycholinguistic revolution was John

B. Carroll's (1964) _Language and thought_. Already there were comments about two of Goldman-Eisler's (1951, 1954) early articles and a chapter dedicated largely to speech production.

The first edition of Hörmann's (1967) German textbook also appeared quite early, particularly early for the European scene. He too referred to one of Goldman-Eisler's (1964) earlier studies as well as to Maclay and Osgood (1959), but there was no reference to Boomer (1965) and no chapter on speech production. Boomer was not introduced even in the later textbooks of Hörmann, but the 1981 and 1986 textbooks had a chapter on _Strukturen der sprachlichen Äusserung_ (The Production of Utterances). Hörmann's use of _Äusserung_ was deliberate; he had no intention of becoming enmeshed in the matter of "sentence production," as Fodor et al. (1974), Foss and Hakes (1978), and David W. Carroll (1986) all entitled their chapters on production. His emphasis was clearly on the spoken utterance, not on sentential units, and he was wise enough not to speak of production without taking modality (speaking vs. writing) into account.

Two other German textbooks must be mentioned. The first is that of Engelkamp (1974). He omitted any mention of the _loci classici_, did not treat temporal organization at all, and treated speech production rather abstractly. Grimm & Engelkamp (1981), however, used all three sources and accepted without question the proposition that "about half the time in speaking is spent in pausing, and these pauses account for the most part for the variance of speech rate (Goldman-Eisler, 1968)" (p. 135; my

79

trans.).

There are two elements in this quotation that have been accepted on the word of Goldman-Eisler. They are both inaccurate and they have both been incorporated into the literature through citations such as this one (as we shall see further) in various textbooks. A glance at Kowal, Wiese, & O'Connell (1983, p. 388) will show that Goldman-Eisler's story-telling data on percentage of pause time/total time were more than two standard deviations greater than the grand mean (33%) derived from the extant archival literature on story telling. The percentage for interview data given there for purposes of comparison and for media data (Kowal, Bassett, & O'Connell, 1985, p. 6) were even lower (all means < 20%). And as to articulation rate, even if it may indeed be in some sense "a personality constant of remarkable invariance" (Goldman-Eisler, 1968, p. 25), articulation rate still varies from setting to setting and from phrase to phrase even within the same speaker. For example, O'Connell (1984b) found great variation in articulation rate in readings of various poems by the same poet or dramatic artist.

The mythology about half the time of speaking being spent in pausing has also been perpetuated in Aitchison (1976, 1982, 1983), Clark and Clark (1977), Ellis and Beattie (1986), Harris and Coltheart (1986), and Hörmann (1981, 1986). The oversimplification regarding articulation rate as "a personality constant of remarkable invariance" has been accepted by John B. Carroll (1964) and Clark and Clark (1977).

Of all the textbooks, perhaps Palermo's (1978) had the most unusual conceptualization of temporal phenomena in speech. They were all subsumed under the heading "Rhythm" (p. 132 f.), instead of being considered under speech production.

Although a number of the textbooks have presented Boomer's (1965) evidence (e.g., Aitchison, 1976, 1982, 1983; Clark & Clark, 1977; Ellis & Beattie, 1986; Fodor et al., 1974; Foss & Hakes, 1978; Garnham, 1985; Herriot, 1970; Paivio & Begg, 1981), none of them has treated his evidence critically. O'Connell and Slaymaker (1984) have concluded that Boomer's contentions must be rejected for the following reasons:

His data themselves are not entirely accurate; it is not at all evident that phonemic clauses can be identified operationally solely from primary stress and terminal juncture; his categorization of words and word fragments is questionable; the tabulation of hesitations by word-boundary positions is biased; the hypothesis itself is implausible, especially in the case of short clauses following a juncture pause; nor is it evident to what extent juncture pauses and hesitations in the first word-boundary position are associated functionally with the preceding clause, the next occurring clause, or the transition itself; finally, he excluded 56% of his data. (p. 202)

Further problems regarding the acceptance of evidence from both Goldman-Eisler (1968) and Maclay and Osgood (1959) will be taken up in the next chapter.

There are several recent textbooks in the psychology of language use that should be examined in more detail. The first of these was first published in English, translated into German, and then prepared as a second edition (Aitchison, 1976, 1982, 1983). Aitchison's division of pauses into "breathing pauses and hesitation pauses of the er. . . um variety" (1983, p. 231) is quite misleading. Some pauses are neither breathing nor hesitation pauses, and breathing pauses can and do co-occur with hesitations. Nor do we necessarily "slow down our rate of breathing when we speak" (p. 231). We may or may not; what we actually do is lower the inspiration/expiration time ratio during speaking. Nor do breathing pauses "account for only about 5 per cent of the gaps in speech" (p. 231; cf. Kowal, 1987). Nor do hesitation pauses "account for one-third to one-half of the time taken up in talking" (p. 231). One emphatic generalization is completely the reverse of the facts: "All researchers agree that speakers do not normally pause between clauses, they pause inside them" (p. 232). Presumably the erroneous generalization is traceable to Maclay and Osgood (1959):

> Yet -- finally -- statistical analysis of the distribution
> of Filled vs. Unfilled Pauses clearly shows that the former
> tend to coincide with the syntactical junctures at phrase
> boundaries, while the latter fall within phrases. (p. 41)

Involved here are not only the definitions of phrase and clause, but a number of artifactual conditions in Maclay and Osgood. These will be taken up in the next chapter.

The final five textbooks to be commented 'upon are all quite recent. Carroll (1986) has made a very plausible, but highly intuitive generalization in his chapter on speech production to the effect that "pauses are the oral equivalent of commas" (p. 270; see also Akinnaso, 1982, p. 105, for a comparable claim). Empirical investigations have indicated that the comma is actually the only type of punctuation mark that is not used consistently for pausing (see O'Connell & Kowal, 1986; Van De Water & O'Connell, 1986).

Ellis and Beattie (1986) incorporated into their textbook a chapter on "The psycholinguistics of speaking" (p. 115). On many topics, their book is refreshingly critical and historical in its orientation. But Ellis and Beattie omitted any mention of Maclay and Osgood (1959), and, as we have already seen, perpetuated the mythology from Goldman-Eisler (1968) that pausing "takes up as much time as the speech itself" (Ellis & Beattie, 1986, p. 19) and uncritically accepted Boomer's evidence that "pauses tend to cluster at or near the beginnings of clauses in spontaneous speech" (Ellis & Beattie, 1986, p. 120). Their contention that "a tip of the tongue state is effectively just a very long pause" (p. 123) is simply not correct. The tip of the tongue phenomenon has nothing to do, in fact, with silence; the term has been consistently used metaphorically. They also disregarded criticisms by Kowal and O'Connell (1985) of their position on cognitive rhythms, reduced Power's (1983) similar criticisms to a "but see" (p. 141) parenthesis, and included references (pp. 139 &

83

149) to nonexistent explanations elsewhere (Chapter 7) in their book. They clearly approved of the approach to speech production that "views speaking as translating thoughts into sentences, words and sounds" (p. 117).

Harris & Coltheart (1986) have already been criticized for their confusion of behavior and the product of behavior in their comparison of speaking and "formal written language" (p. 212). They also accepted quite uncritically the whole apparatus of Garrett's (e.g., 1982) model of speech production that began with meaning instead of ending with meaning: "roughly speaking, a non-linguistic representation of the basic idea the speaker wishes to convey" (p. 209). The model is a classic case of what Reddy (1979) has referred to as the conduit metaphor and Linell (1982) as the translation or recoding theory. But speakers do not translate meaning from pre-meaning; they produce meaning. Harris and Coltheart also presented "Well" (p. 213) as an example of either a false start or repetition. It is neither. Nor are unfilled pauses as such one of the "types of hesitation" (p. 213). Harris and Coltheart also questioned whether "pausing is a necessary part of language production" (p. 214). It is; but the Beattie and Bradbury (1979) experiment, which Harris and Colt-heart used to prove the point, has nothing to do with the logic of the answer. One cannot prove the obvious. There is no evidence in the Beattie and Bradbury (1979) experiment, in any event, that reduction of pauses was responsible for the "very marked increase in the amount of repetition" (Harris & Coltheart,

84

1986, p. 214). Nor is it demonstrably the case that discussions of academic topics typically do not involve "well-practiced utterances" (p. 215). Finally, Beattie and Bradbury made the same mistake as Dell (1986, p. 319) in stopping at "performance limitations" (p. 229) as the source of disfluencies in speech. The specific performance problem is quite obvious: <u>Tempus fugit</u>, time flies.

The next to last textbook to be commented upon is one by Garnham (1985). His chapter was on language production rather than just speech production. He accordingly discussed the sort of equipment needed to record handwriting: "More complex recording techniques (e.g., for forearm muscle activity) are required in investigations of handwriting" (p. 205). But forearm muscle activity is decidedly not coterminous with writing activity. Twirling a pencil absentmindedly between sentences would thoroughly distort such measurements of writing. Garnham also recognized only three methods of studying production: the study of faulty performance (errors, pathology), controlled experiments with normal subjects, and the writing of computer programs. The one method of investigation that is most urgently needed was not even mentioned -- naturalistic observation of genuinely communicative speech in social situations. Garnham too persisted in categorizing pauses among the disfluencies (although inconsistently; cf. pp. 206 & 208). He also understood Wells' (1951) First Law of Slips of the tongue as: "Each speech error results in a sequence of sounds that is permitted in the language being spoken" (p. 208). The underlying assumption was, of course, as it so often has been in traditional psycholinguistics, that the speaker is monolingual. If the speaker is working back and forth between two languages, such a limitation is ridiculous. Nor does latency of response always reliably and validly reflect "the difficulty of formulating a response" (p. 209). There are numerous reasons other than difficulty of formulation, e.g., simple reluctance to speak, that can result in long latencies. Garnham also made use of the conduit metaphor: "Representations are converted into speech or writing" (p. 209). And finally, speakers "use semantic knowledge to construct a literal meaning that can be used to express the intended meaning" (p. 210). But the fallacy in this principle was really only a corollary to the conduit metaphor itself. What has been prepackaged was assumed to be necessarily the literal meaning.

The last textbook to be considered is one by McNeill (1987). What he has presented as "a new approach" omits mention of all but one of the loci classici and mentions that one (Maclay & Osgood, 1959) only in passing. Although McNeill has incorporated a chapter on "Producing and Understanding Speech," the temporal organization of speech has been thoroughly neglected in favor of an abstract concept of "deep time" (p. 1). His neglect of real time is most notable in his incorrect definition of Kozhevnikov and Chistovich's (1965) concept of the syntagma, an articulatory unit bounded mandatorily by pauses. McNeill completely disregarded the pause component and described the syntagma as a meaning unit (p. 129).

And so, we find that there áre many ways of presenting or failing to present the material on temporal organization of speech production in an introductory textbook on the psychology of language use. Most of them have been seriously flawed, all of them have been seriously negligent of the true importance of time in speech production. In this respect, one can hardly rejoice over some sort of recency effect. The more recent textbooks have indeed manifested more interest in the temporal organization of speech production, but they definitely have not manifested a great deal of accuracy in treating the topic.

There is one more aspect of these topical textbook treatments to be considered. From textbook to textbook, the overlap of treatment has been astoundingly minimal; and where overlap does occur, it has manifested all too often the copycat phenomenon.

O'Connell (1987) has investigated the overlap of bibliographies in a number of the recent textbooks considered above. Since Carroll (1986) had a very extensive bibliography (919 entries), it was used as the base of the comparisons. Less than 20% of both Hörmann's (1986) and McNeill's (1987) bibliographical entries (54/278 & 66/373) coincided with Carroll's entries. Extending the investigation to include two more textbooks, Aitchison's (1983) and Paivio and Begg's (1981), reduced overlap to the following six entries: Bever (1970), Chomsky (1957, 1965), Fromkin (1971, 1973), and Sachs (1967).

Considered pedagogically, the lack of overlap must raise the question as to whether there is or is not some central core of instructional material that is mandatory in an introductory course on the psychology of language use -- not to speak of mandatory material regarding the temporal organization of speech production, or indeed speech production, or language production in general. The answer is no! That is to say that, as long as the vast confusion reigns as to what the psychology of language use is all about, and as long as the level of critical analysis remains as minimal as it is at present, the introductory text-books will go on communicating mainly confusion in any event. The lack of overlap in these textbooks is itself perhaps the best proof available that no one has any idea what the basics of the psychology of language use really are.

There is one more source of lack of overlap that should be mentioned. The textbooks discussed in this chapter can be categorized as American, English, or German, depending partly upon authorship and partly upon intended readership. Each of the three types has relied upon a regional (both nationalistically and native-language based) bias in the selection of archival literature to be included for discussion. In other words, despite our protests of internationalism, the psychology of language use remains quite provincial.

Chapter 6

Loci Classici et Res Novae

In the preceding chapter, a case was made for the thorough
inadequacy of current textbooks on the psychology of language use
in regard to language production, and more specifically speech
production and the temporal organization of speaking. Some
indications have already been given there that the three sources
referred to as loci classici are themselves involved in this
inadequacy. Chapter 5 can be looked upon as a tentative diagnosis, if you will; what we need now is an investigation of the
etiology of this pathology: not only what is wrong with the
archival literature in the field, but why it has developed
historically as it has.

All of us need some advice every once in a while. Ordinarily we seek such advice from people who are involved in the
matter at hand, who know the ropes, so to speak. This may be a
first mistake insofar as the expert, almost by definition, has no
distance from the question whatsoever. But at least we seek
advice or clues as to what might be wrong from someone who is au
courant. Going back more than 700 years is admittedly a bit
unusual. Thomas Aquinas (c. 1265/1978) has, however, given some
very insightful advice to a certain Brother John about scholarship: "Choose the way across the brooks and don't plunge at once
into the ocean! One must arrive at the more difficult by means
of the easier" (p. 250; my trans.). Someone should have given
psycholinguistics such sage advice decades ago, but it is not too

89

late to learn from our mistakes. We have been saddled with the headiest of models, theories, and generalizations imaginable in an area of research in which we are still profoundly ignorant of the most basic facts and relationships. It is with this conviction that I undertake to examine some samples from the archival literature regarding the temporal organization of speech production, and in particular the loci classici.

It would be a dreadful mistake to assume that the research tradition in question begins with Maclay and Osgood (1959). It would have been desirable for them to have examined the extant literature in detail, and I am quite convinced that, had they known that their research was not going to be accepted as "an exploratory investigation" (p. 19), but as one of the most important contributions to date, they would indeed have presented the background literature. As things turned out, the background literature was not reviewed until the current decade (Appel, Dechert, & Raupach, 1980; O'Connell & Kowal, 1983). Rochester's (1973) critical review of the literature on pauses in spontaneous speech must also be acknowledged, however, as an important milestone. Butterworth's (1980) chapter, on the other hand, was neither a critical nor a thorough review; Bloch's (1946) was the only pause research predating Goldman-Eisler that even mentioned by Butterworth.

And so, it should be emphasized at the very beginning that Maclay and Osgood did present their evidence in good faith as an exploratory study. Without forgetting that important fact, let us try to analyze the importance of their study as objectively as possible.

With regard to their corpus, it should be kept in mind that it was not continuous discourse at all, but a selection of 163 longer utterances (M - 309 words) by 13 male speakers at a professional conference. Essentially, therefore, the data were monologic, although the setting in principle allowed exchange or interruption. But a further selection was made for the analysis of hesitation pauses, such that only isolated phrases were represented. Hence, no inferences whatsoever regarding hesitation pauses relative to clauses or any other syntactic units more comprehensive than phrases were in principle possible from this subselection of data.

More specifically, Maclay and Osgood wished to test Lounsbury's first hypothesis:

> Lounsbury's first hypothesis was that hesitation pauses will tend to occur at points of highest uncertainty in spontaneously produced utterances. Since, as Fries notes, there are many more members (alternatives) in his lexical classes than in his function-word classes, we should expect pauses of both types to occur more frequently before lexical words than before function words" (p. 32).

Note that Maclay and Osgood were not testing Lounsbury's first hypothesis in its intended comprehensive sense; they were testing only a logical corollary of the hypothesis, a subhypothesis, if you will. In order to test "points of highest uncertainty in spontaneously produced utterances," it is both logically and empirically of absolute necessity that the uncertainty structure of the utterances be available intact. In other words, the phrase structure uncertainty was only a small component of the uncertainty structure of the spontaneous utterances themselves, and it could therefore tell us nothing about the comprehensive distribution of the uncertainty structure as such. This is not to say that incidence of hesitation pauses before lexical and function word classes is not of interest and importance. The evidence has, however, not typically been interpreted realistically in light of the above limitations.

But there are difficulties even with the corpus itself. Maclay and Osgood themselves acknowledged that it involved "after-the-fact interpretations" (p. 25). The first interpretative step was actually taken by secretaries. They were instructed not to clean up the text, but "to produce as literal a transcription as possible" (p. 23) from the tape recordings of the conference. A crucial component of this version is the fact that the secretaries introduced the first segmentation of the text. This segmentation, indicated mainly by punctuation and capitalization in their typed versions, was influenced by whatever variables entered into their perception of the spoken corpus. The secretaries were, in other words, implicitly reporting, among other things, pauses; and we know from more recent literature that:

An appreciable number of false positives and false nega-

tives and over- and under-estimates of duration contami-
nate such reports. The natural language in question, the
native or nonnative proficiency (or total lack thereof) of
the reporter, the duration bracket of the actual pauses,
syntax, syllabic prolongation, loudness, intonation, and
temporal parameters such as articulation rate and mean
duration of actual pauses in the corpus all conspire to
influence these reports. (Stuckenberg & O'Connell, in
press; see also Adams, 1979; Carpenter & O'Connell, in
press; Chiappetta, Monti, & O'Connell, 1987; Duez, 1985).
The reports produced from this first interpretative step
could not reasonably be relied upon to reflect hesitation types
veridically.

But there was a second interpretative step on the part of
the two authors. Independently each used both the conference
tape recording and the secretaries' transcriptions to identify
hesitations. Then, only those hesitations identified by both
authors were included in the analyses. Maclay and Osgood were
convinced that this procedure insured the high probability "that
all hesitations upon which the analysis is based really did occur
at the points indicated" (p. 25). The argumentation overlooked
the fact that the perceptual and reporting determinants that
occasion false positives and false negatives are precisely common
to all the procedures of the experiment. Stuckenberg and
O'Connell (1987), for example, obtained a false positive rate of
16% across all subjects in the identification of pauses. Maclay

93

and Osgood's reliability in identification of hesitations simply did not insure veridicality.

There is one more problem in the Maclay and Osgood study that cannot be ignored. Their definition of unfilled pauses is highly problematic. The category was essentially a garbage category: "These were marked when there was judged to be an abnormal hesitation in speech that could not be referred to the three previous categories" (p. 24). There are two further specific problems with the category of unfilled pauses: (1) Their identification was acknowledged to be dependent on "rate of delivery" of each speaker; (2) They included in altogether unknown proportions both "silence of unusual length" and "non-phonemic lengthening of phonemes":

> UP has two major forms: silence of unusual length and non-phonemic lengthening of phonemes. This is necessarily a matter of judgment on the part of listeners (here, the authors) familiar with the pace and style of a particular speaker. What may be clearly noted as an instance of Un-filled Pause for one speaker would not be so judged for another speaker, say, with a slower rate of delivery. (p. 24)

I have spent a great deal of space on the Maclay and Osgood study because it has had such an important role in influencing subsequent research. What is truly astounding is that the conclusions of Maclay and Osgood were simply accepted without any effort whatsoever at critique. O'Connell and Kowal's (1983)

94

summary can well be made my own here:

> Both the subjective method of identifying unfilled pauses
> and the very small, selective, atypical sub-corpus on
> which analyses are based make the results minimally signifi-
> cant. Undoubtedly the historic influence this research has
> exerted in stimulating further research has been far-reach-
> ing. (p. 235)

Even more recently, Kowal (1987, p. 469 f.) has noted that
what had been universally accepted as the definition of the false
start (FS) in Maclay and Osgood (1959) is not at all in accord
with their actual description, in which the component "following"
(p. 24) the initial segment was referred to as the FS.

With regard to the second of the loci classici, I have
already quoted the conclusions of O'Connell and Slaymaker (1984)
that the entire study must be dismissed as fallacious. Boomer's
(1965) investigation actually took its lead from Maclay and
Osgood's (1959) complaint that "no independent method of defining
encoding units has been developed" (p. 23). Boomer then provi-
sionally accepted the phonemic clause as defined by Trager and
Smith (1951) as fulfilling this need, arguing that his contention
would be confirmed if the hypothesis that hesitations "occur
predominantly at the beginning of these units" (p. 150) were
confirmed.

At this point, he might well have reasoned instead, as did
Brotherton (1979):

> Boomer assumed that planning and speaking must be concurrent

operations in the case of clauses without pauses but in
doing so begged the question of why some clause transitions
were fluent whereas others were not. (p. 194)

Brotherton was, of course, calling attention to the fact that 56%
of Boomer's data failed to manifest hesitations in clauses at
all. This is really the more interesting finding, and Brotherton
was perfectly correct: Planning and speaking are concurrent
operations. But Boomer proceeded to categorize his data inconsistently, array them artifactually, tally them inaccurately,
analyze them incorrectly, and draw from them invalid conclusions
(see O'Connell & Slaymaker, 1984).

But, just as in the case of Maclay and Osgood, the failure
to critique a finding that was not even plausible has been
monumental on the part of psycholinguists. As we found in
Chapter 5, Boomer's findings have been recapitulated again and
again in the textbooks. The archival literature too (e.g., Ford
& Holmes, 1978, p. 35) has not questioned his evidence. Occasionally there has been a hint of something amiss, but no effort
to criticize the original investigation.

The third of our <u>loci classici</u> has undoubtedly been the most
influential of the three. Goldman-Eisler (1968) is conveniently
an overview of all Goldman-Eisler's previous work on the temporal
organization of speech. Her influence has been gratefully
acknowledged by the participants of the 1980 Kassel conference in
dedicating to her the published report of the conference,
<u>Temporal variables in speech: Studies in honour of Frieda</u>

Goldman-Eisler (Dechert & Raupach, 1980).

In addition, I owe Frieda Goldman-Eisler my own personal gratitude. Shortly after the completion of our first experiment on temporal organization in speech production (O'Connell, Kowal, & Hörmann, 1969), I had an opportunity to discuss the manuscript with her in London. She was most encouraging regarding the research and added, to my amazement, that, were she beginning her own research over again, she would begin it with precisely the experimental methods I was using (personal communication, 1969).

In the statement of the problem to be engaged in the overview of her research, Goldman-Eisler (1968) mentioned "the disinclination of experimental psychologists to analyze the complex of conversational behavior or of such skills generally as involve temporal patterns" (p. 2) as part of the

> position of psychology at large. Living speech and language
> as used in spontaneous human communication was placed
> outside the pale of the legitimate area of psychological
> enquiry as indeed were other active pursuits of human
> beings. (p. 1 f.)

She went on to describe the import of her research as follows:

> Pauses interrupting the smooth flow of speech thus became
> the main subject of all further investigation. The ques-
> tion presenting itself was: if activity in conversation,
> if vocal action, is a peripheral phenomenon, might not
> absence of activity indicate the presence of central ac-
> tivity? A technique for studying the relation between

97

speaking and thinking seemed to have been found. (p. 4)

We know now by virtue of hindsight that the heady optimism of 1968 was premature. In particular, "the relation between speaking and thinking" is still resistant to our investigation and understanding. Still, Goldman-Eisler's was a brave beginning, and it had little support from within the ranks of psychologists.

I have already discussed in Chapter 5 two of Goldman-Eisler's conclusions that have found the widest audience through inclusion in textbooks: her convictions that almost half the time of speaking is spent in pausing and that articulation rate is a personal constant. In the following, I would like to limit my critique to several specific points that my colleagues and I have pursued in our research.

The first of these is Goldman-Eisler's generalization that "fluent transitions between sentences are extremely scarce even in spontaneous speech" (1972, p. 111). She understood by fluent transitions those without pauses or with pauses shorter than 0.5 sec. Using this definition, Kowal, Bassett, and O'Connell (1983) analyzed interview data: "The application of this definition to the present data would actually raise the percentage of measured fluent transitions well above 50%" (p. 13).

The second is Goldman-Eisler's statement to the effect that "a large proportion of pauses in spontaneous speech does not fit in with the linguistic structure, and does not serve communication" (1968, p. 31). O'Connell, Kowal, and Hörmann (1969) expressed the conviction that "both filled and unfilled pauses, even when they do not 'fit in with the linguistic structure', are communicative in their function" (p. 63). Evidence from media interviews (Kowal, Bassett, & O'Connell, 1985) and from politicians (Kowal, 1987) has confirmed our conviction. An example from an as yet unpublished analysis of one of the most eloquent passages of oratory of modern times, Martin Luther King's "I have a dream" address, involves a pause of 1.13 sec duration between article and adjective: "the/public-address system." In cases such as this one, the violation of the hearers' expectations is precisely the rhetorical emphasis communicated by the longer than usual pause between two closely related words.

The third of these points brings us back to Kowal, Wiese, and O'Connell's (1983) finding that Goldman-Eisler's percentage of pause time/total time was more than two standard deviations greater than the grand mean in the archival literature on storytelling. The source of difficulty is to be found in Goldman-Eisler's (1961) operational definition of words. All "irrelevant vocal productions, i.e. noise, such as repetition of the same words or other obvious forms of marking time vocally" (p. 167) were excluded from her word counts, but nonetheless entered into the determination of total time. This decision automatically yielded a slower speech rate and shorter phrase length, and correspondingly a higher percentage of pause time/total time, since the time of the "irrelevant vocal productions" was relegated to pause time.

The fourth and final point to be made regarding Goldman-Eisler's methodology is her use of the concept of cognitive rhythms. In her (1968) book, she summarized the research on cognitive rhythms as follows:

> The evidence obtained from spontaneous speech, readings and simultaneous translations confirmed that the successive speech and silence durations can have a regular structure, periods of considerable hesitancy alternating with periods of fluency in a rhythmic fashion. (p. 94)

The controversy regarding the existence of cognitive rhythms lasted almost exactly two decades and culminated in a confrontation between Power (1983) and Beattie (1984) in the pages of Language and Speech. Kowal and O'Connell (1985) have tried to lay the matter to rest. They argued that

> the term itself is a misnomer, that the relevance of articulation rate has been neglected, that fluent and hesitant phases of cognitive rhythms have been assessed both subjectively and intuitively, that the speech-production model underlying the concept is simplistic, and that the empirical evidence is based on an extraordinarily small corpus which has been described inadequately in the research literature. (p. 93)

In the remainder of the present chapter, I would like to discuss several fairly current representatives of the archival literature on temporal organization of speech production. The important point to be made thereby is that current methodology is in no way an improvement over the _loci classici_ that have been criticized above.

The first of these is a monograph by Deese (1984), earlier reported in part as an article (1978) and a chapter (1980). Deese is refreshingly independent of mainstream psycholinguistics and has his "doubts about the value of experimentation in cognitive psychology" (1984, p. 6). In fact, he considers the prospect of understanding the "process whereby some mental activity becomes speech" to be "hopelessly unattainable" (p. 6) with current techniques. Hence, he is opposed to artificial laboratory situations as sources of speech samples, and he criticizes both Goldman-Eisler (1954) and Maclay and Osgood (1959) for asking "speakers to produce spontaneous speech under artificial circumstances" (p. 17). The fact is that neither of these studies involved such artificiality.

Deese made use of subjective estimates of short, medium, and long pauses. He insisted that there were no instances of false positives, the report of pauses where there actually are none (1980, p. 75), and relied on "a high correlation between perceived and physical length of pause (.85)" (p. 74) for an indication of the veridicality of the estimates in his study. He acknowledged, however, that "there is also an interaction that depends upon whether the pause terminates a sentence or occurs in the middle of a clause" (p. 74). Logically, nonetheless, the high correlation does _not_ exclude the occurrence of either false positives or false negatives. The evidence offered above in the discussion of Maclay and Osgood (1959) would indicate that Deese's claims are not justified (see Adams, 1979; Carpenter & O'Connell, in press; Chiappetta, Monti, & O'Connell, 1987; Duez, 1985; Stuckenberg & O'Connell, in press). Once again, reliability cannot be accepted for validity.

Although it does not concern temporal organization as such, it should be noted that Deese's examples of sentences are not in accord with his operational definitions (1984, pp. 24 & 31).

The fact that skilled media personnel (see Kowal, Bassett, & O'Connell, 1985) and politicians (see Kowal, 1987) used filled pauses to good rhetorical effect should also bring into question Deese's generalization that "it is universally agreed that filled pauses are not very elegant" (1984, p. 95). What we are instead dealing with here is simply one more example of The written language bias in linguistics.

A far more important problem involves the operational definition of hesitation pauses. They turn out to be, as they were for Maclay and Osgood (1959), a garbage category:

Hesitation pauses, in what follows, make up a leftover category (as they do in most writing on the subject). That is, they are the pauses that are left over when we have accounted for all of the pauses we can by invoking the most conservative of linguistic standards. I have tried to separate hesitation pauses from pauses that serve some direct linguistic or rhetorical function by invoking three criteria: (1) Does the pause have an interpretation? (2) Does

102

it serve some grammatical function, such as marking the end of a sentence or phrase? (3) Does it make the discourse more easily comprehended (as in marking members of a series? (1984, p. 98)

The combination of subjective estimation and garbage category makes the actual identity of hesitation pauses quite questionable and their function quite mysterious, even though Deese has assumed "that every aspect of the production of speech, save for certain pathologies associated with damage to the brain, is functional" (1984, p. 7).

There is one more rather serious problem regarding Deese's findings. They are presented in two somewhat discrepant tables (1980, p. 78; 1984, p. 101) in terms of disfluencies per 100 words. Since the syl/word index differs dramatically from corpus to corpus and especially from one native language to another, the rate of occurrence per word is not a generalizable index, as the norms for various languages presented by Fucks (1955) clearly indicate. Had Deese included a mean syl/word index for his corpus, the tables would have been considerably more useful.

In view of all these objections, the significance of Deese's findings is hard to evaluate. It can be said in his defense, however, that even his most speculative interpretations are thought provoking and uninhibited by mainstream psycholinguistics.

My rationale for selecting the last empirical study to be critiqued in this chapter is rather idiosyncratic. It happened to be the most recent article to come across my desk, the very day I left Chicago in December, 1986. It was chosen, therefore, because it is the most recent example I could incorporate into this book.

The study is Gee's (1986) investigation of "Units in the production of narrative discourse." My comments, I'm afraid, cannot be in any respect positive. The study was entirely intuitive in its approach, eschewed both descriptive and inferential statistics, was terminologically and operationally vague, logically inconsequential, and poorly written and proofread.

More specifically, the data were divided into two subcorpora. For the first subcorpus, a "prosodic transcription" was available; for the second, "measurements of temporal structures" (p. 391) were available. No cogent argumentation was made from either of these objective sources in the course of the article.

The empirical logic was also seriously flawed, as the following indicates:

> Major transitions or breaks in the plot of a story tend
> to have longer pauses than more minor transitions or
> breaks. If this is indeed true, we can use pausing as evi-
> dence of larger units in the construction of a text or, put
> another way, as evidence of major discourse-level transi-
> tions or boundaries in the text. (p. 393)

The logic is cogent if and only if longer pauses are used by speakers only for "major discourse-level transitions or boundaries". In actuality, the argumentation is circular: "Indeed, this is one way one can find such units in the case of languages which are not written" (p. 393). In Gee's second subcorpus, as a matter of fact, the fourth longest pause was definitely not at a major boundary, but Gee segmented the text there anyway: "children (.980 ms) shouting" (p. 418). Even though the segmentation was inappropriate, the position became a major boundary because of the duration of the pause. It should be noted, however, that the decimals in all of Gee's durations were misplaced. Presumably he intended 980 ms in the present instance.

Although he referred to it three times, Michaels and Collins (1984) was not listed in Gee's references. He also referred to Sabin, Clemmer, O'Connell, and Kowal (1979) as the source of his statement that "at least some elderly people tend to pause somewhat more and somewhat longer than younger subjects" (p. 403), only to go on to qualify the statement. Sabin et al. (1979) had nothing to say about "elderly people" and limited their study to children and adults.

The most objectionable element of Gee's presentation, however, was his failure to use the archival literature on narrative discourse itself. Kowal, Wiese, and O'Connell (1983) spelled out in great detail the data on temporal organization from more than 20 empirical studies in the archival literature. No use was made of these data by Gee.

In Chapter 8, I will take up the use of _line_ by the ethnologists as a unit of oral discourse. For the present, I will simply assert apodictically that the concept of _line_ as used by

105

Gee has no scientific merit and communicates no intelligibility in his analyses. Oral discourse is not organized into lines and stanzas, and the metaphorical terminology that asserts such to be the case throws no light on the situation whatsoever.

In short, Gee's analyses are worthless. A competent professor of freshman composition would have presented a far more insightful, perceptive, and correct analysis of Gee's data-- without the useless nomenclatural impedimenta.

Major research contributions to the archival literature on the temporal organization of speech production have not been impressive in furthering the development of a strong psychology of language use.

Chapter 7

Stranger than Fiction

Allow me to begin this chapter with a brief dialogue and a commentary on it:

> "One more thing," said Humkoke, as he pulled a yellow cookie can off a shelf next to Murke's desk, "what are these snips of tape you have in this can?"
>
> Murke turned crimson. "They're. . . I collect a certain sort of leftovers," he said.
>
> "What sort of leftovers?" asked Humkoke.
>
> "Silence," said Murke, "I collect silence." (Böll, 1958, p. 45; my trans.)

In Heinrich Böll's delightful little satire, <u>Doktor Murkes gesammeltes Schweigen</u> (The collected silence of Dr. Murke), the story of an eccentric gentleman who snipped various types of silences from radio-studio tape recordings is related. Murke complains, however: "There's not much yet; I have only three minutes. But then there's not a lot of silence" (p. 46; my trans.). The collection of spliced-out sections of "sighing, breathing, absolute silence" (p. 45; my trans.) seems to us completely ludicrous. In some sense, however, it is more believable than the anomalies and aberrations to be found in the domain of scientific research on the temporal organization of speech.

Note, too, that the archival literature with which we've been dealing in the last two chapters is not necessarily "fact stranger than fiction" in the sense of "empirical truths astounding in nature." Precious little empirical truth has been culled from the research, and none of it could be termed astounding findings or scientific breakthrough.

I am aware that my own cynicism still remains the real obstacle to credibility. The anomalies and aberrations reported here probably still seem to most readers unlikely or at least highly exaggerated and taken out of context. The picture is being painted by the cynicism itself rather than by the facts of the case!

The present chapter is an attempt to gather together some of the more extreme cases in the archival literature and spell out some of their implications and corollaries, even while continuing the search for etiology. Once again, why does confusion arise in research on temporal organization of speech?

One very important source of confusion is a failure on the part of many researchers to appreciate the complexity of temporal organization. We can use a very simple example to illustrate this complexity, noting as we do that the additional complications of stress, intonation, and pitch variations are being disregarded. Not that they operate independently of temporal organization. But then they don't really _operate_ at all; along with all the other nuances of speech, including the temporal organization, they are operated. That is to say (redundantly, I know), they are used by a human agent for communicative purposes.

Our example, then, can be the simple expression I LOVE YOU.

Let's assume a very shy young man who states it with a bit of pausing. Pauses in speech occur very seldom within words. Pausing will occur, then, after I and/or after LOVE. But one long pause of, say, 1.4 sec is not necessarily the equivalent of two pauses of 0.7 sec, and they in turn are not the equivalent of two pauses of 0.3 and 1.1 sec. Stated so abstractly here, these differences may seem trivial. To the young lady listening for the real meaning of the utterance, the differences would be very critical.

Basically, the offtime component in speaking, pausing, can vary in: (1) position of occurrence, (2) numerosity of pauses, and (3) duration of pauses. These components have not been carefully distinguished consistently in the archival research. Braehler and Zenz (1975) have presented many of these problems in their important contribution on methods of temporal measurement.

The pausing is not, however, the only component of the temporal organization; it is only the offtime component. To return to our simple example, even an expression as simple as I LOVE YOU can be uttered with fast or slow articulation rate or a variable articulation rate. Articulation rate reflects the ontime component of temporal organization. If we were to accept Foss and Hakes' (1978) arbitrary and non-empirical limitation to the effect that "stressed syllables last 200-350 msec" (p. 76), there would not be a large range possible for our shy young man. Fortunately, the data of Van De Water and O'Connell (1986, p. 535) offer us the possibility of syllables well over a half second in emphatic settings. Our as yet unpublished data from Martin Luther King are even more helpful; he prolongs syllables up to 1.37 sec ("and I've SEEN the promised land"). Foss and Hakes have obviously overgeneralized without adequate evidence.

Many factual errors and errors in empirical logic can be traced to misunderstandings of temporal dimensionality. Turner and Pöppel (1983, p. 296) provide a classic example:

⌐A human speaker will pause for a few milliseconds
every three seconds or so, and in that period decide on
the precise syntax and lexicon of the next three seconds.
A listener will absorb about three seconds of heard speech
without pause or reflection, then stop listening briefly in
order to integrate and make sense of what he has heard.⌐

The immediate question that should arise is: "What can happen in 'a few millisconds'?" One cannot breathe in that short a period of time. In fact, our articulatory skills are not finely tuned enough to plan and execute such pauses. Nor are such short pauses even perceptible to the human listener. And as for deciding three seconds worth of "precise syntax and lexicon," forget it. Even the physical measurement of such minuscule durations is possible only with the most sensitive of instrumentation and hardly in the noisy settings of most discourse. Were Turner and Pöppel correct, the expected percentage of pause time/total time would be 0.06%, a far cry from Grimm and Engelkamp's (1981) "about half the time" (p. 135).

The only data that come anywhere near the Turner and Pöppel

norm are those of Glukhov (1975). He has given percentages (based on live radio broadcasts) that range from 4.2% to 2.6% for six different languages (English French, German, Italian, Portuguese, and Spanish). I am convinced that Glukhov's data were somehow misconstrued (perhaps in the process of translation from the original Russian). Were the decimal points to be moved one place to the right, the percentages would be in accord with the archival literature. If Turner and Pöppel and Glukhov are correct, the rest of the world is wrong.

The opposite extreme is no less objectionable. The insistence on the part of Butterworth (1973) that percentages of pause time/total time of less than 20% reflect "either recitation or unconsidered ramblings" (p. 773) is unfounded. Speakers in interviews (Kowal, Wiese, & O'Connell, 1983, p. 388) and media personnel (Kowal, Bassett, & O'Connell, 1985, p. 6) were guilty of neither of these failings, although in all these cases the mean percentages of pause time/total time were less than 20%.

Turner and Pöppel wished to make still more of the three seconds of speaking:

> This fundamental "parcel of experience" turns out to be
> about three seconds. The three-second period, roughly
> speaking is the length of the human present moment. (p. 296)

Van De Water and O'Connell's (1985, p. 399) data from poetry readings and their (Van De Water & O'Connell, 1986, p. 535) data from American radio homilies manifested no case of any overlap whatsoever with the three-second norm of Turner and Pöppel (1983;

111

see Pöppel, 1985).

At another extreme, Esser (1977, p. 145) claimed that his speakers used 63.4% of their time in pausing. The only other claim of such a high percentage can be pieced together from Aitchison's (1983) statements that "around 40 to 50 per cent of an average spontaneous utterance consists of silence" (p. 231) and her additional statement that hesitation pauses "account for one-third to one-half of the time taken up in talking" (p. 231). If the two components are to be considered independent, they would add up to between 60% and 75% of the total time and would leave only 40%-25% as productive ontime.

Hänni (1974) also disregarded the complex dimensionality of temporal organization. He argued that, "If extraneous auditory input during silent pauses fails to disrupt ongoing speech, these same silent pauses cannot be serving the function of planning periods for the speech to follow immediately thereafter" (O'Connell, 1980a, p. 24). But he analyzed only one dimension of silent pauses, their duration. Or, as I have stated in an earlier critique:

> He did not consider at all their frequency or their posi-
> tioning or patterning in the discourse. The argument is
> somewhat like that of a youngster who squeezes one end of
> a balloon and exclaims: "Look! I made it smaller." Obvious-
> ly, the balloon has simply betaken itself elsewhere.
> Similarly, tremendous variation is possible within the
> silent-pause system of a given corpus of speech, without the

slightest change in the mean length of silent pauses.
(O'Connell, 1980a, p. 24)

Grosjean, Grosjean, and Lane (1979, p. 58) and Gee and Grosjean (1983, p. 411) made a similar one-dimensional mistake in their logic. Both articles made use of the same set of "completely isolated passages divorced from any communicative intent or expressive function" (O'Connell, 1984b, p. 19). My more extended commentary on a previous occasion was the following:

Gee and Grosjean (1983) use only mean proportionalities of pause duration, and only those _within_ sentences at that. Actual pause durations are not predicted at all. Further, the model does not engage "temporal organization per se" in any way. At best, only a partial aspect of the temporal organization of _off_-time enters into the correlations offered in support of the model; _on_-time organization does not enter into the correlations at all. Finally, the already isolated sentences used as data base were distorted away from a normal performance by the specific instruction "to read 14 sentences at five different rates" (Gee & Grosjean, 1983, p. 413). In other words, the temporal organization can well be supposed to have been determined not so much by prosodic structure per se as by the specific instructions to _alter_ the temporal organization itself. (O'Connell, 1984b, p. 19 f.)

Once again, the complex dimensionality of temporal organization has been neglected by Grosjean and his colleagues.

Another logical error can be diagnosed in three different studies: Kowal, O'Connell, O'Brien, and Bryant (1975, pp. 553 & 562); Rochester, Thurston, and Rupp (1977, p. 74); and Wiese (1983, p. 186). In all these cases, the same problem was evident: Mean pause durations were presented that undercut the minimum cutoff point for measurement of pauses. If only pauses longer in duration than the cutoff point are accepted into the data base, it is, of course, impossible to obtain a mean that undercuts the cutoff point. The logical distinction between non-occurrence and a genuine zero-entry is sometimes difficult to discern or even notice, particularly when non-occurrence is not frequent. My own hypothesis regarding the origin of these means is that non-occurrences were taken to be zero-entries and incorporated into the calculations of the means. Without access to all the steps of data collection and tabulation in all the cases, my diagnosis remains an educated guess. But even if the etiology may have been something else in one or another of the cases, the occurrence of such illegitimate means is instructive. The danger of not discerning between non-occurrences and zero-entries is, by the way, particularly prominent when automated data collection and computerized analyses are being used.

What cutoff point should be accepted as a minimum in the measurement of pauses has been discussed by Braehler and Zenz (1975), by Hieke, Kowal, and O'Connell (1983), and by O'Connell & Kowal (1984). It has become customary in current research to use a cutoff point between 0.2 and 0.3 sec, after Goldman-Eisler

(1968), to exclude shorter "gaps in phonation" that are "determined by the need to adjust the position of articulation" (p. 12). But some research has used no cutoff point whatsoever (e.g., Henze, 1953; Wilkes & Kennedy, 1969) or, at the other extreme, cutoff points of greater than 2.0 sec (e.g., Siegman, 1979). Such differences in choice of cutoff point alter the percentage of pause time/total time, articulation rate, mean pause duration, and mean phrase length (defined as syl/pause). Hieke, Kowal, and O'Connell (1983) argued that "short pauses (0.13-0.25 sec) are indeed psychologically functional" (p. 212). They opted for the 0.13 sec cutoff point. O'Connell and Kowal (1984) provided normative comparisons using both a traditional cutoff point (0.27 sec) and the suggested one (0.13 sec); with the latter cutoff point, 318 more pauses (1304 > 986) were measurable, and these were on the average 0.11 sec shorter (0.50 < 0.61 sec) than with the larger cutoff point.

If research is to become comparable from one study to another, either a common cutoff point must be adopted or norms such as these for transposition of data collected with variant cutoff points must be developed.

The research shortcomings to be discussed in the remainder of this chapter arise not so much from a misunderstanding of the dimensionality of temporal organization itself but from other logical or methodological errors. It is hardly instructive, for example, to find in the archival literature generalizations regarding various natural languages that are actually character-

istic only of the idiosyncratic performance of a single individual. This is exactly what appeared in Barik's (1977, p. 120)
research -- a classic case of $\underline{N}$ = 1. The same data had been
presented already by Barik (1973, 1975) and they all added up to
much ado about nothing. I will cite here my previous critique of
Barik's research:

> Any valid comparison across natural language systems
> must have as an absolute minimum a comparable data base
> in each of the languages to be compared. This requirement
> sounds so basic as to be trivial as well as easily satis-
> fied. But it is neither. The data base must be adequate
> to be representative of the language in question in such a
> way that its characteristics cannot be attributable to
> speech genre, individual differences in speakers, random
> variation, experimental instructions, or any other identi-
> fiable confounding variable. (O'Connell, 1980a, p. 25)

The logic of Beattie and Bradbury (1979) was aberrant in a
quite different way. They started with an impossible empirical
question about pauses: "Are they also integral to speech in the
sense that spontaneous speech cannot occur without them?"
(Beattie, 1983, p. 34). Since one simply cannot speak over any
considerable span of time without pausing, the question becomes
chimerical. But the logic of the experiment carried out by
Beattie and Bradbury was in addition highly implausible.
In the crucial condition, subjects were given a light signal
contingent upon pauses of 600 msec. Subjects were told that the

116

light was a signal that "their story-telling was particularly poor at certain points" (Beattie, 1983, p. 34). Beattie and Bradbury interpreted the subsequent decrease in pauses and increase in hesitations as follows:

> Hesitations would seem to be an integral part of speech in
> every sense -- subjects cannot produce spontaneous speech
> without them, although speakers do seem to be able to
> substitute repetition in speech for unfilled pauses, when
> required. (Beattie, 1983, p. 35)

The interpretation was completely unfounded and implausible. The subjects obviously did not know what they had done wrong and were thoroughly disoriented by their unsuccessful efforts to "improve" to the satisfaction of the experimenter. This is at least a plausible reason for their "repetition" -- a simple search for what they had already done wrong.

By now, the reader should not be surprised by anything. Fliess (1949) even developed an essentially psychoanalytic taxonomy of pauses, including urethral-erotic, anal-erotic, and oral-erotic silences. Again, I cite from a previous critique:

> The first of these included ordinary interruptions in
> expected locations, the second disruptive pauses, and the
> third a temporary replacement of verbalization by silence
> -- whatever that might be. The article is great entertain-
> ment for a rainy evening, but its empirical logic is de-
> plorable. (O'Connell & Kowal, 1983, p. 230)

Mahl (1958, p. 349) contended, in a similar vein, that the

117

individuals who use the most filled pauses were weaned early, had strict parents, and are compulsive.

Mahl and Fliess were writing three and four decades ago. It is disappointing, however, to find that such basic and serious errors are still being made in research design. Butcher (1981) in his otherwise fine study of the speech pause, for example, expected speakers to speak "at a normal rate" while wearing "a rubber anaesthetics mask. . . which covered both nose and mouth and was fitted with a. . . gauze filter" (p. 65). Speakers at the slow rate and the fast rate, however, did not wear comparable equipment.

Researchers can obviously become so involved in the details of their research that they indeed cannot see the forest for the trees. This is the only way Foppa (1984; cited in Cranach, 1986) could have questioned "the possibility of communicating the intention to speak, except of course through the spoken word itself" (p. 163). And it's the only way Garrett (1982) could have thought that "the target of utterance is, in fact, grammatical speech" (p. 21). Both these pronouncements are patently absurd. The fact of the matter is that "the goal of making sentences is to know what exists" (Cahalan, 1985, p.15). The myopia occasioned by research involvement is sometimes testable by a moment's reflection -- or a bit of common sense.

Fact is indeed sometimes stranger than fiction. But the facts about empirical research are not the same as empirical

118

truths culled from research.   We are left with a multitude of regrettable instances of the former and all too little of the latter.

Part Four

Some Unlikely Partners

The topics to be discussed in the following four chapters--
writing, punctuation, the poetic line, and poetic oral readings
-- have an extrinsic bond among themselves in that all of them
have been neglected in psycholinguistic research. But they can
be and should be re-integrated with the main body of research on
the psychology of language use.

Writing, to start with, is one of the tools used in turn for
speaking; one writes things down in order to speak them out. A
speech is written to be read aloud; a play is written to be
dramatized aloud. And whether one reads the written aloud or
silently, one uses the punctuation as a tool too, a means for
clarification of units or segments.

Strangely enough, in the battle for supremacy as unitizers
of poetry, punctuation dethrones the sacred cow of poetry -- the
poetic line; and the theory of lineation -- requiring a pause
after every line in the oral reading of poetry -- proves empirically unsupportable.

The written, finally, comes alive in one more way: in oral
readings of poetry. It turns out that the literary critics have
long neglected the richness of the spoken word in their intuitive
ruminations on the written poem.

120

Chapter 8

The Basic Manual-Visual Medium

Chances are that not even the initiated are quite sure what the actual topic of this chapter is supposed to be. The title is deliberately offbeat in an effort to disrupt a bit of functional fixedness. The topic is, of course, writing.

It is of interest to recall that, in modern linguistic and psycholinguistic research, there has been on the one hand a massive implicit underlying conceptual bias in favor of written language, as Linell (1982) has so well called to our attention in The written language bias in linguistics, and on the other hand an explicit theoretical bias against writing as a subordinate, less important system, to the extent that writing has been excluded from the pale of psycholinguistics (see Chapter 2; Clark & Clark, 1977, p. vii; Dell, 1986, p. 283). As Ong (1969) has pointed out, both literacy and "hypervisualism" have been historically responsible for much of the shifting in biases. And as Ong (1982) has further pointed out, "Freeing ourselves of chirographic and typographic bias in our understanding of language is probably more difficult than any of us can imagine, . . ." (p. 77).

The paradox is that, despite the written language bias, research on writing has been chronically and thoroughly neglec- ted. In this regard, Levelt's observation (1983b) that "Mother Psycholinguistics has one deprived child: the study of the speaker" (p. 278 f.) was completely off the mark. But to continue his metaphor, I think the reason the observation was so far from the facts is very simple: Mother Psycholinguistics has never acknowledged writing as one of her children. Mother has erred and Levelt has erred.

One might have thought that comparisons between writing and speaking would eventually have been undertaken simply to compare modalities. Instead, there has developed over the past two decades an extensive and excellent research tradition concerned with a manual-visual medium that has nothing to do with writing in any direct way. It is surprising that American Sign Language (ASL) has become so popular as a research field, when the manual-visual forms used by billions more people have hardly been touched. The point is not made as an objection to ASL research at all, but as an observation on the lack of writing research itself.

The ASL research has already changed linguistic views regarding the very definition of language; it appears no longer tenable to claim that language must include in its definition the element of vocal production, as Brown (1987, p. 2) has recently called to our attention. But then, this development too might have been expected to stir some related interest in the psychology of writing and in some comparisons with speaking, with a view to throwing more light on both (as well as on ASL). Given the extensive use of writing throughout the world, it would seem a shame not to look for at least some moderately instructive comparisons between writing and speaking.

Writing is stereotypically, but not essentially or necessarily or universally, used for communication with readers who are removed in time and place from the writer. Writing is also a subordinate and derivative mode of communication not shared by many people of the world who speak very complex oral languages quite fluently.

The differences between writing and speaking make comparison indeed a formidable task. Not only are the motor skills different in the two cases, but writing is also accompanied by instrumental adjuncts such as stylus, pen, pencil, typewriter, and word processor, whereas amplification is the only major instrumentation associated with speaking. The temporal organization of the two is also subject to different demands. The writer (and the reader) can ply back and forth in a text at will, whereas the speaker's words are heavier burdens to both speaker's and hearer's memory: _Verba volant, scripta manent_ (The spoken flies away, the written stays put). This characteristic of permanence also establishes the priority of the written for legal, official, archival, and morally binding purposes. Correlatively, a certain dignity and an aura of normative correctness have associated themselves more properly with the written.

Akinnaso (1982, 1985) has recently undertaken to analyze the differences and similarities between spoken and written language. Unfortunately, the effort bogged down in taxonomic and empirical confusion. For example, Akinnaso claimed that "everyday colloquial speech lacks authority because it originates with specific individuals and is bounded by the particularities of time and space" (1985, p. 341) and that, "at the prosodic level, . . . the variety of intonational possibilities available in everyday conversational language is highly constrained" (1985, p. 341). Even a youngster might well respond: "My Daddy doesn't have any trouble with either!" Akinnaso has concluded that:

> To remain with the hypothesis that written language is dif-
> ferent from spoken language comes dangerously close to a de-
> nial of the lexical, syntactic, and semantic substratum
> shared by both discourse types. (1985, p. 350)

But the articulatory, prosodic, and temporal differences between speaking and _writing_ must still be taken into account. Akinnaso has not distinguished clearly between _the written_ on the one hand and _writing_ on the other, as I shall further discuss in Chapter 16.

There are also, of necessity, partly different principles of unitization operative in speaking and writing. The writer may go on writing while he or she breathes; the speaker finds it impossible to continue speaking while breathing. Similarly, when the writer runs out of "surface," he or she has to do something different. If one is writing in a circle (e.g., a Mayan on a Central American stone), there may be simply a gradual shift. Most of us are familiar with a rather more abrupt shift called the end of the line.

When I was a boy, I used to defy the end of the line (and page) in my impatience and would make a left turn (upwards) and

124

then carry on with something analogous to what rat runners sometimes call "wall hugging". I would ascend the right margin and branch left again over the top of the page upside down. This anecdote is not meant to be mere indulgence of childhood memories. I haven't received a letter like that since the one from a well educated, adult woman on the day on which I first drafted this passage (January 12, 1987). And I still do my "wall hugging" in hand-written drafts and on postcards. We resist the tyranny of the line -- and analogously, of the page.

In recent years, an unusual phenomenon has occurred within ethnology. A number of ethnologists (see Gee, 1986) have begun to use the concept of a line as a principle of unitization in oral narratives. Gee (1986, p. 395) himself has adopted the analogy and has provided criteria for identification of lines. Many would think of this as an innocuous metaphor used with reasonable justification. Linell (1982) would, of course, see in it just one more case of The written language bias in linguistics. I too find it quite objectionable. It is a meaningless metaphor in that the criteria used by the ethnologists apply only to "sense lines" and lines of poetry, and even in these cases only in a suggestive and approximate way. The unit does not apply at all to the line units I so happily defied as a child. These arbitrary prosaic entities, multiplied by the billions in our midst daily, carry no unitary sense whatsoever. They are defined geographically by page width, print (or script) size, and spacing -- and by nothing else. Hence, the use of line by the ethnologists in the sense described above is not innocuous at all; it is a pseudo-unitization that relies on a misunderstanding of what lines are and do for a living in a literate tradition. The appeal to the written analogate as the ground for the metaphorical usage is ad hoc, vague, and misleading. <u>There are no lines in oral narratives</u>!

But there are lines in writing. In speaking, we can adjust our breathing within limits, but the line is in itself inflexible. Paradoxically, it is at this very moment in history rapidly disappearing precisely among those for whom it is most important, namely among those who write the most. The word processor has suddenly decreed the death of the line as well as the page itself as psychological work entities.

There is a quiet little tragedy hidden in this development. The fad can already be seen developing. We must study the psychology of (let's call it) "user friendliness". This is not intended as mockery; there are all sorts of things about computer usage that can be legitimately categorized as within the psychology of language use. No, the tragedy is that we haven't even begun to study line usage so as to learn something about writing. And now it's too late; we are not to produce anymore in terms of lines.

Of course, this is a bit of an exaggeration for purposes of contrast. We will have lots of lines around for a long time to come. I will have more to say about the poetic line as well in Chapter 10.

For the moment, I wish to return to the question of a comparison between speaking and writing. It is my conviction that the failure to engage writing in psycholinguistic research has been only partly because of the unavailability of instrumentation for the measurement of writing in real time.

My thesis is perhaps analogous to Linell's (1982) diagnosis of _The written language bias in linguistics_. There is evidence from the tremendous interest in recent years in "the written," that researchers really think they are getting at _the psychological processes of writing_ through the written. They are therefore convinced that they need not examine writing itself. This fallacy is, of course, related to the overwhelming need to teach writing in the schools. In mass education (and that is what we are talking about with reference to the United States and many other western nations), writing is taught at most levels.

For the present purposes, I wish to concentrate on the secondary level and higher education level, where writing is almost entirely taught by reference to _the written_. What I mean by this is that teachers and professors seldom, if ever, observe students' writing performance or behavior itself. Improvement is expected from discussion of what is to be written (usually for no real readership, by the way) or of what has been written, and papers are returned with an abundance of rubrics for correcting the text or for the next composition. Except to argue for a better grade, no one ever looks at the corrections!

In terms of Bühler's (1927) criticisms of modern psychology,

127

this preoccupation among researchers and educators alike with the written instead of with the writing is a concentration on "the products of human endeavor" rather than on "the integrated behaviors of human organisms" (p. 29; my trans.). The difference is of crucial methodological and theoretical importance.

In recent years, a fad called "writing across the curriculum" or WAC (see, e.g., Fulwiler, 1984) has been invoked as a remedy for these educational woes. But WAC is actually based on a minimum of vague research, much speculation, and a great deal of hype. Somehow it has become the focus of the crusade to appeal to the conscience of educators that something must be done to improve the writing of young people. The reason it is doomed beforehand to failure is that it relies uniquely on feedback to the writer at successive stages of production, i.e., between productions. The fact that the method is to be delegated to various departments ("across the curriculum") does not introduce any new principles of solution, but simply delegates the method in many instances to professors who do not write well themselves, or who are not interested in teaching writing, or who do not know how to teach writing, or some or all of the above.

What is lacking in all this is very simple: Writing itself must be engaged. Educationally, however, such an engagement would require a tremendous dedication of both time and energy--more than anyone in the WAC camp has even had the courage to acknowledge, much less even roughly to estimate. As long as educators and researchers are basically convinced that operating on the written can save the writer, the real patients, the writers, will continue to die while the surgery on their compositions is going on. For quite recent considerations on The psychology of written composition, see Bereiter and Scardamalia's (1987) volume under that title.

There are methods available, however, for the analysis of writing in progress. One such method has been proposed by Flower and Hayes (1980, 1981; Hayes & Flower, 1980). Their basic faith has been that protocol analysis "is a powerful tool for the identification of psychological processes" (Hayes & Flower, 1980, p. 3). Protocol analysis was defined by them as "a description of the activities, ordered in time, which a subject engages in while performing a task" (p. 4). More specifically,

> In a verbal, or "thinking aloud" protocol, subjects are asked to say aloud everything that occurs to them while performing the task, no matter how trivial it may seem. (p. 4)

The procedure actually sounds more like classical psychoanalysis, doesn't it? Kowal and O'Connell (1987b) have provided a critique of this application of protocol analysis. In brief, the verbalizations themselves massively alter and even distort the ongoing writing. Writers are unable, in any event, to verbalize their "activities" underlying their writing "performance". There is a very basic problem here in that, as Ericsson and Simon (1984) have put it: "Processes can only be implied from the information in STM, which does not. . . usually include informa-

129

tion about process" (p. 227). The protocols were in any event relatively retrospective and extraordinarily cumbersome as a research device. For example, Hayes and Flower (1980) have described a protocol of 15 pages and 5 additional pages of notes for "a page of completed essay" (p. 20).

Kowal and O'Connell (1987b) have also critiqued the direct methods of studying writing. In the sense intended, protocol analysis would still be considered an indirect method. The direct method obviously must involve painstaking observation of ongoing writing itself. The objections to protocol analysis already make it quite evident that "the processes," whatever they may be, are very opaque to observation. But we can observe the macro-level of the act of writing as it develops before our eyes. And although instrumentation for such accurate observation and measurement was for many years problematic, video-cassette-recorder (VCR) methodology is now available. Even with such equipment, however, analyses are quite meticulous, and on this score alone, it is hardly surprising that indirect methods are still preferred.

And so, there has not been much research with the direct method to critique. In their summary of the entire tradition, Kowal and O'Connell (1987b) have provided the following:

To sum up the studies on temporal aspects of writing we can state that the designs have included comparisons of various writing tasks on the one hand and comparisons of writing with speaking on the other hand in terms of the

130

overall time course. In only one study (Spittle & Matsuhashi, 1981) were comparisons made between temporal aspects within a given text. All of the studies were concerned with writing rate or pause time or both; all neglected articulation rate and revising. The prevalent aim of the research has been to obtain clues to the internal processes of planning as they differ according to language modality or writing task. Our critique of the methodological approaches used in the design of the studies as well as in data analyses has made it clear that for the most part the research questions have not been settled. (p. 121 f.)

Van De Water, Monti, Kirchner, and O'Connell (1987) have heeded the warnings of Kowal and O'Connell and have carried out a research project in which four-minute narratives were spoken or written and then recalled a week later (in the same modality as previously). Except for the modality itself, all else was constant across conditions, including the 0.1 sec minimum for pause measurement. The authors found that:

Speakers took only a fourth of the time taken by writers, but spoke more than half again as many syllables as writers wrote. Mean durations of pauses for writing and speaking were equivalent (1.00 ≅ 0.97 sec, respectively), but the respective distributions of pauses differed dramatically: In writing, a far greater number of pauses per syllable led to shorter phrases (segmentation between and even within individual words), whereas speaking was characterized by

fewer pauses per syllable and consequently longer phrases
(segmentation between syntatic units).   Pauses at syntactic
positions (i.e., after punctuation) were the least frequent
ones in writing, although the longest in mean duration.
(p.99)

In terms of real time usage, therefore, speaking and writing
were found to be dramatically different.   The word was clearly
the basic element of unitization or segmentation in writing.   The
word was not the basic element of unitization or segmentation--
again, in terms of real time usage -- in speaking.   Multi-word
phrases, often syntactic, were.   The methodology used by Van De
Water et al. (1987) was, like protocol analysis, cumbersome, but
it gave far greater promise of quite valuable and reliable data.
For example, one may no longer proclaim, to the obvious advantage
of producers of dictation equipment, that "People speak seven
times as fast as they write" (Ohem, 1987, p. 18; my trans.).   Van
De Water et al. found that both articulation rate and speech rate
were less than six times the corresponding rates in writing.   The
application of their methodology to educational and developmental
research problems concerned with writing would seem to be quite
hopeful.

Research on writing, despite all the prejudice against it,
has a rightful place within the psychology of language use.   It
is not at all a domain intractable to research methodology; it
has simply been neglected until now.

Mother Psycholinguistics abandoned a promising youngster.

Chapter 9

Pointing at Structure and Meaning

If writing has been neglected in psycholinguistic research, what is one to say about punctuation? What a silly thing to be concerned about! Who cares how people use punctuation anyway! Such expostulations may indeed sound anti-intellectual and uncalled for, but they are the literal reaction of an anonymous reviewer of one of my recent manuscripts. As always, there were quite sufficient grounds for more reasonable objections he or she might have raised; but she or he chose the irrational one.

Webster's ninth new collegiate dictionary (1983) has defined punctuation as "the act or practice of inserting standardized marks or signs in written matter to clarify the meaning and separate structural units" (p. 955). The original Latin, punctuare, means simply to point. A writer points, or points up, or pinpoints structure and meaning with signs or marks called punctuation. One should add that there are other typographical techniques that serve the same purpose (e.g., paragraph and chapter divisions, blocking, italicization).

Does the writer divide things up for him or herself? Certainly not typically. Punctuation is most commonly inserted into text for others, readers separated in time and place, who will process the written material silently. Sometimes too, the punctuation is made use of by someone who wishes to read aloud intelligently, rhetorically, expressively -- someone who wishes to communicate to still others the message structure, the meaning of the original writer and/or the message of the reader himself (through the _words_ of the original author). Punctuation is meant to clarify message structure.

What have linguistics and psycholinguistics had to say about punctuation? Virtually nothing. As Waller (1980) has put it, "It is hard to find one modern general linguistics textbook that even mentions punctuation" (p. 247). Kainz (1969) called it "a background phenomenon. . . at the periphery of the language system and not the focus of research" (p. 218; my trans.). Smith (1982) contended that "Punctuation does a rather poor job of representing how speech actually sounds" (p. 154). The reason, of course, may be that it is not the function or job of punctuation to represent "how speech actually sounds." The citations should suffice at least to indicate that punctuation is not a burning question for researchers of the psychology of language use.

And yet, punctuation is used to clarify. Is this not in itself an invitation to research? The generic question is _how_ punctuation serves to clarify. Let me exemplify. Recently I read the first draft of a dissertation and deleted in the process approximately 100 supernumerary commas. Had they remained, would they have _interfered_ with a reader's understanding of the dissertation? Undoubtedly they would have. The story exemplifies, however, an entire research area of interference on the one hand and clarification on the other. Punctuation marks are like people giving directions: Some help, some hinder. But how can we

134

learn to tell the difference?

Some things can be explained more easily in one language than in another. Excuse my use of a German anecdote to such purpose. A few years ago, on the occasion of the wedding of my German colleague Richard Wiese, his teenage nieces Andrea and Sandra teasingly came up with the following: ER WILL SIE NICHT. I print it here in uppercase letters and without internal punctuation to emphasize its semantic potentialities. In the teasing, nuptial, oral context of intersubjectivity, the youngsters came up with two prosodic versions, translatable as: (1) He wants to marry her, but she doesn't want to marry him; (2) He does not want to marry her. The play on words relies on the written ambiguation of sie. If one were to take into account the possible reading Sie (with initial uppercase letter), the potential meanings could be multiplied even more. Let's limit ourselves to sie. Literally, the translation would be: He wants she (her) not -- nominative or accusative.

In such cases, the linguistic importance of a comma in the German becomes quite evident. The sentence had been ambiguated in the first instance by being written -- by having its prosodic and temporal organization stripped away. Then, by a reversal of the process of ambiguation -- disambiguation -- the sentence had to be clarified by use of punctuation. Some semantic potentialities are thereby eliminated. Note that I do not speak of the exclusion of only one semantic potentiality. The nominative sie still allows for a multitude of nuanced understandings, even

135

after a corresponding multitude of nuanced understandings has been shorn away by the exclusion of the accusative. But the comma does serve its function here of clarifying potential meanings by "separating structural units". In the oral versions (again, plural because there are many legitimate oral renditions), this function is fulfilled by means of prosodic and temporal organization. In other words, it is the subtraction of prosodic and temporal elements in the written modality that necessitates the use of punctuation for clarification.

This is not to say that an exact, one-to-one relationship between the oral elements (prosodic and temporal) on the one hand and punctuation on the other exists. In fact, herein reside important unanswered empirical questions: What are the relationships? What functions of prosodic and temporal organization can be and are taken over by punctuation and which perhaps remain inadequately represented in the written modality or represented by some other markers or devices?

By way of parenthesis, it is extraordinarily important in such matters to be quite precise about what varies and what does not. An example of this importance can be found in Perkell and Klatt (1986) in the preface (written by Lindblom, Perkell, & Klatt) to Invariance and variability in speech processes: "Variability in the acoustic manifestations of a given utterance is substantial and arises from many sources" (p. ii). There is no "variability in the acoustic manifestations of a given utterance". There is a confusion here in the level of word usage. In other words, despite the experts' wish to use the term otherwise, there is only one acoustic manifestation of a given utterance. If English is to have any meaning at all, "a given utterance" is acoustically quite determinate (see Foss & Hakes, 1978, p. 16). It is not legitimate to use concrete, determinate expressions to stand for abstractions. The latter is what was intended in this passage. My objection is not meant to be petty quibbling. We are addressing means of clarification and the avoidance of confusion; the shifting of levels of word usage is a frequent source of confusion in scientific discourse.

To return to the question of the relationship of prosodic and temporal elements on the one hand and punctuation on the other, hypotheses regarding possible relationships of the latter two (temporal organization and punctuation) are to be found in the archival literature throughout the past several centuries. I would like to engage these, without any claim, be it understood, that the prosodic relationships to punctuation are any less important or do not interact on their own part with temporal organization.

O'Connell and Kowal (1986) have sampled such hypotheses (dating back to the year 1692) regarding temporal organization and punctuation for four different languages (English, French, German, & Hungarian):

> The only common element in all these is the hypothesis
> that pauses at periods are longer than pauses at commas;
> otherwise there is not agreement, either across languages

137

or within a given language. (p. 94)

The empirical question then becomes: Does the variety of hypothe-ses reflect a genuine randomness in language use with respect to temporal organization and punctuation? Or can orderliness be found in these relationships by means of empirical investiga-tions?

O'Connell and Kowal (1986) and Van De Water and O'Connell (1986) carried out parallel investigations of German and American radio homilies in order to answer these questions. The homilists read from their personal manuscripts. Pauses were objectively measured (Siemens Oscillomink L and F-J Electronics FFM 6502) to a minimum cut-off point of 0.13 sec and were categorized accord-ing to corresponding punctuation positions in the original manuscripts. The hypothesized relationships and the empirical findings of the two studies can be summarized as mean durations of pauses at the various punctuation positions, measured in seconds:

Hypotheses	P	>	?	>	!	>	.	>	:	>	;	>	--	>	,	> null
German	1.65		1.14		1.09		0.98		0.72		0.65		0.59		0.47	0.36
American	1.68		1.31		1.18		0.99		0.72		0.63		0.89		0.55	0.54

The only exception to a consistent sequence in order of magnitude was occasioned by one American homilist who clearly used dashes functionally as sentence dividers, i.e., as periods. Not all successive differences were significant; but some punctuation marks clearly served to separate major structural units and some served to separate minor structural units. The null positions were simply defined as between-word positions where a pause occurred, but no punctuation occurred. These were consistently the shortest pauses, indicating for the most part clarification of meaning rather than separation of structural units as such.

Hence, across at least two major languages, the relationships of punctuation to temporal organization were found to be quite similarly orderly. These two studies did not investigate prosodic organization. German punctuation accounted for a greater percentage of pause time than did American (91% > 76%), a finding quite in keeping with the mandatory use of commas at between-clause positions in German, but not in American English. Correspondingly, the percentage of all punctuation marks that were commas was twice as much in German (55% > 26%) as in English. Hence, proportionally more pause positions were comma positions in German than in American (36% > 17%); however, in both German and American English, commas accounted for a high percentage of the punctuated positions where no pause occurred (95% & 82%).

In this respect, commas were used most variably and most stylistically of all punctuation types. To suggest, then, as Carroll (1986) recently has suggested, that "pauses are the oral equivalent of commas" (p. 270) is entirely contrary to these empirical findings. Akinnaso (1982) has also overgeneralized to the effect that commas "signal" pauses (p. 105).

Punctuation marks -- and in particular the major punctuation

139

marks: exclamation and question marks, periods, colons, semicolons -- do "separate structural units". Paragraph positions should be included along with the major punctuation marks; paragraphs are major locational markers, even though they are instances of macro-typography rather than of punctuation marks as such.

Do these findings imply that reading aloud involves a syntactic analysis of the text on the part of the reader? It is hardly surprising, given the syntactic bias of psycholinguistics over the decades, that such an inference has been made. Brown and Miron (1971) have stated the position most clearly. They concluded that "fluent oral readers tend to pause at grammatical junctures" and that "pause durational values in oral reading actively reflect an 'understanding' of sentence structure" (p. 665). Interestingly enough, they analyzed only lexical and syntactic predictors of pause location and duration. They did not analyze the relationship of pauses to punctuation at all. The same is to be said for Butcher (1981), Goldman-Eisler (1972), and Grosjean and Collins (1979). Such neglect of evident cues, obviously usable by the reader without further search, analysis, or inference, can only be explained in terms of the experimenter's bias in favor of an inference dictated both by the experimenter's own knowledge of the syntactic structure of the text and by a theoretical syntactic bias. Both are clear violations of empirical logic.

Use of punctuation was an adequate explanation of the pause

location and duration effects in all these studies. This brings us back to the learned, social nature of language use. Simply stated, we have learned from our language community how major and minor punctuation marks are used to "separate structural units". We use them accordingly. Oral reading does not demonstrably "reflect an 'understanding' of sentence structure," as most of the research would have us believe. A citation from Knobloch (1984) characterizes Brown and Miron's conclusion quite well:

> A psychological fallacy that -- crudely stated -- directly attributes to the speaker, as a prerequisite for speaking, the product of theoretical considerations on the part of the linguist regarding language structure. (p. 300; trans. from O'Connell & Kowal, 1986, p. 97)

O'Connell and Kowal (1986) have added their own commentary to that of Knobloch:

> Our current research knowledge does not in fact allow us to discern what the inferred active understanding of sentence structure might be. Whatever it may prove to be, it ought not be naively identified with the formal syntactic analysis made by the researcher. (p. 97)

Before leaving these two studies (O'Connell & Kowal, 1986; Van De Water & O'Connell, 1986) altogether, one more observation is in order. It is something of a coincidence, but it returns us to the cynicism of Chapter 1. In both articles, after corrected page proofs had been returned to the journals in question, changes were somehow introduced into the text at the final stage

141

of printing. In one instance, Table 1 (O'Connell & Kowal, 1986, p. 94) was rendered unintelligible by the arbitrary deletion of an entire column of eight punctuation marks (periods). In the other, the figure captions for Figures 1 and 2 (Van De Water & O'Connell, 1986, p. 536 f.) were arbitrarily reversed. Both editors were greatly embarrassed and immediately agreed to insert a notice of the erratum.

The point in this anecdote is not to argue that _we_ do not make mistakes; that would be a supremely silly assertion. It is indeed upsetting that changes can occur after final proofreading, but it would be a shame to leave the matter at that. Perhaps the real point can only be discerned if scientists step back a few paces from pride of authorship; for there really is a further lesson to be extracted. We become so frightfully incensed at both stupidity and irresponsibility. We feel constrained always to find someone to blame for any and all misadventures, and it just so happens that "_we_ were right". Behold the very essence of the intellectual snobbery to which we are all prone. It so happens that scientists, scholars, and the well educated are equally as peccable and fallible as the rest of the human family. We all share the heritage!

I wish, finally, to conclude this chapter on punctuation with a brief consideration of one more episode. Butterworth (1975) asked independent judges to divide transcripts of speech like ideas. He wanted them "to look for semantic units without too many preconceptions as to structure" (Butterworth, 1980, p.

142

165). The logical problem with the experiment was that the transcripts were already pre-divided into "structural units" (Webster's definition of punctuation once again, 1983, p. 955). There was no good methodological reason for Butterworth not to delete the punctuation (and any other clues to structural unitization, e.g., initial uppercase letters) from the subjects' transcripts, if he really wanted subjects "to look for semantic units without too many preconceptions as to structure".

Having misquoted my (O'Connell, 1977, p.311) criticisms regarding the methodological problem (Butterworth, 1980, p. 165), Butterworth (personal communication, 1981) replied to my letter in which I had called the misquotation to his attention, only to say that he still didn't understand why I objected to his procedure in the 1975 research. At this point, I'm afraid I can only suggest that readers who are sufficiently interested in the methodological question go back to the Butterworth (1975) study and decide for themselves what is to be said about the research.

To conclude this chapter, then, let me insist that punctuation is important for research on the psychology of language use in at least two respects: (1) Punctuation is an untapped area of research in its own right; the extant evidence indicates that punctuation is an important clue that is used by readers in an orderly way "to clarify the meaning and separate structural units" (Webster's, 1983, p. 955); (2) Punctuation must not be overlooked as an important clue used by subjects, even when the

143

research is intended as an investigation of other independent
variables.

Chapter 10

Lining Up Words

"Lining up words" seems hardly the proper diction to apply to poetry. School children and soldiers are peremptorily told to "line up." And yet, part of the poet's writing task is to muster words into poetic forms, to put them down on paper one after another, to line them up.

But there are a number of ways of "lining up words." One of them has been investigated by Levelt (1981b) in a speaking task. He has referred to it as "linearization" (p. 305), and it is just that: the speaker's task of arranging words one after another. The same task occurs in writing as well. But there is another type of lining up that is peculiarly characteristic of poetry. It involves not only the arrangement of words one after another, and not only the arrangement of words into geographical lines according to the limitations of the writing surface, but more specifically the arraying of words in poetic lines.

Literary scholars have dedicated voluminous discussions to the characteristics and uses of the poetic line. Entry into that domain of discussion -- meter and rhythm, rhyme and diction -- is hardly my intention. For the psychologist of language use, the poetic line poses many empirical questions that can be legitimately engaged without on the one hand demeaning poetry by contact with empirical science and on the other without posing as a literary scholar. I would like to navigate somewhere between Scylla and Charybdis in this respect.

In most poetry of the western world, a poetic line can be accurately described as "a horizontal array of words with punctuation as determined by the author" (Van De Water & O'Connell, 1985, p. 398). It would certainly be permissible (After all, what is not permissible for the poet?) to array letters and/or words vertically or diagonally or in whatever construable constellation the poetic intention dictates; but these are not the ordinary conventions of the poetry we are accustomed to reading. In this respect, poetry, like all other language use, is a social convention, and the expectations of readers partly determine how a poet feels free to communicate with them.

Fussing over a definition of the poetic line may seem to be unwarranted; on the face of things, it is a fairly simple concept. However, there is obviously something very special about the lines "as determined by the author" in poetry. The line itself serves as part of the poetic convention and subserves the communication of the author's poetic intentions.

Some would go so far as to say that the line is part of the definition of poetry, or even that it _is_ the definition poetry. In this vein, Hartman (1980), for example, has asserted that "Verse is language in lines" (p. 11). But he did not stop there. Somehow, a pause at the end of every poetic line became part of the definition as well:

There is a dichotomy -- not a spectrum -- between verse and prose. Lineation distinguishes them. . . . verse is harder to read than prose. One reason is that unless one wilfully

ignores lineation, one pauses at the end of each line.

Whatever else this pause may do, it forces the reader to

slow down and pay more attention to what he is reading.

(p. 52)

Johnson (1986) intended the same thing -- the mandatory nature of

the line-end pause in poetry -- in the following statement to the

effect that the reader must "attend to the junctural integrity of

the poetic line" (p. 5). Perhaps Turner and Pöppel (1983) have

been the most explicit about the mandatory pauses in the reading

of poetry:

The LINE is preceded and followed by a distinct pause (not

necessarily a pause for breath), which, despite the pre-

sence of other pauses within the line divides the verse

into clearly identifiable pieces. (p. 286)

These are very strongly worded normative characteristics of

poetry, if we are to take them at all seriously. Turner and

Pöppel were so emphatic as to assert additionally "the extraordi-

nary prevalence of the 3-second LINE in human poetry" (p. 293).

It should now be clear why and how these normative or

definitional matters become part of the legitimate domain of

research in the psychology of language use. It is simply an

empirical question as to what readers actually do with poetry.

Do they "aim for at least one pause per line, usually line

final," as Dillon (1976, p. 12), yet another literary scholar,

has asserted? And is it an empirical fact that "the poetic line

147

constitutes a unit of temporal programming in at least some languages, including English" (Lehiste, 1984, p. 9)?

One could, of course, argue that, even if empirical evidence from all varieties of readers (including the poet, dramatic artists, literary scholars, ordinary adults, and children) were to indicate that everybody reads poetry otherwise (i.e., without consistently pausing at line-ends), it would not answer the real question, namely how should poetry be read. I find it difficult to take this real question seriously, but such was indeed the response of Johnson (personal communication, 1985) when I sent to him a manuscript copy of Van De Water and O'Connell (1985).

There is one more objection to be considered before proceeding to the actual psychological research on the reading of poetry. It is related to the objection of Johnson mentioned in the previous paragraph, but relies on a further sophistication called the "performative fallacy" (Hartman, 1980, p. 38; see also Wimsatt & Beardsley, 1959, p. 587): the use of any particular performance or sets of performances to identify a poem. It would, of course, also be contrary to the principle of multiple semantic potentialities, as enunciated in Chapter 4 above, for me to claim that any single performance or any number of performances constitute the poem. In other words, the problem to be found in this formulation of the performative fallacy is not in the identification of a poem as such, but in an implicit corollary: that performance cannot be used at all to provide clues as to the intentions of the poet or to reflect understanding (or lack of understanding) of those intentions on the part of various readers.

Hartman, I think, was following just such an implicit corollary when he added a footnote to the effect that he was in any event less interested in acoustical than in psychological facts (p. 52, footnote 2). Paradoxically, he then proceeded to develop his argumentation as if he were indeed talking about honest to goodness silences of real readers. For example, "Surrounded by silence, each line becomes responsible for maintaining some internal rhythmic integrity" (p. 56), sounds very much like Johnson's "junctural integrity". Hartman continued to speak of "a reader" and asserted that one must "listen to the poem" (p. 56). But what reader? Whose readings can help the literary scholar's understanding in this matter? And how could a psychologist of language use, for example, check such readings?

It becomes fairly obvious after a while that there are no oral readings in question at all, but only Hartman's literary intuitions. But instead of centering all our attention on Hartman, I would like to broaden the target. I am quite convinced that we are dealing here with a prevalent type of literary intuition based almost entirely on silent readings of poems. Even in such instances as are truly based on the reading of a poem aloud, however, there is no archival record of the reading, much less any objective analysis of the record, or argumentation from such an analysis.

All this could be read as an attack on the intuitions of

literary critics as such. I would rather see it as an argument regarding the _limits_ of literary intuitions.

There are some assertions that actually require attention to empirical detail. The "prevalence" of line-end pauses is of such a nature. It can only be judged accurately from actual readings. And if all varieties of readers fail to give evidence of such prevalence, or if only the readers who can reasonably be assumed to be less competent (e.g., children and ordinary adults) manifest such prevalence, to the exclusion of those who can be assumed to be more competent (e.g., the poet, dramatic artists, literary scholars), then a "should pause at line-ends" becomes a meaningless abstraction and a groundless principle of poetic theory.

If I turn now to empirical evidence, it should be clear what kind of evidence my colleagues and I have used. Over the past decade, we have analyzed recordings of 49 performances by poets and dramatic artists and 240 performances of adults and young readers of various descriptions.

The corpus of readings consisted of poems in four languages: English (E), French (F), German (G), and Italian (I). The number of different poems by each poet and the language of the poems are both noted in parentheses in the following: Cummings (4, E); Frost (2, E); Heaney (9, E); Jarrell (1, E); Lowell (6, E); Montale (3, I); Nemerov (8, E); Rilke (3, G); Roethke (8, E); Saba (1, I); Verlaine (1, F & 1, E trans.); and Williams (2, E). The summaries and conclusions that follow are based on the following sources: Chakoian and O'Connell (1981), Funkhouser (1978, 1979a, 1979b, 1982), Funkhouser and O'Connell (1978, 1984, 1985), O'Connell (1980b, 1982a, 1984b, 1985), O'Connell and Kowal (1984), and Van De Water and O'Connell (1985).

The principles summarized in the most recent of these publications (Van De Water & O'Connell, 1985) have given an overview of our findings:

> (1) The poetic line is <u>not</u> the unit of performance. (2) Punctuation is a major contributor to unitization. (3) Line-end and punctuation combined (or stanza, where used) best predict pause placement and duration. (4) Use of some very long pauses (> 1 sec) characterizes expressive readings; indiscriminate use of pauses at line-end positions characterizes nonproficient or unexpressive readings. (5) Wide variability of articulation rate and pause duration characterizes the range of expressiveness of skilled readers. (6) There is no single best way of performing a poem. (p. 398)

Let me review some of the empirical evidence underlying these conclusions one by one.

(1) With regard to the line-end pauses, there was only one case in our entire corpus of readings by poets themselves and by dramatic artists, in which every line-end was marked by a pause of measurable duration ($\geq$ 0.13 sec). The actual case constitutes almost a reductio ad absurdum for mandatory line-end pauses. It was a two-line poem read by the poet himself, Nemerov's <u>Power to</u>

the People, with one line-end pause.

Cummings might serve as a far more typical example. He paused up to four times within lines, and also spoke up to four lines without a pause. Only one other poem in the entire corpus had even an average of one pause per line, Westphal's reading of Rilke's Der Panther (in German), and even in this case, three of the eleven lines were without either medial or line-end pauses.

The search for the unit of performance is chimerical in any event. There is no doubt that the poetic line is one of many elements that contribute to the unitization (or from another perspective, the segmentation) of a poem; but the poet is not constrained to use the line according to rules fashioned from the abstract and unfounded oversimplifications of literary intuitions.

(2) The second principle asserts that punctuation is a major contributor to unitization of performance in oral poetry readings. What is intended here is "the relatively greater importance of punctuation over lineation for the prediction of pauses, and consequently for the temporal unitization of oral readings of poetry" (Van De Water & O'Connell, 1985, p. 397). The evidence for this conclusion is particularly clear in Van De Water and O'Connell (1985). More than 98% of all punctuated positions were used for pauses in Heaney's readings of his poetry, whereas less than half of both the stanza positions and the line-end positions were used for pauses if they were not punctuated. The other unpunctuated positions were used for

152

pauses even less often.

Since many poems are not divided into stanzas at all, the data have been analyzed into four categories so as to apply to all the poems in our corpus: punctuated line-end positions, including, of course, punctuated stanzas where they occur (PL), punctuated midline positions (P), unpunctuated line-end positions (L), and unpunctuated midline or null (N) positions. There are two aspects of "unitization of performance" that can be tested from these data: (1) the percentage of available positions used for pauses, (2) the duration of the actual pauses occurring at the respective positions. For both these response measures, the hypothesis compatible with our principle is the same: PL > P > L > N.

The data of O'Connell (1982a, 1985) and of Van De Water and O'Connell (1985) have been specifically analyzed with these hypotheses in mind, and they have confirmed the hypothesis in terms of both response measures. If the percentages and durations of pauses from these studies are weighted so as to give the four languages used (English, French, German, and Italian) equal weightings, the following data emerge for the two response measures for the respective positions: (1) 96% > 62% > 44% > 4%; and (2) 1.12 > 0.62 > 0.57 > 0.48 sec.

The other articles cited above are in complete accord with these data, but only the more recent studies included formal analyses in these terms. The descriptive data given here have been summarized from the articles to provide an overview without

153

cluttering the picture with great detail. In summary, the line-end position (lineation itself) alone was not as predictive of pause placement as was punctuation alone or punctuation in conjunction with line-end position. Moreover, when pauses did occur at unpunctuated line-end positions, they were shorter than the pauses in any other category with the exception of the unpunctuated midline (N) positions.

(3) The third principle simply emphasizes the fact that it is the combination of line-end (or stanza-end) and punctuation that maximizes predictability of both percentage of available positions used for pauses and of the duration of the actual pauses. Throughout our corpus, in both group data and the data from poets and dramatic artists, a higher percentage (c. 90%) of available punctuated line-end positions was marked by pauses than any other position, and these pauses were longer in duration than those in any other positions. Even a performance that was not particularly expressive, for example, Frost's reading of his Dust of Snow, contained a stanza pause longer than any of the other pauses (0.77 > 0.63 > 0.47 > 0.37 = 0.37 > 0.30 sec; Funkhouser, 1982). Another example, hardly unexpressive, but performed at a rather rapid pace (an articulation rate of 5.14 syl/sec) to portray a merry-go-round, was Quadflieg's reading of Rilke's Das Karussell (in German). Even in this accelerated instance, the mean duration of stanza pauses relative to all others was more than twice as long (0.84 > 0.41 sec).

(4) For the discussion of longer (> 1 sec) pauses, I wish

154

to revert to my childhood memories of <u>Aesop's fables</u> once again. I can still visualize the two pictures: one with a single tree in the forest circled by a yellow ribbon; another with a whole forest of trees each circled by a yellow ribbon. The literal word of the promise to "circle the right tree with a yellow ribbon" had been kept, but the spirit of the promise had been violated. A second story I remember is the classic one about the boy who called "wolf" too often and laughed when concerned neighbors came running. When the wolf finally did appear, neighbors were no longer concerned. The first story involves simultaneity, the second story involves succession in time; they can both serve as an analogy for longer pauses. The principle of perceptual salience and hence of rhetorical usefulness of longer pauses that becomes relevant here is that of segregation. Longer pauses are useful rhetorically insofar as they are perceptually segregated and therefore salient. When one can no longer "tell the forest for the trees," can no longer single out the longer pauses, they have become lost in numerosity and are no longer capable of functioning rhetorically. As with any other attention getting device, be it yellow ribbons or "wolf" or any other, overuse of longer pauses defeats the rhetorical purpose.

And so, there is nothing magical about longer pauses, and certainly nothing automatic about the salience of a pause greater than one second in duration. The overall temporal organization in which these pauses are embedded is extremely important in this respect. Nonetheless, competent speakers (in the present instance, poets and dramatic artists reading poetry) do use longer pauses differently from the ordinary reader.

O'Connell's (1982a) analyses of readings of Verlaine's L'Automne by nonnative speakers of French have provided an extreme example. A total of 22 of these readers used only 24/236 or 10% longer pauses. By way of contrast, the French dramatic artist Périer read the same poem with 3/6 or 50% longer pauses. Similarly, the German actors used 17/67 or 25% longer pauses across the board (even though Das Karussell must reflect continuous rapid motion).

O'Connell and Kowal (1984) found a striking confirmation of this usage in women native speakers of German who were judged to be more expressive than all other groups of readers in their experiment:

> An examination of the total number of pauses > 1 sec in duration suggests that the disproportionate number of longer pauses is partly responsible for listeners' impressions of expressiveness on the part of the German women; their 16 pauses > 1 sec in duration are more than the total number of such pauses in the three other groups taken together. The finding is in accord with the findings of Clemmer et al. (1979), O'Connell (1980b) and Chakoian and O'Connell (1981) regarding the expressiveness of longer pauses. (p. 311)

For the sake of completeness, it should be added that longer pauses can be just the opposite, i.e., a sign of lack of competence rather than an indication of rhetorical usage. Two of the nonnative speakers of French can serve as examples of this tendency. All their pauses were longer than one second in duration. These subjects were rated, however, as the very worst of all the readers because their pauses were obviously a function of their inability to articulate French correctly without great effort in their formulation. As was said above, there is nothing magical about any particular duration.

The least competent readers, in fact, were characterized in their readings by a sort of indiscriminate use of pauses at line-end positions. This is actually the inverse of Dillon's (1976) hypothesis of a pause per line as appropriate segmentation of a poem, and it is also a direct challenge to Hartman's (1980) and Turner and Pöppel's (1983) contention that lineation defines poetic performance.

As it turns out, readers who slavishly paused at the end of every poetic line were among the readers rated the worst. Cummings' Dying is Fine can serve to illustrate this phenomenon. In the O'Connell and Kowal (1984) research, both native speakers of English and nonnative speakers (Germans) read the poem. It contains 21 unpunctuated line-end positions. One American reader paused at 20 and one German reader at 15 of these positions. The overall effect of such a rendition was a painfully staccato, childish doggerel. Otherwise, the relatively proficient native speakers paused at an average of only 2.5 of these unpunctuated line-end positions, and the less proficient Germans at an average

of 6.2. The latter number is actually quite close to cummings'
own number (7) of pauses at unpunctuated line-ends in reading his
own poem. But the similarity of performance is misleading in
this simplified form. Once again, the Germans were simply less
proficient in the language and were using the pauses for trouble-
shooting and without properly discerning their function, whereas
cummings himself was reading with extraordinary expressiveness.

(5) A reminder is in order before discussing variability of
articulation rate and of pause duration in the readings of
skilled readers. The hypothesis is that they do so in keeping
with the meaning of the poem. But the principle states not a
necessary or mandatory means of expressiveness, but an optional
means used by competent readers (and speakers more generally as
well). A speciously similar variation could well be occasioned
by a succession of phrases, some of which were very familiar
(hence easily articulated) and some of which were quite unfamil-
iar (and hence, perhaps quite difficult to articulate) for a nonnative or very incompetent speaker.

For the skilled readers, however, the variability was
rhetorically functional. In Williams' reading of his poem The
Catholic Bells, for example, he ranged from an articulation rate
of 5.88 to 1.01 syl/sec across phrases (defined in units of
syl/pause), a difference of 4.87 syl/sec (Funkhouser & O'Connell,
1985). On the other hand, in the course of reading four Italian
poems, Vittorio Gassman's corresponding ranges of articulation
rate were only 2.36, 2.08, 1.92, and 3.55 syl/sec. In Quad-

flieg's readings of Rilke's <u>Der Panther</u> in German, the range was a moderate 3.33 syl/sec; but interestingly enough, the fastest and slowest articulation rates in the reading (6.02 & 2.69 syl/sec) both occurred in the same line: "<u>ist wie ein Tanz von Kraft</u> (0.9 sec pause) <u>um eine Mitte</u>". The rhetorical contrast between the two parts of the line was most dramatic. His reading of Rilke's <u>Das Karussell</u>, on the other hand, maintained the merry-go-round pace throughout and never slowed below a 4.06 syl/sec articulation rate. In all these cases, the unit for which individual measurements of articulation rate were made was the temporal phrase, defined as the syllables articulated between any two pauses (or syl/pause). Kowal (1987) has referred to these as <u>articulatory</u> phrases.

The average articulation rate for an entire poem revealed yet another style of variation from poem to poem and reader to reader. Stability was, of course, common. Roethke, for example, read four of his poems in two versions with an overall range in mean articulation rate (over the eight samples) of only 0.92 syl/sec. Across eight of his own poems, Nemerov's articulation rate was stable within a range of only 0.99 syl/sec, and cummings' across four poems within a range of 0.64 syl/sec. However, some other expressive options can readily be seen in a comparison of <u>Das Karussell</u> and <u>Der Panther</u>, each read by both Quadflieg and Westphal. Both actors read <u>Der Panther</u> with exactly the same articulation rate (3.60 syl/sec), but <u>Das Karussell</u> with unusually different rates (5.13 > 3.98 syl/sec).

Articulation rate reflects only ontime. Turning to offtime or pause time, we find in these same four readings an even more striking stylistic variation. In this case, the more dramatic difference in mean pause duration occurred in Der Panther (0.56 sec), rather than in Das Karussell (0.29 sec), from one actor to the other. The comparable ranges across various readings of their own poems by the poets were the following: Nemerov (0.75 sec), Roethke (0.51 sec), cummings (0.28 sec), Lowell (0.40 sec), and Frost (0.06). Most of this within-reader variation -- Frost is the obvious exception with a surprisingly stable mean duration of pauses from poem to poem -- is more than two standard deviations greater than the variation across readers for all the groups mean durations available from ordinary readers in the published literature. There is, with the exception of Frost, virtually no overlap between the poets and dramatic artists on the one hand and the members of the ordinary groups on the other hand in this respect. In other words, the dramatic variation in mean duration of pauses on the part of the poets themselves and dramatic artists is to be interpreted as the skilled use of this option to reflect rhetorically the mood and thrust of the individual poem.

(6) According to Clark and Clark's (1977) principle of the "ideal delivery," an artistic performance is a classic case in which one performance is to be considered the correct one. The sixth principle enunciated above is directly contradictory to this concept of "ideal delivery." The best empirical evidence

160

from our corpus to support this conclusion is the repeated performance of the same poem by the poet himself or by competent dramatic artists. In Roethke's repeated readings of four of his own poems and in Quadflieg's and Westphal's performances of _Der Panther_ and _Das Karussell_, there was abundant evidence of dramatically different readings. In fact, in all of them, the occurrence and duration of pauses in various positions varied from one version of the poem to the other rather dramatically-- whether the second version was by the same reader or by another reader. Roethke, for example, used 11% more time in pausing in one version of _The Waking_ than in the other, and a mean pause duration one third of a second longer. In _Elegy for Jane_, he used 22 pauses in one version, 34 in the other. Westphal took 24 sec more time to read _Das Karussell_ than did Quadflieg. Frost, as usual, sang out of chorus; his two readings of _Provide, Provide_ were almost identical in every available descriptive statistic. But then Frost has been noted for his monotonous, droning quality: "The impression is. . . that Frost often simply talked through many of his poems" (Funkhouser, 1978, p. 192).

It is not incidental that the various findings from this corpus of poetry readings were comparable across the four languages sampled. Pause usage in poetry, very much like the punctuation usage and corresponding pauses found in radio homilies, as reported in Chapter 9, is quite orderly and rhetorically functional on the lips of competent readers.

The theories of speech production presented within the

mainstream tradition of psycholinguistics over the past several decades (see O'Connell & Wiese, 1987) have had nothing to say about such phenomena of real speech. The theory of the ideal delivery turns out to be instead a theory of sentence production. In actuality, an appropriate performance depends on much more than sentence structure, and the sentence is by no means the unit of production (see O'Connell, 1977). The poetry readings show quite clearly that there is no single "correct" way of executing a sentence.

The principles or conclusions enuntiated and explicated in this chapter are certainly compatible with a general statement to the effect that performance structures of sentences are task specific. Hence, the contrary position of Grosjean, Grosjean, and Lane (1979) should be carefully examined here: "The performance structures of sentences are not task specific. The linguistic surface structure of a sentence is a good predictor of the pause durations" (p. 58).

How is it possible that researchers can assert such diametrically opposite conclusions? It must be said as forthrightly as possible that the data of Grosjean et al. are based on the reading of completely isolated passages without any communicative intent and no expressive purpose whatsoever. More recently, Gee and Grosjean (1983) set out to pull everything together: to "unify the various determinants of pausing into a linguistically and psychologically relevant system" (p. 431). Using the same data that Grosjean et al. had used, they came to the conclusion that:

> The prosodic model is shown to have a wider domain of
> application than temporal organization per se, accounting
> for parsing judgments as well as pausing performance, and
> reflecting aspects of syntactic and semantic structure as
> well as purely prosodic structure. (p. 411)

That their "prosodic model" reflected syntactic and semantic
structure was hardly surprising; the model itself incorporated
both into its rules for structural derivation. But these same
rules are not independent of the rules used in parsing judgments.
In other words, the logic is circular.

When it comes to pausing performance, however, it is a vast
overgeneralization to say that it is accounted for by the
prosodic model. What Gee and Grosjean (1983) had actually
predicted were only the mean proportionalities of pause duration,
and even these only _within_ sentences. They could predict
absolutely nothing about actual pause durations from these data.
Further, the model did not engage "temporal organization per se"
in any way. At best, only a partial aspect of the temporal
organization of _offtime_ entered into the correlations offered in
support of their model; _ontime_ organization did not enter into
the correlations at all. Finally, the already isolated sentences
used as data base were distorted away from a normal performance
by the specific instruction "to read 14 sentences at five
different rates" (Gee & Grosjean, 1983, p. 413). In other words,
the temporal organization could well be supposed to have been

determined not so much by prosodic structure per se as by the specific instructions to _alter_ the temporal organization itself. Given this limitation in addition to an already impoverished and artificial situation, the only framework remaining to the reader as a basis for temporal organization was that of the sentence. It is, frankly, an impertinence on the part of these authors to make such bold assertions from such a limited and distorted data base.

Support for our conclusions in this chapter has come unexpectedly from Russian research by Aleskandrova and Shishkina (1982). O'Connell (1984b) has cited their conclusion that "syntactic pauses are fairly fixed in neutral, communicative-pragmatic texts, but optional in poetry" (p. 20).

All the evidence indicates that temporal organization in poetry readings is extremely complex, while at the same time quite orderly. Poetic pauses turn out to be good, law abiding citizens, even if they do not array themselves one per line obediently, as Dillon (1976) and others after him would insist, or without systematic differences in duration, as Meinhold (1967) described them.

There are many ways of "lining up words," and most of them go far beyond sentence structure. Poetry readings prove to be good data for demonstrating this fact as well as for demonstrating how nuanced temporal organization can be and really is in actual language use.

164

Chapter 11

Richer than the Page

Poetry probably would not have become a research area for me, had not Linda Funkhouser decided to use the pausological methodology to analyze a number of poems in her doctoral dissertation at Saint Louis University (Funkhouser, 1978). A few years later, I began studying poetry readings myself. I asked faculty members of both the English Department and the Drama Department at the University of Kansas to read cummings' Dying is Fine and Williams' The Botticellian Trees. This was the beginning of my adult poetic education.

What does one learn from such research? Well, first of all, that fellow faculty members don't like to perform experiments for psychologists. It is interesting to note, when the chips are down and they are the guinea pigs, what attitudes toward our research emerge in their questioning and post-experimental conversations. Somehow we have taught our colleagues that we are devious: that we investigate other matters than we say we are investigating.

I must say quite honestly that I blame the social psychologists most of all for this image, although it is perfectly obvious that they have not established it without substantial help from the rest of us. It was fortunate for me that I had not planned to do the research with the help of a graduate student. I am quite sure the professors would not have agreed to participate in the experiment under such an arrangement. As it was, I

165

went to the office of each professor at her or his convenience and did the tape recordings there.

I began with the expectation that English professors would read poetry eloquently. I was disappointed in this expectation. Sometimes it was amusing or surprising. One of the English professors read the last line of <u>Dying is Fine</u> as "(forgive us, o life! the Death of sin," instead of "(forgive us, o life! the sin of Death." One of the English professors, who taught cummings and had published a text about poetry, insisted that the same poem was to be read as "dying is fine) but Death <u>question mark</u> o baby. . ." He was quite serious about <u>reading</u> the "question mark." Suddenly, I found myself asking myself: "What do people really know about poetry?"

Obviously, the professor in question really thought that cummings wanted the poem read that way and actually taught students to read cummings accordingly. But apparently, it never occurred to him at all to ask how, perhaps, cummings himself read this poem. I don't think he really cared; it was not relevant to the poem.

This apparent disinterest in the performance of poetry was the great surprise I experienced in dealing with the English professors in the experiment and for years afterwards among the English professors with whom I have discussed the matter. One of them insisted that modern English (I'm sure he meant to include American) poetry is written to be read silently. Of course, I mentioned this to other English professors, and occasionally received looks that communicated rather clearly the conviction that I was indeed a country bumpkin. One even wrote to inform me that "no one holds this" (but see McLuhan, 1964, p. 261).

All this has to be related to the way in which the English professors read the poetry. The drama professors read the poems with great expressiveness; several even apologized that they would have done it better with a bit of practice. The English professors, by and large, read the poems as if they were grocery lists -- to my great horror and profound disappointment. Not that it was empirically a problem at all; actually it led to clear differences between the two experimental groups, something an experimentalist can always be grateful for. But what did it say about the oral reading of poetry in our institutions of higher education? Indeed, what did it portend regarding the oral eloquence that has always been part of our tradition of education in America? As a Jesuit priest, my own educational roots are in the tradition of the Ratio Studiorum of 1599, with its strong emphasis on eloquentia as a primary goal in education. And so, I found the experience unsettling, to say the least.

From other quarters too, I found evidence of neglect of poetry. O'Connor (1982) has put it as follows: "Probably at no time in the history of linguistic thought has the study of poetry been as far from its proper central position as it is today" (p. 143). In terms of curricular emphasis, the same would have to be said; in neither secondary nor higher education is the proper concern for the oral reading of poetry in evidence.

167

The problem is, however, not merely the neglect of poetry, but the neglect of the entire domain of oral use of language in anything more than (or other than) the most informal peer-group situations. Emphasis on such old-fashioned activities as debating, elocution, oratory, drama, media work, and even class-room presentations is seldom found. There is no time for such luxuries; "content" is much more important; the opportunities are there anyway on an extracurricular basis! The neglect of oral use of language is also not unrelated to the profound neglect of foreign languages in America. All this is just as wrong as it would be to claim that "writing across the curriculum" (which is indeed misconceived) is unimportant because writing skills can be learned elsewhere. Oral eloquence is neglected at every level and in every aspect of its importance for modern life.

In one of Funkhouser's (1979b) early articles, a discussion of Jarrell's The Death of the Ball Turret Gunner, she made a very modest claim for the use of pausological methodology for literary critical purposes:

> A methodology which adds some measure of the spoken
> voice of the poet and other readers has added several in-
> sights into the poem and has raised some questions about
> its performance, about Jarrell's intentions, and about its
> meaning for current readers. (p. 401)

Her claim was perfectly correct and the more impressive precisely because of its modesty. Funkhouser was not saying that we have revolutionized literary criticism, but simply that the oral readings of poems are an important element of literary criticism that has been seriously neglected. Given the truth of this claim, why is it that the method has not been used by others, at least since Funkhouser has shown the way? There is really no mystery as to the answer, but it is nonetheless interesting in terms of disciplinary preoccupations. Psychologists of language use are simply not interested in poetry on the one hand; and on the other side of the equation, literary scholars are certainly not interested in measuring anything. It should be said in this connection that Funkhouser's methodology (and my own) does indeed involve measuring. The meticulous nature of the analyses of temporal organization of speech from level recordings is a very serious impediment to anyone with a bias against the physicalistic and statistical procedures of modern psychology.

One of the first things the methodology occasions is the repeated (well nigh ad nauseam) exposure of research personnel to the oral version of the poem. In plain English that means that we have to listen to the readings of the poem bit by bit over and over again as we go about localizing and measuring the duration of pauses. This turns out to be a considerable advantage in the long run, for the simple reason that failure to hear the poem is precisely the problem in modern literary criticism.

One begins to hear things, not imagined things, but previously unnoticed performance characteristics. For example, it took both Linda Funkhouser and myself a number of years before we finally realized that Williams, in reading his The Botticellian

Trees, added an additional component to line 27: "quick with desire l'" rather than simply "quick with desire." One begins to notice, in fact, many changes from the printed text. Williams was particularly prone to this practice. In his _The Catholic Bells_, for example, he altered six words in four different locations of the poem (see Funkhouser & O'Connell, 1985, p. 54 f.).

Far more valuable, however, are those characteristics of the oral performance, particularly in the case of the poet's own oral readings, that tell us something about the poet's intentions and the communication of those intentions to the audience, something that simply cannot be discovered by analyzing the written poem. The reason for this discrepancy is not hard to find; the prosodic components important in the oral reading are completely lacking in the silent reading, though some of them may be paralleled in an impoverished way by typographical characteristics of the poem.

One of my favorite examples of this application of the pausological methodology comes from Funkhouser's (1979b) discussion of _The Death of the Ball Turret Gunner_. It is important to note that the literary critics had, previously to her discussion, not granted the word "loosed" in line three of the poem,

"Six miles from earth, loosed from its dream of life,"
any special import. In Jarrell's own reading of his poem, "loosed" is: (1) isolated by the use of pauses before and after the word; (2) emphasized by use of a pronounced surge of loudness (the greatest measured amount of acoustic energy relative to all

170

other words in the entire poem); (3) prolonged to become the longest single syllable in the entire poem; (4) mispronounced as /luwzd/. None of the English professors who read the poem and none of the ordinary adults who read it did any of these things with the word "loosed". Funkhouser construed Jarrell's intention in line three as follows:

> For Jarrell, the understated horror of the physical details
> is secondary to the impact of the gunner's awakening from
> child-like innocence to reality. Line three marks not only
> the gunner's ascension from the earth, but his loss of
> youthful dreams and hopes of what life will bring. (p.
> 402)

Funkhouser also called attention to "the subjective impressions of the critics who note the difference in pace established in line 3" (p. 390). The point to be made in this regard is that none of them were aware of the actual nuances of this "difference in pace" as realized in the oral reading of Jarrell. Needless to say, they were also unaware of Jarrell's play on the word "loosed."

Funkhouser's (1979a) treatment of cummings' Buffalo Bill's also provides an instructive example of the effectiveness of temporal analyses of oral readings. As she pointed out (p. 236), the critics are in general agreement that "onetwothreefourfive" in line six of the poem,

"and break onetwothreefourfive pigeonsjustlikethat,"
was run together in order to indicate a speeding up of the pace.

171

The English professors who read the poem in Funkhouser's research also seemed to be convinced that this was the function of the running together of the words. Interestingly enough, both cummings and the control group of ordinary adults read the run together words quite similarly. Whereas the professors averaged 1.20 sec for "onetwothreefourfive," cummings used 1.70 sec and the ordinary adults 1.65 sec, or 42% and 38% more time than the professors' average time.

Funkhouser has commented that the discrepancy exemplified by these comparisons "has not been dealt with previously in literary commentary on 'Buffalo Bill's' or in general discussion of Cummings' use of spacing" (p. 237). She also spelled out quite clearly the literary critical alternatives posed by these discrepancies:

> Yet this incongruity looms so large in light of Cummings'
> reputation as a reader of his own poetry as to make it im-
> possible not to discredit either the critics who take spac-
> ing as an oral cue to speed, the professors who follow the
> critics' view in performing the poem, the spacing technique
> that Cummings used in the poem, or Cummings' performance of
> this line. (p. 237)

In other words, no matter how one interprets these data, some-thing has to give. The intuitions of the literary critics are not so infallible as to stand in spite of such empirical evi-dence.

At this point, we establish contact once again with our

previous chapters. For, although cummings did not use his own devices "of spacing and capitalization as reliable performance cues for his own reading" (Funkhouser & O'Connell, 1984, p. 123), he followed punctuation as a cue for pausing "quite conventionally" (p. 123). He also used an extraordinarily slow articulation rate "due to nonphonemic syllabic prolongations" (p. 123). Funkhouser and O'Connell were not amiss in their reading of the temporal data from cummings' own readings of his poetry as "providing a rich resource for stylistic analysis, especially analysis of the fulcrum and of Cummings' visual techniques" (p. 123).

The paradox in all this is that it is nothing new. Some would still agree with Ehlich (1983): "Texts are eo ipso written. They are the given of the literary scholar" (p. 24; my trans.). But there is no reason whatsoever to limit the literary critic to the textual. Ong (1982) has put it as follows:

> But the textual mentality was relatively unreflective.
> For, although texts are autonomous by contrast with oral
> expression, ultimately no text can stand by itself indepen-
> dent of the extratextual world. Every text builds on pre-
> text. (p. 162)

Both I. A. Richards (1929), in his Practical criticism over fifty years ago, and Robert Frost (1964), in correspondence with Sidney Cox, had suggested the application of such physical measurements as were already in use by psychologists to get at the actual temporal organization of poetry (see Funkhouser, 1979a, p. 219).

173

McLuhan has emphasized the importance of the oral version of poetry as follows: "Radio and gramophone and tape recorder gave us back the poet's voice as an important dimension of the poeteic experience" (p. 53).

The inertia of literary critics or their total disregard for the enrichment available from oral readings of poetry leads us back once more to The written language bias in linguistics of Linell (1982). Apparently, it has affected the intellectual world far beyond the narrow confines of linguistic analysis. In today's technological academe, the use of such methodologies-- or, perish the thought, collaboration with someone in another intellectual discipline -- is convenient to anyone who has the zeal for enrichment.

On second thought, perhaps that last sentence is quite a bit oversimplified. Collaboration with scholars in other disciplines is easier said than done. It requires far more humility and adaptability on an intellectual plane than most of us are capable of. I can speak from the experience of having published a variety of articles in conjunction with sociology, linguistics, English literature, and dramatics professors. Our various nomenclatures include identical terms that refer to different realities and different terms that refer to the same realities; our presuppositions and assumptions are not the same; we do not have the same goals in research; we do not share the same pathways (methodologies) to our goals; and we still have trouble finding publication outlets that are genuinely open to interdisciplinary research. Dare one suggest additionally that we do not universally respect one another and one another's disciplines and convictions? After all, we are right.

Beneath all of this, perhaps the humility to acknowledge that we do have something to learn from other disciplines (that there are aspects of the very area that I am researching that I do not understand, and that someone else may be able to tell me about) is the most essential prerequisite to collaboration with someone from outside the pale.

I'm sure it sounds like a very strange thing to say, but I am going to assert it. I am convinced that many academicians profoundly lack the virtue of docility, the ability to be taught. Many of them also lack the basic zeal for learning, studiositas, to get out of their tired old ruts. By the way, many of them aren't even aware that they call themselves acamedicians much of the time instead of academicians (just as a number of American academicians -- one of whom was giving colloquia at various American universities on the subject -- refer to the German Habilitation as Halibitation without being aware of it).

In any event, poetry is one of those cherished human institutions that will never be brought to life by tired old techniques and methodologies. Poetry must be read aloud in order to come to life. Anyone who might imagine, for example, that my appreciation for the poetry of cummings or Williams or Heaney or any of the other poets that we have analyzed has been dulled by dint of the very massive exposure, would be mistaken. The poems have come to life more and more for me, as I heard them again and again, even though some of the readings were admittedly less than aesthetically pleasing. Similarly, the longer I played and replayed short sections of Martin Luther King's magnificent "I have a dream" address, the more overwhelming his eloquence became for me through its very sound. Anyone who has ever measured pauses will know that it is quite an accomplishment to be emotionally overwhelmed in any positive way during that meticulous process.

Poetry is indeed richer than the page and deserves better than to be left to languish on the page.

Part Five

A Few Abstract Considerations

The four chapters in this portion of the book bring us to several considerations that have arisen from the research on temporal organization of speech: gradualism, disfluency, perceptual nonveridicality, and rhetoric. They are admittedly abstract notions, but they encapsulate important and neglected characteristics of the spoken word. All of them are corollaries of the temporal enmeshment of speaking, and all of them have been quite neglected in modern psycholinguistics, despite their importance for the development of an accurate and useful psychology of language use.

It is a truism to say that speech proceeds through time. And like many other important truisms, its neglect can lead to fallacy and error. In complex, dialogic situations, time is the arbiter who decides what can be accomplished. Two or more individuals face off, bringing to their conversation partially overlapping cognitive, affective, experiential, value-imbued, goal directed intersubjectivity. It is only gradually, in time, that anything can develop from this setting. It is a social give and take -- speaking and listening -- during which and through which dynamic change takes place.

Time is not, in this sense, one of the tools of the trade. It is not a means to be used in the same sense as the other tools of language usage are means. Rather, it is constitutive of the contingent metaphysical setting in which all the tools are put to work. The old scholastic definition of time -- _mensura motus secundum prius et posterius_ (the measure of motion according to before and after) -- has always seemed to me to be somehow unfair -- too simple for such a difficult concept. And yet, time is not reducible to dimensionalities other than the motion of physical objects in space. This reducibility to motion is also the ultimate source of our propensity for spatializing time. But time is _not_ space, even if measurable only by means of moving spatialized objects. It must be accepted on its own terms as part of the psychology of speaking and listening. Hence the basic importance of _gradualism_.

The concepts of _fluency_ and _disfluency_ are also closely related to time. Whether we speak of the development of fluency in our mother tongue or in one or more foreign languages, we are dealing with negotiations of discourse that require time in different ways -- depending upon the level of fluency. And all the expertise underlying an individual's fluency is time-related in its application. Even were the child to be endowed with the proper cognitive accoutrements, keeping pace with an adult conversation would be impossible. The parallel experience of the nonnative speaker of a given language is also quite familiar: The fluent conversation moves on; the nonfluent foreigner gropes and falls behind.

The third chapter (Chapter 14) in this section is the only part of the book in which receptive, perceptual processes are focal. It is largely methodological in the sense that a preoccupation with pause reports arose not from interest in perception per se, but from a concern that the purely perceptual assessment of pause occurrence and pause duration was not veridical. The nonveridicality turns out to be far more complex than I had imagined when I began to engage the problem, and this complexity has serious implications for further research on temporal organization of speech, as well as for our evaluation of the archival research that relied on perceptual assessment.

The last chapter in this section (Chapter 15) relies very largely on the research of Sabine Kowal (1987), whose Habilitation was just being completed as this book was taking shape. The Habilitation is rather peculiar to the German academic system, a postdoctoral monograph to be published before the author is ordinarily eligible for a professorship. The Deutsche Forschungsgemeinschaft has supported this research and has thereby generously, albeit indirectly, contributed to the present book. Because of Kowal's analyses of political speech, the present treatment of rhetoric can be extended beyond the poetic, media, and homiletic research that has constituted my own rhetorical research.

The concept of rhetoric is closely related to the concept of eloquence, and both come very close to the heart of this book. Our speaking becomes optimally communicative when our rhetoric becomes worthy of the term eloquence. Indeed, eloquence bespeaks a certain dignity in keeping with the human spirit, whereas rhetoric, left to itself, or rather to ourselves, can and does easily subserve unworthy goals. In other words, the goal of this book is, however ineloquently, to foster eloquence, genuine communication, rather than any pretentious simulation thereof.

The mention of goals also brings us right back to means and to the Organon model of Bühler; for, without being incorporated into a comprehensive finality, means are meaningless precisely because only proximate. Without being incorporated into a comprehensive finality, language use is -- just as the use of any other proximate means -- ultimately meaningless and empty. In this respect, language -- let it be said once again -- is not unlike any other tool to be used by human beings to accomplish a goal.

Chapter 12

"On the Gradual Working-Out of One's Thoughts in the Process of Speaking" (Kleist, c. 1806/undated, p. 975; my trans.)

The chapter title above is also the title of Kleist's short essay written over 180 years ago. I'd like to work-out my own thoughts by citing and commenting on several passages from the essay.

Kleist began as follows:

If you want to understand something and can't figure it out by pondering, I would advise you, my dear ingenious friend, to speak of it to the next acquaintance who happens by. It certainly doesn't have to be a bright fellow; that's hardly what I have in mind. You're not supposed to ask him about the matter. No, quite the contrary; you are first of all to tell him about it yourself. (p. 975; my trans.)

Kleist added almost immediately that he does it himself. After brooding unsuccessfully over something for hours, he turns to his sister and simply says it and it becomes clear.

Perhaps the first thing to note about Kleist's suggestion is that it goes contrary to the conduit metaphor (Reddy, 1979, p. 290) or translation or recoding theory (Linell, 1982, p. 145 f.). Kleist was characterizing the productive, creative nature of speaking. He was obviously not talking about reading something out, nor about packaging thoughts into words. In fact, that was precisely the process -- the pondering and brooding -- that hadn't worked. It was, on the other hand, precisely the process

181

of interacting with a friend, of facing his sister, that was productive. Speaking is in this sense an intelligent dealing with reality. Note that the cognitive component is not some separable, "relatively autonomous" (Levelt, 1983b, p. 279) module. The speaking itself is an intelligent social activity, the integrated activity of a human agent. The speaker does not understand what he begins to say, and that's precisely the point: That's why he is to say it, in order to come to an understanding by speaking. It is not a process of "giving linguistic shape to the message (formulation)" (Levelt, 1983b, p. 278), nor is it a process of "translating thoughts into sentences, words and sounds" (Ellis & Beattie, 1986, p. 117). Quite the contrary, it is a process of finding the message by speaking.

The fallacy of considering spontaneous speech as a process of reading off from within (intus legere) is extraordinarily widespread. What is needed, and what Kleist is describing, is:

A philosophy and practice of communication which is finitely open-ended, or heuristic, that is, open-ended until that exact moment in which it has "found" what it wanted to say after extensive trial-and-error. (Chouinard, 1985, p. 51)

In this respect, the terminology that describes spontaneous speech as productive in contrast to reading, which is reproductive, is most appropriate (even though reading too must similarly be a learning as one goes). The rest of this chapter, then, will deal with spontaneous or productive speech.

The inevitable question arises almost immediately: What

182

about the _hesitancy_ of spontaneous speech? Is hesitancy the cost of productivity? In other words, is hesitancy a diminution of efficiency and effectiveness? The reader will recall that this was Dell's (1986) basic position:

> Why is the language-production system error-prone? The main reason, I feel, is that the system must be productive. That is, it must allow for the production of novel combinations of items" (p. 319).

But, let us return to Kleist's version of what happens as he speaks:

> I mix in some unarticulated sounds, prolong transitional words, use some redundant apposition, and avail myself of other tricks to extend the discourse in order to win the requisite time to construct my ideas in the workshop of my mind. (p. 976; my trans.)

Is this a classic description of disfluency in action?

It is to be carefully noted that Kleist did not use the term _hesitancy_ (_Verzögerung_ in the German) at all. A gradual working-out (_allmähliche Verfertigung_) is a process of production, building, fabrication. Disfluency was the furthest thing from Kleist's intentions, and the term "error-prone" is equally foreign to his thoughts.

The problem seems to have arisen historically in that Lounsbury (1954) described _hesitation phenomena_ in a most confused and confusing fashion. In his section heading, _Pausal, Juncture, and Hesitation Phenomena_, he set pauses off from the

183

other two categories, but his description was then worded: "Hesitations which interrupt the continuous flow of speech are anything from very brief pauses to extended periods of halting, often filled with 'hemming and hawing'" (p. 98). In other words, at least some pauses must be considered hesitation phenomena. Note that _all_ pauses, even juncture pauses, "interrupt the continuous flow of speech" by their very nature, though it is quite clear in the context above that Lounsbury intended only "hesitation pauses" (p. 99) and not "juncture pauses" (p. 98). Perhaps he should have used the word "disrupt" instead of "interrupt" to describe hesitations. O'Connell and Kowal (1983) have commented on Lounsbury's influence as follows:

> In fact, the historical sense of American pausologists typically extends no further back in history than Louns-bury. Finally, Lounsbury's purely speculative characteri-zation of juncture and hesitation pauses was partly in terms of syntax, partly in terms of the purpose they serve for speaker and/or hearer, and partly in terms of duration. The confusion has led to much unnecessary controversy. (p. 233)

But the legitimate functions of these phenomena, as envi-sioned by Lounsbury and by Maclay and Osgood (1959) and others who followed in their footsteps, were essentially encoding on the part of the speaker and decoding on the part of the hearer. The research stimulated by Lounsbury was characteristically transi-tional probability research at the level of words. Rochester

(1973) has critiqued this tradition and has concluded that "the transition probability studies seem to support only a linear model in which pauses are dependent on moment-to-moment lexical choices" (p. 58).

The encoding legacy of Lounsbury is, then, one of proximate planning, certainly not one that emphasizes intentional communication or rhetorical expression. But how are we to know that pauses are limited to the function of planning? How can we tell that the speaker is not intentionally pausing for the special needs of a hearer or for a specific rhetorical effect? How are we to know that the speaker is not distracted by something else going on at the time of the pause (externally or in his own mind)? How are we to know that the speaker is not taking time out to think back on what he or she has just said, or on what reaction the message has just elicited from the hearer? The answer to all these questions is, of course, that we don't know. And the only reason the questions weren't being asked in the early research was that the research was entirely misconceived. Anything remotely resembling ecological validity was missing in most of the research, and the relevance of naturalistic observation, at least as a supplement to laboratory experimentation, was not acknowledged. Maclay and Osgood (1959), for all their other deficiencies, were a welcome exception to this criticism.

Some pauses may well be genuinely hesitant. But it is absolutely impossible to be certain that a pause is hesitant from its duration alone, as Lounsbury (1954) claimed, insofar as

185

juncture pauses "were in the order of a hundredth of a second or less in length" (p. 98). And in experiments in which there are typically no realistic context and no genuine communication to a listener, the potential uses of pauses (other than for hesitation) are reduced to banalities.

The terminology has stuck nonetheless. Chafe (1980a, b), for example, included all pauses as hesitation phenomena, even though he acknowledged:

> We may even find, when we study comprehension in relation to these phenomena which we are too prone to regard as infelicities, that they not only enable the speaker to express his ideas more effectively, but also enable the hearer to assimilate them more effectively too. (1980b, p. 170)

The real infelicity seems to have resided in the use of a term that implied disruption and disfluency for a phenomenon that is most certainly neither synonymous nor co-extensive with disruption and disfluency -- namely the pause. For example, it should be obvious that breathing is not in itself hesitation; yet breathing pauses automatically become hesitation as soon as all pauses are categorized as hesitation. Similarly, it is absurd to refer to silence used for emphasis (of something about to be said or of something just said or, for that matter, of something going on during the silence) or for a major transition to a new train of thought as hesitation.

Whence this impatience and carelessness in throwing everything silent into the same pot and calling everything in the pot

186

hesitation? I think there are at least two salient factors involved in this tendency.

The first of these factors is the perceptual fact that the only pauses which, so to speak, call attention saliently <u>to themselves or to their proximate environment</u> are those which actually <u>are</u> disruptive. Pauses that efficiently <u>subserve</u> emphasis, transition, structure, and/or nuance do not call attention to themselves. In our everyday experience, we do not advert to such phenomena at all. Put another way, the most efficient pauses are those that are silent in every sense of the word -- unnoticed. This silent salience is completely compatible, it should be noted, with the expressiveness of long pauses in keeping with principle (4), as enunciated in Chapter 10.

The second factor in our tendency to throw all pauses into the hesitation pot is once again <u>The written language bias in linguistics</u> (Linell, 1982); however, not only in linguistics, but also in native speakers of any language who are literate. We are so impressed by the orderliness of written text that the implicit comparison of written text and spontaneous speech becomes compelling. We have said previously that this comparison is an apples and oranges comparison that is completely unwarranted. But we generally fail to reflect on what actual writing is like and fail to make use of the proper comparison between writing and speaking in similar situations.

Indeed, when the proper comparison is made, as in Van De Water et al. (1987, p.101), the percentage of pause time/total time is significantly <u>greater</u> in writing than in speaking (42.2% > 34.1%). Such a finding cannot, of course, be generalized to every comparative setting of writing and speaking, but it indicates very clearly that spontaneous speaking is definitely not more "hesitant" than comparable writing.

There are two characteristics of pauses that are important for us to keep in mind if we are to avoid thinking of pauses as hesitations: (1) Any given pause may serve a number of functions simultaneously; and (2) Many of these functions are optional, i.e., they may be fulfilled by means other than pauses.

(1) The multiple simultaneous functions of pauses may be referred to as multi-determination. The most obvious case is the breathing pause. Since it occurs inevitably, the most efficient thing to do with it is to position it (and prolong or shorten it) so as to segment discourse as needed. But there is likewise no reason why, for example, a pause marking a major syntactic segment cannot at the same time indicate additionally a rhetorical emphasis or a semantic nuance.

(2) The speaker may choose to make use of <u>ontime</u> means instead of pausing at a given point in time to accomplish the same purpose. Stress, intonation, and acceleration or deceleration of articulation rate are all options that can be used to change the speech patterning to communicate emphasis, nuance, irony, metaphor, and many other effects, instead of pausing to accomplish the same effects.

The two characteristics work hand in hand, as some examples

will indicate. Funkhouser and O'Connell (1984, p. 98 f.) provided some from cummings' reading of his own poem "In Just Spring." In the following a slash is used to indicate a line-end; pause durations are indicated in seconds in parentheses. Only the words remain the same in the three repetitions:

Lines 4/5   balloonman (0.73) / whistles (1.13) far
                 (1.23) and wee (2.00) /

Lines 12/13   balloonman whistles (1.30) / far and wee
                 (1.50) /

Lines 21/22/23/24 balloonMan (1.00) whistles (1.43) /
                 far (1.03) / and (1.53) / wee (poem end)

In addition, the horizontal/vertical positioning of the words was different in each case in the printed version of the poem, and the use of upper and lower case quite idiosyncratic (e.g., in line 21 above). The only relatively stressed words in these excerpts were the first occurrence of "balloonman" and the last two words of the entire poem, "and wee". Articulation rate also varied greatly from one occurrence to the next of the same word. Cummings was obviously tremendously flexible in his pause usage with respect to both multi-determination and option. In fact, the only position consistently followed by pauses was "whistles". All the other positions were marked either by pauses or by shift in articulation rate, line format, stress, intonation, or a combination of these means. Van De Water and O'Connell (1986) gave the example of a melodramatically punctuated position in a speaker's manuscript, "an exclamation mark followed by a double

189

quotation mark, followed in turn by a dash" (p. 534), where the speaker made no pause whatsoever. Finally, Van De Water and O'Connell (1985) found that Seamus Heaney marked only 8/17 of all his unpunctuated stanzas with pauses, even though they were clearly positions of major importance. The ontime means of marking were evidently considered by him to be sufficient in these cases.

Both these characteristics, multi-determination and option, indicate the contribution of pausing as "tools of the trade." The Organon concept of language use is thus extendable to means that have not been part of the traditional armamentarium of linguistics. Pauses are an essential part of language use. Temporal organization is thus part of the deliberate, purposeful use of means in social settings for the optimizing of communication. That pauses are used in an overlearned and habitual fashion does not diminish the importance of these considerations. In this respect, they do not differ from the more traditionally acknowledged linguistic means of language use.

In view of the vast flexibility in pause usage that I have analyzed above under the rubrics of multi-determination and option, the analysis of pause structures of isolated sentential units can now be seen in a more realistic light. And the contention of Grosjean, Grosjean, and Lane (1979) in this regard becomes more than questionable:

The performance structures of sentences are not task specific. The linguistic surface structure of a sentence

190

is a good predictor of the pause durations. (p. 58)

The isolated sentence, read in the laboratory under profoundly distorting conditions, may indeed yield the "performance structures" of which Grosjean et al. speak, but it is equally true that "the little lame balloonman whistles far and wee". Somehow, I find myself more willing to listen to him.

The critical reader will have noticed by now perhaps that all the examples of multi-determination and option, with the exception of the obvious one of breathing pauses, have been taken not from spontaneous speech, but from reading. In reading, there are reference points to be found in the repetition of the same words and phrases, and in punctuation and page format. These are the advantages of the reading examples used above.

What reference points might we use to exemplify or demonstrate the use of multi-determination and option in spontaneous speech? For a number of years now, researchers -- generally for quite other reasons than an interest in multi-determination or option -- have found such reference points by analyzing the speech corpus so as to prepare a written text with punctuation that reflects syntactic and semantic structure. In most such cases, insufficient information is given to the reader to judge whether the written text accomplishes what it is supposed to. However, where the details have been adequately presented, it becomes clear that this method of discovering the structures of spontaneous speech is a failure.

Several examples of these attempts can be presented. The

only criterion used in their selection was that they present sufficient detail for us to make a judgement. Goldman-Eisler (1972), for example, argued that "the hierarchy of syntactic structures is reflected differentially in the pause structure of spontaneous speech" (p. 103). Syntactic structure, however, was defined by a secretary's use of punctuation. Goldman-Eisler acknowledged the secretary's "use of punctuation to be influenced by the intonation" (p. 104), but failed to note that it is equally plausible to assume that her punctuation was influenced by the subjective perception of pause structure. In other words, Goldman-Eisler's logic is completely circular.

Chafe (1980a, b) has provided a second example. Although he acknowledged that "intonational, hesitational, and syntactic" (1980a, p. 14) factors are not reliable predictors of idea units, he proceeded to set off as sentences such units as "OK" and "Um- - let's see" (1980b, p. 172), while insisting that other sequences of 53 syl and 92 syl (p. 174) were unitary sentences. He accomplished this inconsistency by the de facto acceptance "of falling pitch contour as 'sentence-final' intonation" (p. 173). And so, he came up with some quite implausible sentence units.

A third example is to be found in Deese (1984). The criteria (perceptually identified) used in preparation of transcripts included words, stress, pauses, and rate of speaking. Yet, Deese accepted units such as "WHEN YOU HAVE ACTUAL SPECIFI-CATIONS" (p. 21 f.) as sentences.

O'Connell (1977) has provided other examples of similar

192

procedures used to discover the structures of spontaneous speech and has concluded:

> The concept of <u>sentence</u> and consequently the use of the sentence as an empirical unit are extremely complex and problematic. A universal prescientific concept has been erected into a scientific universal by various implicit metamorphoses. We would all do well to pursue some of the logical implications and empirical ramifications of our use of the concept <u>sentence</u> and be very suspicious of circularity in our identification or isolation of sentences -- particularly those of other people. (p. 313 f.)

Similarly, Akinnaso (1982) has observed that

> Discourse analysts have recognized the non-applicability of the notion of sentence to the analysis of natural conversational data, and have suggested an alternative unit of analysis under the various names of "information unit" (Halliday, 1973), "utterance chunks" (Gumperz, 1977), and "idea units" (Kroll, 1977; Chafe, 1980, 1982). (p. 105)

Ludwig (1983), on the other hand, has denied "that sentences in written texts are necessarily different from those in spoken texts" (p. 65; my trans.).

Identifying other people's spoken sentences -- or "units" or "chunks" -- is not only <u>like</u> reading other people's minds; it is a clear case of trying to do so. Desirable as it might appear to be to have clearly identifiable reference points in spontaneous speech in order to demonstrate the occurrence of the phenomena of

193

multi-determination and option, it appears to be logically and empirically very difficult to do so.

But let me return once again to the "gradual working-out of one's thoughts." The German word _Verfertigung_ proves of interest in yet another way. The adjective form _fertig_ has a broad range of meanings; among them, one finds the notions of finished, complete, accomplished. All these notions carry with them at least a strong connotation of the definitive. In the present context, this connotation of the definitive suggests further "the last word" on a given topic, something that could be printed out in black and white, so to speak. I think one must heartily disavow such a suggested surplus meaning, both in Kleist's essay and, more importantly, in human speech. Interestingly enough, the essay itself ended with "to be continued" (p. 980; my trans.). And since there is no evidence that Kleist either had or implemented any intention to do so, we can accept the phrase symbolically.

The spoken word is never "the last word," but rather always part of the ongoing, contingent, developing, intelligent dealing with reality on the part of humankind. We are always _in mediis rebus_, literally in the middle of things, never quite finished (_fertig_). Chouinard's "_exact_ moment in which it has 'found' what it wanted to say" cannot, therefore, be accepted in the sense of "the final word," nor did he intend his statement in that sense.

A more appropriate metaphor would be a strobe flash atop a tall city building. The world is suddenly -- but only momentarily -- enlightened by its brilliance. Neither the strobe flash nor a spoken utterance enlightens permanently and definitively. The written language bias in linguistics has left us, nonetheless, with an impatience to say it all and be done with it -- to get it down on paper. But more realistically, nothing is truly worth saying unless it leads -- gradually (allmählich) -- beyond itself to wonderment at the transcendent mysteries of the universe and of the human condition. It is precisely in this sense that Chouinard (1985) has referred to poetry as "not only a puzzlement, but a puzzling" (p. 31).

The very notion of wonderment or puzzlement suggests silent awe, an attitude of listening rather than of proclaiming. This in turn suggests the dialogic, and we are then far beyond the considerations of Kleist. But listening must be present even in monologue. The speaker is simultaneously the listener, and that is indeed part of Kleist's secret. We learn from ourselves when we address others -- if we are listening. And if the stance of listening is already present in our monologic speaking, then we are ready to listen to others in turn.

Some would accept as a working assumption the principle that "Planning must take up time not used for phonation" (Butterworth, 1980, p. 158). But speaking itself is a far richer phenomenon than that; not only do we plan during our speaking, we listen as well, not only to ourselves but to many other ongoing, shifting contextual circumstances.

Concluding a chapter with such glowing wonderment over

speaking may pose a further problem, however. What about those who think otherwise, who are content with their beautiful, finished prose, and who care not one bit for "transcendent mysteries". My advice to such as these is to stop speaking, stop conversing. They have nothing more to say; they have said it all. These are the ones who love to answer questions (sometimes without finding out what the real question is), instead of asking more questions. The basic pathology is that they still haven't found the real questions, and their answers are therefore necessarily banalities: "Confusion is a critical component of creativity" (Chouinard, 1985, p. 137). And so, speaking is the process of working-out our thoughts gradually -- in time -- with one another. The tool is always to be used in the service of a transcendently creative goal.

Chapter 13

Babel Now: An Essay on Fluency and Disfluency

Let me begin this chapter with a quotation from Walter Cronkite. In a television interview of President Reagan, Cronkite wished to introduce a rather blunt question suggesting a parallel between Soviet intervention in Afghanistan and American intervention in El Salvador. The final portion of Cronkite's lead-in was as follows: "what what's where where's the where why isn't that a parallel situation" (Kowal, Bassett, & O'Connell, 1985, p. 15). Printed as baldly as it is here, it does not <u>look</u> very complimentary. It is difficult, in fact, to imagine one of the top TV anchormen in the world being so. . . . Perhaps the reader would care to supply the appropriate adjective. Was Cronkite being inarticulate? Disfluent? Hesitant? Ineffective? Did he make himself look silly in this situation? The question is, of course, unfair precisely because the total context is needed to make any judgement. Suffice it to say that President Reagan's reaction was not to bristle and not to refuse to answer the question on the ground that it was an impertinence. Quite the contrary; he laughed aloud and replied jovially and at length. I suspect too that, had we inquired of TV viewers immediately after the program, they would have agreed that Cronkite had been his usual friendly, articulate self, completely in command of the situation.

Anecdotes have limited value for proving the ultimate nature of fluency, but there is a point to be made. Whatever properties

197

we wish to associate with fluency, they must take into account the purpose of a given utterance or type of utterance and the context in which the utterance occurs. To come to the question of fluency with a bias, for example, in favor of some a priori definition of "the well-formed sentence" would be absurd. It might, in fact, leave us with only one alternative: to acknowledge that Cronkite was being hired for a handsome salary by a national network to be inarticulate.

If we choose to operate out of The written language bias in linguistics (Linell, 1982) to pursue the nature of fluency, we are liable to get nowhere because the written shears away the very prosodic, temporal dynamics that contribute to fluency in speech. Suddenly we are right back to the one correct reading, the ideal speaker, and the whole crypto-normative array of written language principles.

Perhaps some of the differences between the written page and the spoken word might be pinpointed as follows. While I am silently reading sentences from the written page, typically nothing else in the ambient context is contributing to what is going on in the reading. The reading is relatively timeless, at least in the sense that whatever time constraints are present are extraneous to the text. In speaking, the situation is entirely different. In the midst of any one of my sentences, all sorts of things might happen. My interlocutor might, for example, nod assent or wave dissent. Someone might join the conversation or leave. I might simply realize that there is a nuance or a fact missing, or that something was not quite correctly stated, or that the microphone level is wrong. Note that well-formedness in these sentences _must_ be something quite different from the well-formedness of written sentences if the former are to be _part of the ongoing context of the speaking itself_. Were they to be well-formed in the same sense as written sentences, we would not even need a coroner to pronounce them _dead_. _Fluency in the spoken modality does not have a one-to-one relationship to well-formedness in the written modality._

Let us pursue this matter just a bit further; for it is quite clear that the well-formedness of the written modality can still claim normative prestige. We do not think of the Cronkite utterance as well-formed when we _see_ it, and that's why I mentioned above that it doesn't _look_ good. When it is removed from its oral setting, it really does _look_ silly. The reason is that it isn't meant to be _looked at_ at all.

But the other side of the coin is just as revealing. The only reason why written well-formedness looks so good is paradoxically because it not only _looks_ dead, _it is dead_. Rommetveit (1974), crediting Birdwhistell (1971), described this aspect of the written text eloquently:

> Birdwhistell argues that what is preserved in typed transcripts of face-to-face dialogues is in fact only 'the cadaver of speech'. And an essential part of what is lost in the transcription has to do with what Roman Jakobson refers to as meta-linguistic operations, i.e. with shifting

> premises of communication conveyed by, for example, body movement, gesture, facial expression and tone of voice. What is made known by speech when it is 'alive' can hence, according to Birdwhistell, only be assessed by a joint exploration of the 'integrational' and the 'new informational' aspects of the entire, multifaceted process of interaction. (p. 62)

Linguistic theory and above all <u>The written language bias in linguistics</u> have, however, done a superb job of cosmeticizing the cadaver. We hardly notice the deadness. Hence derives the frequency with which the apples and oranges comparisons between the written and the spoken recur again and again in the literature.

Let us return to Kowal, Bassett, and O'Connell (1985) and their analyses of both Walter Cronkite's and Dan Rather's television speaking. I assume that most readers would be willing to agree that we are dealing with expert speech in these cases. It is also clear that both speakers chose to speak spontaneously in their interview questions of President Reagan instead of reading off questions. This does not imply that the questioning was not prepared, only that the wording was not predetermined. This allowed Kowal, Bassett, and O'Connell to compare the interview performance of the two speakers to their reading performance in other settings.

The findings give us some insights into the differences between the fluency derived from well-formed written sentences and the fluency characteristic of spontaneous speech.

Except for the fact that less than half of all pauses were between-sentence pauses, the readings of both Cronkite and Rather were by and large in keeping with the characterization of ideal delivery:

> Both speakers articulated rapidly. . ., made use of only a small amount of pause time, produced no vocal hesitations, and paused regularly between sentences but did not pause within syntactic phrases. Pauses between sentences were clearly longer than pauses at other positions, thus helping the listener to better understand the sentence structure. (p. 10)

This description is in stark contrast to that of the interview performances:

> The spontaneity of both speakers was characterized by pauses of longer duration, by vocal hesitations of all three types, and by a distribution of off-time (in terms of duration and position) not dictated exclusively by syntactic constraints. (p. 11)

The three types of hesitations mentioned above, by the way, are the classic filled pauses, repeats, and false starts. The point must be made emphatically, with Kowal, Bassett, and O'Connell, that the characteristically spontaneous interview performance described above was not disfluent on that account. The deviation from ideal delivery clearly "reflects an alternative norm for effective communication" (p. 11). The speaker's communicative

201

intent and his or her moment to moment adaptation to the interlocutor and to the overall setting take precedence over the ideal of "the grammatical integrity of the sentence" (p. 12).

Even a quite generic or commonsensical notion of development might suggest that the fluency characteristic of adults is not the same as the fluency characteristic of children. Nonetheless, we do not ordinarily think of children as disfluent. Their speaking skills are partly determined by a number of component motor skills and partly by complex cognitive and social skills.

How the development of these various skills affects the temporal organization of speech has been the preoccupation of a number of researchers in recent years, notably Kowal, O'Connell, and Sabin (1975); Sabin, Clemmer, O'Connell, and Kowal (1979); and Starkweather (1980). For our present discussion, the data given by Kowal et al. in their Table II (p. 200) and Table 1 (p. 199) can serve as a summary. In the experiment, 12 boys and 12 girls at each grade level (K, 2, 4, 6, 8, highschool sophomore, highschool senior) were asked to tell a story aloud in response to a series of cartoon frames. Only the data for the two extreme levels are given here in order to pinpoint the magnitude of change:

Response Measures	Kindergarten	H. S. Seniors
$\underline{M}$ Number of syllables	80.3	116.5
$\underline{M}$ Speech rate (syl/sec)	2.15	3.84
$\underline{M}$ Phrase length (syl/pause	5.5	10.0
$\underline{M}$ Pause duration (msec/syl)	293	89

Number of filled pauses	32	29
Number of false starts	60	29
Number of repeats	48	12
Number of parenthetical remarks	3	70
Number of subordinate conjunctions	14	67

The most basic change evident in these data is the increase in amount spoken. The descriptive detail and narrative development of the kindergartners were quite primitive in comparison to those of the highschool seniors. But both pause frequency (as reflected in the phrase length or syl/pause) and pause duration (msec/syl) decreased dramatically, contributing to an equally dramatic increase in speech rate. The evidence regarding the various vocal hesitations is equally clear. Filled pauses remained stable across these levels, but false starts and repeats diminished appreciably. The category of parenthetical remarks includes such fillers as "you know, well, sort of, like"; these increased greatly across these levels. Finally, the category of subordinate conjunctions is included to provide an indication of a parallel development in the complexity of the utterances.

Is it reasonable, however, to consider the fluency of the highschool seniors as adult fluency? This was precisely the question engaged by Sabin, Clemmer, O'Connell, and Kowal (1979) in using the same experimental task with college seniors and alumni (average age of 25). Their findings (p. 44) for these two additional groups were indeed comparable to those for the highschool seniors, although speech rate declined slightly in the two older groups from the younger subjects' rates.

There is, then, a very notable shift in the temporal organization of speech over the gradeschool and highschool years and a leveling off in adulthood. In his review of these findings, Starkweather added a discussion of ontime and argued for the importance of developmental changes in articulation rate:

> A second aspect of fluency is the rate of speech. Rate results from the combined effect of the frequency and duration of pauses and the frequency of syllable production. Of these two elements, pauses are considerably less important in determining rate than syllables. (p. 193)

Starkweather's concept of fluency was essentially defined in terms of effort:

> Fluent speech is effortless, and yet speaking requires some minimal effort. The virtual effortlessness of fluent speech seems to be of two types, one reflecting the fact that we do not need to think very much about the breathing, voicing, articulation, semantics, or syntax of speech production -- it happens almost automatically. The other type of effort is muscular.
>
> Although clearly part of what we mean by fluency, the very small amount of thinking time devoted to the planning and execution of speech has been studied very little for the obvious reason that thinking is difficult to observe.

(p. 189)

A decrement in effortfulness parallel to the development of muscular, articulatory skills does indeed seem to be a component of the changes noted in children's fluency as they grow older. But "the very small amount of thinking time devoted to the planning and execution of speech" is by no means the only other consideration relevant for fluency. The social, affective, communicative elements are equally important. It is noteworthy that consideration is seldom given to the fact that speakers are also listening and observing at the same time. The dichotomy of fluency into "effort of mind and effort of muscle" (p. 192) is clearly inadequate.

There is another problem with Starkweather's formulation. The real reason why "the very small amount of thinking time devoted to the planning and execution of speech has been studied very little" is not "the obvious reason that thinking is diffi-cult to observe". The reason is far more basic than that: There exists no such time. That is to say that, contrary to the conviction of many researchers who voice the same reasoning as Starkweather, "the planning and execution of speech" simply does not have a "small amount of thinking time" allocated to it. The very concept of isolable thinking time is fallacious!

But let us return to the general question of adult fluency once again. The fluent adult is fine in terms of both effort-lessness and ability to communicate so long as he or she remains at home. One of the most profound sadnesses of the human condition is our inability to communicate with one another: Babel, the chaos of words.

In this context, I cannot resist the temptation to relate an anecdote from 1972, when I found myself in a train compartment enroute from Heidelberg to Munich. Part of a group of students had rejoined me in Heidelberg -- four lovely young women. There was one other person in the compartment, a quite handsome young Turkish gentleman. He was intent on engaging my students in conversation, and I was equally intent on hovering protectively and paternalistically. He had perhaps 20 German and 10 English words at his disposal. He persisted charmingly and enthusiastically in what I had at once prejudged to be a flirtatious conversation. By the end of our journey, however, he had made it very clear, with many gestures and his basic vocabulary of 30 useful words, that his marvelous enthusiasm had as its source the recent birth of his first child. He was on his way home from Norway where he had been earning money for his new family. Despite my deep embarrassment, the beauty of our "primitive, disfluent" dialogue was perfectly clear to all five of us. Or rather, quite evidently, to all six of us!

Apart from pathological speech itself, the struggling of nonnative speakers to master communication is perhaps the prototypical case of human disfluency. Hence, the temporal organization of nonnative speech is of central importance to our study of fluency. In one of the classic early experiments of Cattell (1886), he engaged temporal organization of foreign languages:

> The rate at which a person reads a foreign language is
> proportional to his familiarity with the language. For
> example, when reading as fast as possible the writer's
> rate was, English 138, French 167, German 250, Italian 327,
> Latin 434, and Greek 484; the figures giving the thousandths
> of a second taken to read each word. Experiments made on
> others strikingly confirm these results. The subject does
> not know that he is reading the foreign language more slowly
> than his own; this explains why foreigners seem to talk so
> fast. This simple method of determining a person's famili-
> arity with a language might be used in school examinations.
> (p. 64 f.)

It has always been surprising to me that no one in the interim of
100 years has adopted Cattell's suggestion. In fact, the
analysis of temporal organization in second-language learning has
been rather thoroughly neglected.

Our first research in the area made use of the German story
paragraphs from O'Connell et al. (1969) and was reported in
Kowal, O'Connell, O'Brien, and Bryant (1975). Subjects with no
German at all, with four to six college semesters, with graduate
coursework, and with a native German background read the stories
in German and retold them in English. A summary of the significant findings from the readings will contribute to our discussion. Going from least to most proficiency in German, the mean
response measures shifted as follows (p. 553):

Number of pauses: 33.8 > 18.1 > 9.7 > 7.6

Speech rate (syl/sec):   2.01 < 3.40 < 3.55 < 4.12

Phrase length (syl/pause): 4.0 < 8.0 < 12.0 < 16.6

And in the stories told after the readings, one response measure in particular was significant:

Number of syllables   39.0 < 60.6 < 85.6 < 91.9

The most notable similarity between these shifts in fluency in adults at various levels of proficiency in a language on the one hand and shifts in fluency over developmental levels on the other hand is to be found in speech rate. In both cases, it shifted from c. 2 syl/sec to double that rate. Both the second-language and the developmental data also indicate that, under otherwise unchanged conditions, more fluency yields more speaking, whether in telling a story from cartoons or retelling a story just read. Note that in the readings this response measure (number of syllables) was not relevant because there was virtually no variability in this measure.

The very last mean entered above is also of interest: the mean number of syllables spoken by the native speakers of German in retelling the story just read in German. This retelling was in English. In this respect, this one mean is asymmetrical with all the others: In this one instance, the retelling was in a nonnative language, English. Despite this fact, having read the original story in their native language and being proficient in English as a second language, these native speakers of German retold the story in more syllables than any of the native speakers of English.

Wiese (1983) used a similar design involving cartoon stories spoken by native speakers and nonnative speakers of both German and English. Several of his response measures indicated significant differences between stories told in a nonnative language and stories told in a native language:

M Response Measures	Nonnative	Native
Pause duration (msec):	1100	770
Speech rate (syl/sec):	1.95	3.25
Articulation rate (syl/sec):	3.67	4.57
Phrase length (syl/pause):	4.4	8.3
Filled pauses/100 syl:	5.7	2.4
False starts/100 syl:	1.7	0.7
Repeats/100 syl:	2.2	0.7

Wiese's nonnative-native differences are not as dramatic as those found by Kowal, O'Connell, O'Brien, and Bryant (1975) by reason of his design. His subjects were relatively proficient in the nonnative languages used in the experiment. Nonetheless, the decrease in pause duration and frequency and the corresponding increase in speech rate from nonnative to native speech are appreciable. The increase in speech rate was contributed to by a corresponding increase in articulation rate. In other words, both the offtime and ontime components of fluency are different in nonnative and native speech.

Phrase length in native spontaneous speech (Wiese, 1983;

Kowal, O'Connell, & Sabin, 1975) was much shorter (8.3 & 10.0 syl/pause) than phrase length in the reading data for native speakers (16.6 syl/pause) in Kowal, O'Connell, O'Brien, and Bryant (1975). Such long phrases and the corresponding infrequency of pauses reflect the reproductive nature of reading, in particular of reading done for an experiment, but without salient rhetorical, communicative, or expressive intent.

The fact that filled pauses, false starts, and repeats occurred far more frequently in Wiese's nonnative speech data suggests once again the possibility of a completely negative view of such phenomena -- as "to be deleted" disfluencies. Hieke (1981) has taken a quite different approach, according to which hesitations

> form an integral part of speech production in the positive
> sense, a view quite in opposition to the attitude that there
> is fluency on one hand and hesitancy on the other. Not only
> are hesitations a normal component of fluency if they occur
> in moderation, but now pauses and the other hesitations can
> actually be considered wellformedness phenomena rather than
> disfluencies, at least as far as they serve as devices by
> the speaker to produce more error-free, high-quality speech.
> (p. 150)

He then proposed a new classification for hesitation phenomena:

1. Stalls (silent pauses, filled pauses, prospective
repeats, syllabic prolongations).

2. Repair (false starts, retrospective repeats or bridging).

(p. 154)

Hieke (1984) has subsequently called attention to a number of ontime phenomena that must be counted as markers of fluent speech and has questioned (Hieke, 1985) both current concepts and current practices of oral fluency evaluation:

> A satisfactory definition of fluency has not been offered up to now, perhaps because much of the work in this area rests on rather shallow empirical grounds. Sufficiently sophisticated instrumentation to subject the properties of speech to very fine analysis has not been available for long, and the void in conceptual frameworks which could have provided direction has always aggravated the situation further. (p. 136)

He then proposed a componential approach, based in part specifically on the research on temporal variables in speech, instead of "the holistic viewpoint now predominant" (p. 135).

In light of all the current confusion regarding fluency and disfluency, the following statement by Garrett (1982) is of interest:

> A priori, a break in the fluency of utterance may be regarded as an indication that the rate of speech output has overrun the rate of decision making either about what we will say or how we will say it. (p. 23)

In fact, there is nothing a priori about Garrett's contention; instead, it is only a rather undifferentiated expression of ordinary folk wisdom. And, additionally, there is no empirical

211

evidence that a break in fluency is always accompanied by a "rate of speech output" that "has overrun the rate of decision making either about what we will say or how we will say it". Distraction, for example, -- simply thinking about something else in the midst of an utterance -- has nothing to do with "what we will say or how we will say it," but it can certainly occasion "a break in the fluency of utterance". It is simply not the case that "the rate of speech output" is part of the problem of disfluency in every instance. Garrett's overwhelming preoccupation with the "rate of planning processes" (p. 23) has led to a distorted concept of fluency and disfluency.

As Hieke (1985) has summed up the situation, a great deal of work remains before we can "replace the present rather squishy prose descriptions" (p. 140) of fluency -- so as to be able to speak fluently about fluency.

Chapter 14

Listening for Pauses

In actuality, one can neither listen _for_ nor _to_ pauses as
such. For years now, I have replied facetiously, when asked
about my area of research, that I investigate "contextualized
nothing." And, indeed, pauses are perceptible only insofar as
they are contextualized. But they are not really only nothing;
they are not simply silences, but intervals of silence occurring
between speech. We are, of course, capable of estimating the
duration of an interval of silence between audible signals or of
judging whether or not such an interval has occurred. These are
fairly straightforward psychophysical or psychoacoustic questions, but they are not the questions of primary interest for a
psychologist of language use.

There are two clearly distinct questions of interest for the
researcher of temporal organization of speech.

The first concerns the use of pauses in various speech
contexts on the part of the listener. _Use_ in this setting does
not mean reporting pauses, nor adverting to them; it simply means
that the pauses make a difference in the understanding of an
utterance. Pauses can either help or hinder in the process of
conveying intended meaning of a speaker to a hearer. Whether the
listener is aware of this introspectively, whether he or she is
able to report it retrospectively or reflectively, may well prove
important questions in their own rights. But neither question
addresses directly the psychological question: the potential

functions of pauses in the meaning and understanding of speech. It is an extraordinarily complex question, involving nuances of fluency, rhetoric, and many other influences. We are nowhere within range of an answer, and the answer cannot be a simple one in any event.

We must be very clear about the empirical logic involved: For the listener not to be able to report a pause does not prove that he or she has not made use of a pause at that moment; much less does it prove that no pause occurred at that moment. And indeed, reporting a pause at a given point in time does _not_ prove _eo ipso_ that a pause occurred at that moment. It is possible, in other words, for false negatives and false positives to be reported. And it is also possible to err by overestimation or underestimation of the duration of pauses even when occurrence is veridically reported.

The second question of interest to the psychologist of language use is a methodological one: Is it reasonable to use reports of pauses as a veridical reflection of pause occurrence and/or pause duration in research?

Note that in the setting of the first question the listener is listening to oral discourse. It is only in that sense that he or she is listening _to_ pauses. In the setting of the second question, the listener is listening _for_ pauses _for the purpose of_ identifying occurrence and/or estimating duration. The questions are clearly related; in principle, we might, for example, be dealing with the same set of actual pauses. But the two questions are vastly different one from another, and the answers may be just as disparate. Put yet another way, when one instructs an experimental subject to listen for pauses, one is asking him or her to do something that listeners to oral discourse do not typically do at all, and to thereby neglect the listening for meaning that is typical. Our preoccupation in the present chapter will be primarily with the second of these questions, the methodological question: the veridicality of experimenters' or instructed subjects' estimates of pause occurrence and/or pause duration, i.e., their correspondence with physically measured actual pauses.

A research example in which the two questions were confounded may serve to clarify the difference. In her monograph Makrosyntax der Gliederungssignale im gesprochenen Französisch (The macrosyntax of segmental markers in spoken French), Gülich (1970) summarized her methodology with respect to pauses as follows:

> We have conceptualized the segmental elements at sentence
> boundaries and the markers of hesitation as signals of the
> speaker for the hearer. What the ear of the hearer per-
> ceives is therefore critical for our observations, not what
> an instrument records. It would be inappropriate to want
> to correct the subjective auditory perception by means of
> an objective instrumental recording. (p. 277; my trans.)

One point that must be made at this juncture is that we do not know "what the ear of the hearer perceives." Gülich seems to

assume that the ear of the subject listening to the oral discourse and the ear of the experimenter listening for pauses
perceive the same thing. Similarly, one might assume that the
ear of the speaker and the ear of the hearer perceive the same
thing. Both assumptions further imply a one-to-one correspondence between pause perception and pause report. Short of
measuring the objective occurrence and duration of pauses, such
assumptions are the only alternative; however, they completely
bypass the most important empirical questions. In any event, it
is not a question of wanting "to correct the subjective auditory
perception," but of using appropriate data to answer questions.

We have already discussed the use of perceptually identified pauses in the research of Maclay and Osgood (1959) and of
Deese (1984). The history of such usage goes back far beyond
these two studies.

One of the earliest studies is that of Cowan and Bloch
(1948). Although they had at their disposal a record of the
measured actual pauses, they defined pauses perceptually:

> The term 'pause' in all that follows is to be understood
> as meaning a perceptual pause only (including those judged
> to be present but not shown in the physical record). (p.
> 96)

Their ten subjects were in complete agreement, however, on only
56.6% of the pauses. Hence, the above definition was limited
further: "A pause is perceptually present only if five or more of
the ten observers report it" (p. 90). But even this did not

suffice to eliminate false positives and false negatives:

Even in the case of those pauses which lie above our
arbitrary criterion, a comparison of the observers' reports and the physical record shows that some of these
'perceptual pauses' were located at points where there was
no actual interruption of the physical speech energy, and
that on the other hand some relatively long interruptions
of the physical energy were not detected as pauses. (p. 92)

The authors acknowledged the problem mentioned above concerning
the purpose of listening:

Since the attention of the observers was divided between
pause detection and perception of context meaning, the in-
terfering factors which gave rise to the illusion of a pause
are probably for the most part linguistic. (p. 90)

Nor was there agreement among the observers as to which of their
"perceptual pauses" were long and which were short. Lack of
unanimous agreement in this regard characterized two thirds of
the pauses: "Our observers found no consistent psychological or
psychophysical basis for a discrimination of long and short
pauses in the material they worked with" (p. 94). Throughout
their discussion, Cowan and Bloch assumed that there is a one-to-
one correspondence between reported pauses and perceived pauses.
Finally, the tally of number of pauses in Cowan and Bloch's Table
I (p. 90) does not add up.

What I find astounding is that Cowan and Bloch were still
willing not only to make use of their "perceptual pauses," but to

generalize quite sweepingly:

> If speech pauses set off syntactic phrases in accordance
> with accepted linguistic usage, as they do most of the time,
> they present no problem to the observers. If, however,
> there is no objective pause at a point where there is a
> strong linguistic reason to expect one, observers may
> actually be led into reporting a perceptual pause. Simi-
> larly, if an objective pause occurs within a phrase where
> there is no linguistic reason to expect it, observers may
> fail to notice it even when it is of considerable dura-
> tion. This is, of course, a very broad explanation, which
> overlooks important contrast factors of pitch and intensity
> at the points in question; but it appears to be generally
> valid as far as it goes. (p. 92 f.)

Descriptive and inferential statistics were not given, however,
to justify these generalizations.

Even before the Cowan and Bloch research, Newman and Mather
(1938) had used their own impressions of where pauses occurred.
They simply listened to phonographic recordings and noted pauses
without adverting to any methodological problems. Hahn (1949)
too eschewed objective measurements of pausing. Her rationale
was almost a preview of Gülich's later reasoning: "To judge the
vocal and articulatory aspects of speech, one cannot set up
objective measures. The experience of the person making the
evaluations must be the basis for the acceptance of the judgments" (p. 338).

Perhaps the use of perceptual identification of pauses in these early studies is understandable because of the lack of a critical tradition in the archival literature at that time. But Kowal (1987) has listed more than a dozen later studies from the sixties, seventies, and even the eighties, in which the use of perceptually identified pauses continued to be uncritically accepted as quite adequate for the study of pauses in speech production. In other words, these studies continued to assume that actual pauses used in speech production can be veridically identified and are validly and reliably reflected in pause reports of experimental subjects or experimenters.

There have been a number of efforts to study systematically the relationships between actual pause occurrence and perceptual identification and report. The methodologies, however, have differed from one study to another so much that the findings are hardly comparable. Boomer and Dittmann (1962) artificially spliced in hesitation and juncture pauses and instructed subjects to judge sentences as same or different with respect to pauses. Their approach was basically psychophysical:

> A common psychophysical definition of threshold by paired
> comparisons is that point at which 75 per cent correct
> discriminations are made -- that is, halfway between chance
> and perfect discrimination. Thus defined, the thresholds
> would be about 200 msec. for hesitation pauses and somewhere
> between 500 and 1,000 msec. for juncture pauses. (p. 217)

These findings were exactly the opposite of what Cowan and Bloch

(1948) would have predicted, but Boomer and Dittmann did not even mention the Cowan and Bloch research.

Martin (1970), on the other hand, made use of two judges and defined scorer-spectrograph agreement as follows: "Each silent interval recorded by machine and marked by at least one scorer was counted as scorer-spectrograph agreement; the overlap was 90.0%" (p. 76). A moment's reflection will make clear that such an index rises with the number of scorers, instead of making use of scorer overlap as a source of reliability of measurement. In other words, it errs in the direction of including false positives.

Rochester (1975/76) emphasized that the roles of grammar, semantics, and prosody in pause perception are not yet understood. She summarized the work of Cowan and Bloch and Martin as follows:

> The work. . . suggests a dichotomy in pause judgment dependent on duration. Long pauses are always detected and no further variables are needed for explanation, while detection of short pauses (50-200 msec in Cowan & Bloch's work; 50-110 msec in Martin's study) depends on linguistic cues. (p. 3)

Butcher's (1981) summary was couched in terms of the tone group:

> Whereas breaks between tone groups are not heard by 75% of listeners until they are approximately 220 ms long, breaks within tone groups are heard by the same proportion of

listeners when only 80 ms long. (p. 205)

Adams (1979) has added to the conviction of complexity of pause perception by emphasizing the influence of variability of syllabic duration, of acoustic energy, and of vocalic quality in the report of pauses.

In the archival research reviewed up to this point, two distinct sets of variables have been thought to influence pause reports.   One set included physical variables (e.g., syllabic duration, acoustic energy, vocalic quality, in addition to actual pause duration itself); the other set included variables conse-quent upon linguistic knowledge (e.g.,syntax, semantics).   The latter can be controlled by using subjects who do not understand the language being spoken, or varied by using groups of subjects whose proficiency in the language being spoken differs systemati-cally.

Chiappetta, Monti, and O'Connell (1987), Stuckenberg and O'Connell (in press), and Carpenter and O'Connell (in press) have all made use of this distinction between physical and linguistic variables to investigate pause reports.   The archival literature suggests that the linguistic variables should affect the veridi-cality of reports of the shorter pauses.   These recent studies operationalized shorter pauses as $\leq$ 0.3 sec and used a cutoff point of 0.13 sec for minimum measurable duration of pauses.   The archival literature also suggests that the longer pauses should not manifest any differences due to proficiency level in the language used in the experiment.   But what if proficient native speakers of a language find it difficult to prescind from their knowledge of the language, when asked to listen for pauses? In this event, even longer pauses might manifest differences due to proficiency level in the language used in the experiment.

Chiappetta et al. (1987) used native speakers of Italian and American nonspeakers of Italian. Both groups underestimated frequency of occurrence and overestimated duration of pauses. The nonspeakers' duration estimates were significantly closer than were those of the Italians to the actual durations. When percentages of actual pauses correctly reported were broken down according to language group and duration bracket, the following pattern emerged for three duration brackets:

Group	≤ 0.3 sec	> 0.3, < 1.0 sec	≥ 1.0 sec
Italians	46.0%	82.5%	92.9%
Americans	25.0%	93.7%	93.8%

In other words, a facilitative effect of knowledge of the language listened to appeared in the shortest duration bracket for the percentage of actual pauses correctly reported. There also appeared an inhibitory effect in the middle duration bracket; the Americans were more accurate than the native speakers. Here the inability to prescind from the linguistic features of the corpus seemed to have distracted the Italians from the reporting task. There were no differences in the longest duration bracket, but some quite long pauses were not reported, contrary to the insistence in the archival literature that longer pauses are always reported.

The research of Stuckenberg and O'Connell (in press) did not confirm the facilitative and inhibitory effects of Chiappetta et al. (1987), but found instead overestimation of occurrence and underestimation of duration. German and English corpora were listened to by both German and American native speakers. Germans reported a higher percentage of actual pauses than Americans. A higher percentage of actual pauses was reported in native than in nonnative passages. Americans reported a higher percentage of actual pauses in English passages, whereas Germans' percentages were the same in both languages. The lower percentage of the Americans in the German passages was clearly related to their lack of knowledge of German, whereas the Germans were all proficient also in English. American women reported more false positives than American men, whereas German men reported more than German women. Americans and Germans both reported more false positives in English than in German.

Stuckenberg and O'Connell's (in press) findings indicated an extraordinarily complex dependency of such perceptual reports on an impressive array of independent variables. There were altogether 3104 actual pauses to be reported; reports included 515 false positives and omitted 337 false negatives. The evidence in this research against veridicality of perceptual reports of pauses would appear to be quite massive.

Carpenter and O'Connell (in press) used the same methodology with a small corpus of French poetry. Pauses were reported by both native speakers of French and native Americans. An additional condition was included to enhance linguistic effects: The text to be marked was presented to half the subjects in each group in poetic format with the author's punctuation and to the other half of the subjects in uppercase letters without either poetic format or punctuation.

Both occurrence and duration were underestimated. Two interactions were significant: (1) More pauses were correctly reported by native speakers of French with the punctuated format, whereas more pauses were correctly reported by native speakers of English with the unpunctuated format; (2) Men reported more false positives with the unpunctuated format, whereas women reported more false positives with the punctuated format. Almost all pauses of medium and long duration (95% & 97%) were correctly reported, whereas only 2.5% of the short pauses were correctly reported. Of all reported pauses, 38% were false positives; i.e., they did not correspond to actual pauses in the reading. In both punctuated and unpunctuated formats, these false positives corresponded by and large to positions of salient syllabic prolongation. Correspondingly, the articulation rate of the reading was quite slow (3.23 syl/sec). Of the false negatives, 96% were failures to report short pauses ($\underline{M}$ = 0.16 sec; all at midline and unpunctuated positions in the punctuated format). The first of the two interactions (native language by punctuation format) clearly indicated a use of linguistic cues where they were available.

A recent study by Duez (1985) used a methodology similar to

ours with a French corpus of interviews of politicians. The percentages of actual pauses correctly reported in her three conditions were: 28% for normal speech, 27% for inverted speech (distorted by spectral inversion), and 85% for synthetic speech (a constant frequency vowel sound with the on-off sequences of the original speech). The study can be looked upon as a removal of linguistic cues by stages: semantics and syntax from the inverted speech, then prosody as well from the synthetic speech. Only the temporal on-off pattern remained in the synthetic speech -- a strictly psychophysical or psychoacoustic task. Her low percentages for the normal and inverted speech tasks were partly due to the presence of hesitations, which were entirely absent from the speech corpora (readings) used by Chiappetta et al. (1987), Stuckenberg and O'Connell (in press), and Carpenter and O'Connell (in press). Duez reported of false positives only the fact of their occurrence and indicated that a separate analysis would be presented in a subsequent publication.

The conclusions to be drawn from all these recent studies must clearly be: (1) that the archival literature that has relied on purely perceptual assessment of pause occurrence and/or duration is not to be accepted without question; (2) that both physical and linguistic characteristics of a corpus influence pause reports in complex ways; (3) a great deal more research is needed to isolate the complex effects of these various independent variables. Meanwhile, the warning expressed by Stuckenberg and O'Connell (in press) in their concluding statement should be heeded:

> The use of perceptual reports for the identification of
> pause occurrence and the estimation of pause duration, to
> the exclusion of instrumental measurement, is not justifi-
> able. The practice has led to questionable data and mis-
> leading interpretation of data for many decades. (in press)

Chapter 15

One of the Performing Arts

Most of us would likely classify drama as one of the performing arts. Speaking in general, on the other hand, would not fit stereotypically under the same umbrella. But what about speech genre such as poetry readings, homiletic eloquence, political discourse, and media expertise? They all involve at their best the skillful use of speaking in a way that surely transcends our everyday notion of adult native fluency. Despite our negative stereotyping, there is much to argue for their inclusion as members of the community of performing arts. The present chapter addresses the temporal organization of these skills.

In a number of respects, reading in an experimental setting can be considered the most primitive, artificial, and distorted use of language that fluent adults can engage in. Typically there is no genuine audience, no interest on the part of the speaker in communicating (since an adult experimental subject must assume that the experimenter already has read the material to be used in the experiment), and nothing to be learned from an experimental text that is usually prosaic pap. Reading is always the reproduction of a given text rather than unencumbered creativity or spontaneity.

But even experimental reading can illustrate differences between ordinary adult fluency on the one hand and professional or artistic skill on the other. Clemmer, O'Connell, and Loui

227

(1979) solved the prosaic problem by making use of a rather dramatic passage from St. Paul's "First Letter to the Corinthians" (1 Cor. 13: 1-13). Three experimental groups, representing levels of experience and training in dramatic art, read the passage. Two other groups of adults and professional dramatic artists rated the readings as significantly different in keeping with the three levels of dramatic experience and training. Interestingly enough, the discriminating rationale of these ratings was not basic reading mechanics or even basic clarity, but rather emotional portrayal and apparent grasp of the intended sense of the passage. The untrained group spoke with a slower articulation rate (4.46 < 4.80 syl/sec) and used shorter phrases (7.6 < 8.8 syl/pause) than the other two groups, but used the same percentage of pause time/total time (41%). The group with the most dramatic training and experience used many more pauses of longer duration (> 1.2 sec) than either of the other groups. This usage can quite plausibly be interpreted as an effective rhetorical use of longer pauses to interpret a dramatic passage.

There is no reason to think of the control group in this experiment as disfluent; they were college graduates who read quite well. Their high ratings on basic mechanics and clarity reflected this adult fluency. The differences are instead to be found precisely in the skills of the dramatic artists. It should be noted that the Clemmer et al. (1979) research did not make use of famous professional artists at all, but was still able to uncover quite systematic differences due to advanced skills.

A similar comparison of ordinary adult fluency and professional speaking skills was made by Clemmer and Carrocci (1984). They used students in an introductory broadcasting course, university broadcasters, and professional broadcasters to compare newscast and editorial reading. The most dramatic difference from the study of Clemmer et al. (1979) was that the broadcast setting was characterized by use of less than half as much pause time/total time (15% < 41%) as was the experimental reading setting. The percentages of the professional newscasts were the lowest (11%). In general, the percentages are quite comparable to those of Cronkite and Rather in broadcast reading and interviewing (Kowal, Bassett, & O'Connell, 1985, p. 6). The time constraints of the broadcasting situation obviously made for a very careful use of time. Accordingly, increased expertise was reflected in shorter and less frequent pauses, quite in keeping with the needs of the broadcast situation. But only the professional group adapted their temporal organization notably from the newscast to the editorial: by increasing percentage of pause time/total time (11% < 16%), decreasing articulation rate (5.20 > 4.88 syl/sec), increasing mean pause duration (0.51 < 0.57 sec), and decreasing phrase length (21.4 > 14.8 syl/pause).

The fact that professional broadcasters were thus able to shift very efficiently from newscasts to editorials manifests variability even within the narrow constraints of the broadcast situation. If we return now to the radio homilies mentioned in Chapter 9 (O'Connell & Kowal, 1986; Van De Water & O'Connell,

1986), that variability can be further engaged.

The most striking variation in the radio homilies compared to the data from professional broadcasters is that the percentage of pause time/total time never fell below 21% in the homilies, whereas it was always less than 20% in the professional broadcasts. Similarly, the shortest phrase length among the professional corpora in Clemmer and Carrocci (1984, p. 124) and Kowal, Bassett, and O'Connell (1985, p. 6) was 12.5 syl/pause, whereas all but one of the phrase lengths of the homilies were shorter. The longest was only 12.9 syl/pause. In other words, the homilists, despite the time constraints of the broadcast situation, paused more often than the professional broadcasters.

There are two considerations that are relevant to these paradoxical findings: (1) The homilists were professional clergymen, not professional media personnel; (2) The purpose of their speaking was quite different from either newscasting, editorializing, or interviewing. Their purpose was the classical rhetorical one of convincing, persuading, and eliciting emotional response from an audience. Such rhetorical purpose or intent was certainly less salient in the newscasts and interviews, and even in the editorials of media professionals.

Even a relatively commonsensical hypothesis is able to predict that quite dramatic differences might be found between poetry readings by ordinary adults on the one hand and the poets themselves on the other. In this case, we are not only dealing with professionals, but with professionals who have an intimately

230

personal interest in what they are reading.

Funkhouser and O'Connell (1978) compared readings of their own poetry by cummings, Jarrell, and Frost with readings of the same poems by adults. Combining the means for the three poems, Funkhouser and O'Connell (1978) found poets' articulation rate much slower than that of the adults (3.18 < 4.19 syl/sec) and their phrase length much shorter than that of the adults (6.8 < 12.3 syl/pause). Although half of the adult group consisted of English professors, their readings were not significantly different from those of the other adults.

Since these findings are exactly the opposite of the first study considered above (Clemmer et al., 1979) and equally reliable, some further considerations are in order. The temporal organization of the poets' readings can be described as extremely slow and interrupted relative to the adults' readings. Why? First of all, we must underline once again that we are not dealing with disfluency on the part of the control groups and certainly not on the part of the poets; both the poets and the professors read all the poems without errors of any kind, and their data, as well as the data of the other adults, are quite in accord with the data of Kowal, O'Connell, O'Brien, and Bryant (1975) and of O'Connell (1980b) for adult poetry readings.

The difference between the Clemmer et al. (1979) study and the Funkhouser and O'Connell (1978) study is one of speech genre. If it is true to say that the passage from St. Paul is not prosaic, it remains equally true that it is prose. The dramatic level of lyric poetry and its demand for an expressive rendition are essentially different even from those of dramatic prose readings. In comparison with the other readers, only the poets themselves seemed able to engage the lyrical expressiveness required by the poetic genre and to take the time needed to do so. The finding that the English professors read poetry much as did other educated adults, but not as did the poets, was surprising, but incontestable. They did not read the poems expressively.

All these considerations have now set the stage for a review of Kowal's (1983a; 1983b; 1987; Kowal & O'Connell, 1983) study of political speech. Her preoccupation with professionally successful speaking in comparison with ordinary adult fluency has been similar to my own thus far in this chapter. She chose to investigate in depth two German and two American politicians whose careers gave sufficient witness of professional success. The corpus consisted of readings (selections from media speeches) and interview replies to media interviewers. The focus of the research was on the spontaneity of the interview setting relative to the reading setting. The four speakers chosen were Jimmy Carter, Ronald Reagan, Helmut Schmidt, and Franz Josef Strauß. All samples in the corpus were collected during or shortly after the 1980 elections when all four were frequently engaged in media appearances.

As our first comparison of her data, we can make use of the fact noted above that the available data from professional broadcasts always showed a percentage of pause time/total time less than 20%. Kowal's percentage of pause time/total time for the four speakers in the two situations (readings and interviews) can be examined in view of this preliminary criterion:

Speaker	Percentage of Pause Time/Total Time	
	Readings	Interviews
Carter	34.5%	26.9%
Reagan	18.4%	28.4%
Schmidt	19.4%	22.1%
Strauß	19.5%	20.3%

All the percentages for readings were within the limit given for professional broadcasters, with the clear exception of Carter, qui extra choro cantabat. All the interview percentages, on the other hand, are clearly over the limit. These data are all in the native language of the speaker. There was an interesting exception to this generalization: For Helmut Schmidt a corpus of interview speech in English was available. In this instance alone, an interview percentage was below the limit (19.4%).

Schmidt's English interview percentage of pause time/total time was not notably out of line; in fact, it was the same percentage as the one for his German readings. If we were looking for significant differences here, we would have to be disappointed. What is interesting is what is hidden behind this percentage.

Schmidt speaks excellent English. Nonetheless, some shift in the characteristics of his nonnative English under the

pressure of journalists' questioning might reasonably be expected. Two comparisons with his German interview data tell the
story. In comparison with the German, Schmidt's articulation
rate in English was much slower (4.39 < 5.40 syl/sec) and his use
of filled pauses in English was much greater (4.90 > 1.27 filled
pauses/100 syl). The proportion of these filled pauses <u>within
syntactic phrases</u> in his English interview was twice the proportion in those positions in his German interview (45.9% > 22.8%).
His English interview data were thus characterized by the slowest
articulation rate and the highest rate of filled pause use in the
entire research. By way of contrast, his filled pause rate in
his native German interview data was the lowest of the four
speakers.

The fact that Schmidt's filled pause rate is the highest in
English and the lowest among the speakers otherwise may suggest
to the reader a difference due to the language itself (German or
English). This is clearly not the case in these data. The
highest rate of filled pause use was in Strauß's interview in
German. In other words, both the highest and the lowest filled
pause rates were represented in the German interview data; the
Americans were intermediate in this regard.

Hans Hörmann (see 1981, p. 118) was chronically convinced
that Americans use more filled pauses than other speakers. A
discussion at the International Conference on Reading in Milan,
Italy in 1982, where the data on Schmidt's English interview were
presented (Kowal, 1983b; Kowal & O'Connell, 1983), strongly

leaned toward the same view. There is no evidence in this corpus that such is actually the case, nor is there any other evidence to that effect in the archival literature.

We have already seen many instances in which temporal organization of speech is quite flexible; various means can be used interchangeably or optionally to accomplish the same purpose or serve the same function. Filled pauses enter into this pattern of usage along with many other temporal devices. Schmidt's English interview manifested just such a function of filled pauses in conjunction with a slow articulation rate to avoid the high percentage of pause time/total time typically to be expected in a nonnative speaker. A similar equivalence was noted by Johnson, O'Connell, and Sabin (1979) in comparisons of English and Spanish corpora:

> A comparison of the parenthetical remarks and filled pauses proves particularly heuristic. Both the frequencies and the percentages of subjects contributing to those frequencies strongly suggest the use of certain parenthetical remarks in Spanish (e.g., este, pues, bueno) and filled pauses in English for equivalent functions. (p. 349)

Grosjean and Deschamps (1975) found a similar compensatory use of drawls instead of filled pauses in French and vice versa in English.

I'd like to return once more to the percentages of pause time/total time in Kowal's (1987) reading and interview data (23.4% & 23.5%). In view of the hypothesis that "planning must take up time not used for phonation" (Butterworth, 1980, p. 158), we should expect, ceteris paribus, that the interview responses on the part of the politicians would require a relatively greater percentage of pause time. Such is clearly not the case. Either something else is different across the two conditions or the hypothesis does not hold for these data.

The data of Szawara and O'Connell (1977), on the other hand, would seem to be quite in accord with such an hypothesis: Radio homilies read from the authors' manuscripts manifested a significantly smaller percentage of pause time/total time than did impromptu live homilies (29.4% < 37.9%). In this case, however, one cannot exclude the possibilities that the broadcast vs. live or the formal vs. informal situations were responsible for the differences.

The data of Kowal, Bassett, and O'Connell (1985) paralleled Kowal's reading and interview design closely, but showed mixed evidence. Cronkite used a smaller percentage of pause time/total time in the interview, Rather a higher percentage.

In any event, Butterworth's hypothesis that "planning must take up time not used for phonation" is not clearly confirmed in any of these instances. Another finding relevant for the Butterworth hypothesis has been reported by Kowal and O'Connell (1987a). Their evidence indicated that other processes must sometimes take up time not used for phonation. When experimental subjects had to tell a story while (rather than after) watching Chafe's (1980a) pear film, percentage of pause time/total time

236

almost doubled (61.9% > 32.7%). But neither ontime nor number of syllables produced differed across the two conditions of the experiment. In other words, there was not more need for planning in the one condition than in the other. The difference was clearly one of perceptual overload, not one of planning. Finally, Ford and Holmes' (1978) comment also speaks to the Butterworth hypothesis:

> The amount of disruption and silent pausing before clauses probably does not correspond with clause complexity and processing load during clauses. It seems that the function of pauses and hesitations in speech may not merely be for planning what is to be said next -- their face validity as indicators of planning may be misleading. (p. 50)

To return once again to Kowal's research, it should be noted that mean pause duration and phrase length were also comparable in her reading and interview data: 0.72 & 0.69 sec; 12.1 & 11.3 syl/pause. There were also no differences in these measures across the two languages. The only significant differences were from speaker to speaker. Kowal has referred to analyses at the level of mean percentages of pause time/total time, pause duration, and phrase length as macro-analyses. They are useful in their own right, but they may also obscure more nuanced differences. For that reason, she has pursued another level of analysis, which she has called micro-analyses.

A micro-analysis of the detailed distribution of pauses of various durations in the readings and interviews, for example, yielded very systematic differences:

   (a) The percentage of shorter pauses (< 0.50 sec) is higher
   in the interviews than in the readings (40.2 > 31.3%);
   (b) The percentage of longer pauses (1.07 - 1.30 sec) is
   twice as high in the readings as in the interviews (14.6% >
   7.2%); and (c) Extremely long pauses (2.00 - 3.17 sec; 1.8%
   of all pauses) are used in the interviews, but they do not
   occur at all in the readings. (Kowal, 1987, p. 163; my
   trans.)

Kowal interpreted the relatively greater use of longer pauses in
the readings as a rhetorical device. Such usage was not characteristic of Butcher's (1981, p. 73, Fig. 3) readings relative to
spontaneous speech; but Butcher's experimental readings were read
without rhetorical intent. In English and French interviews,
Grosjean and Deschamps (1975) had found c. 95% of all pauses less
than 1 sec and none over 2 sec in duration; Kowal found instead
c. 87% less than 1 sec and some pauses longer than 3 sec in
duration.

   A similar micro-analysis of phrase length indicated that:
   The percentage of shorter phrases (1-3 syl) is twice as high
   in the interviews as in the readings (19.0% > 8.0%); and the
   percentage of extremely long phrases (37-63 syl) in the
   interviews is 1.4%, whereas phrases of that length do not
   occur at all in the readings. The highest percentage of
   phrases (60.2%) in the readings is 4-12 syl long. (1987, p.
   165 f.; my trans.)

Kowal has critically reviewed the research on breathing pauses in speech. In particular, she faulted Fodor, Bever, and Garrett (1975) for overinterpreting the archival literature in this regard. Their summary conclusion from the research was as follows:

> There are two striking facts about respiration during speech: first, in fluent speech, people tend strongly to breathe at major constituent boundaries; second, in nonfluent speech, they tend not to breathe at hesitation points. (p. 425)

Kowal's own mean findings can be summarized as follows:

Breathing Pause Response Measures	Readings	Interviews
Frequency/min	11.4	12.7
Percentage of all pauses	64.7%	59.8%
Duration (sec)	0.76	0.73
Percentage within phrases	1.1%	10.3%

Before proceeding to discuss these micro-analyses, let me give Kowal's own summary of the most important findings:

> The frequency and duration of breathing pauses are stable individual characteristics. Reagan, Schmidt (in his own native German), and Strauß are quite different from one another in this regard. Frequency and duration of breathing pauses do not shift notably with the exigencies of spontaneous speech in comparison with reading. Position of breathing pauses in both readings and interviews is mainly determined by constituent structure -- a finding that should not

239

be too surprising, given the limited options for breathing positions. Finally, the politicians breathe quite consistently at those positions in their utterances where hesitations are to be expected in terms of planning processes.
(p. 185; my trans.)

In other words, she found considerable individual differences, confirmed Fodor et al.'s (1975) first generalization (locations at constituent structures), and disconfirmed the second of their "striking facts" (non-occurrence at hesitation points).

The durations of the breathing pauses shown tabularly above were longer in both readings (0.76 > 0.50 sec) and interviews (0.73 > 0.66 sec) than the corresponding non-breathing pauses. The final tabular entry above indicates the percentage of breathing pauses occurring within syntactic phrases. These are the hesitation positions not predicted by Fodor et al. (1975).

We have already reviewed in Chapter 12 the problems of operationally defining syntactic units in spoken discourse. Because of these problems and because of Clark and Clark's (1977, p. 261 f.) prescriptions regarding pause position in ideal delivery, Kowal chose to identify the two extreme positions, between sentences and within syntactic phrases, and to define the intermediate positions only as residuals. Clark and Clark's prescriptions have been summarized by Kowal, Bassett, and O'Connell (1985) as follows: "Between-sentence positions are always to be marked by pauses, within-syntactic-phrase positions never" (p. 5). To check the validity of these prescriptions, the

240

intermediate boundaries between clauses and between phrases need not be more specifically defined. In order to gain a better appreciation of her logic in these comparisons, Kowal's mean data on the distribution of pauses across these positions in the readings and interviews can be summarized as follows:

Positions	Readings	Interviews
Between sentences	35.4%	26.1%
Within phrases	3.4%	15.1%
Other	61.2%	58.8%

There is another distribution of importance with regard to these positions. It is the percentage of available positions marked by pauses in each of these categories. The distribution is as follows:

Positions	Readings	Interviews
Between sentences	97.5%	76.2%
Within phrases	1.2%	5.9%
Other	15.7%	13.1%

In the readings, sentences were almost always marked by pauses, and the pauses in these positions were the longest. Their omission was used rhetorically. Pauses at the intermediate (other) positions were about half as long as sentence pauses and constituted the majority of all the pauses. Pauses within syntactic phrases occurred seldom and were the shortest of all position pauses.

The interview data showed a very different picture. A notable portion of the pauses shifted from between-sentences to within-phrases positions. Correspondingly, a smaller proportion of the available between-sentences positions and a larger proportion of the within-phrases positions were used for pauses. There were no significant differences in duration of pauses at these positions in the interviews. Omission of a pause between sentences occurred in the interviews mostly when the two sentences were closely related in their content. The occurrence of pauses within phrases was the result of hesitation, emphasis, or both.

The distributions of pause durations between sentences were quite different in the readings and interviews:

Whereas the duration of the pauses between sentences in the readings is approximately normally distributed with a mean of c. 1 sec, the duration is displaced in the direction of short pauses under the condition of spontaneous speech. (p. 274; my trans.)

One must be careful to distinguish the distribution of pause time itself from the distribution of pauses and proportions of positions marked by pauses. In terms of the distribution of pause time itself, Kowal's data showed the following pattern:

Positions	Readings	Interviews
Between sentences	47.6%	28.3%
Within phrases	1.4%	14.0%
Other	50.9%	57.6%

Again, shifts in the proportionate distribution of pause time are to be noted from readings to interviews. The pause time between sentences was diminished by almost 20% and the other categories correspondingly increased.

We have noted already that there were no differences in articulation rate between readings and interviews in Kowal's data. In the micro-analyses, means and standard deviations of articulation rate/phrase (not syntactic phrases, but articulatory phrases, defined by syl/pause) were calculated for each reading and interview sample. These standard deviations were used as the derived measure and mean standard deviations were calculated for speaker and speaking condition. There were no speaker differences, but the mean standard deviation of these standard deviations was in all instances much smaller in the readings than in the interviews (0.79 < 1.27). In other words, articulation varied from phrase to phrase much more in the interviews than in the readings.

Another micro-analysis indicated that articulation rate was significantly slower in long ($\geq$ 20 syl) phrases than in short ($\leq$ 5 syl) phrases (4.35 < 5.68 syl/sec). And in the distribution of articulation rate/phrase, "the proportion of phrases $\leq$ 4 syl/sec in articulation rate is almost twice as high in the interviews as in the readings (26.6% > 15.0%)" (p. 338; my trans.).

It is difficult to summarize Kowal's (1987) monograph adequately. She has spent almost two decades investigating the temporal organization of speech and the past six years on the research represented in this monograph. Her incisive and perceptive criticisms of the archival research literature bring into question far more "striking facts" and assumed verities than I have been able to engage in this presentation of her findings, or for that matter, in the present book.

Her emphasis of professional speaking has led her to an emphasis on speech genre by a fairly simple logic: It is the professionals who are capable of clearly differentiating genre in their delivery, whereas ordinary adult fluency does not suffice in this regard.

Finally, her willingness to engage in meticulous analyses and to seek out new micro-analyses in order to discover the nuances of rhetorical usage is a contribution of considerable importance to the study of the temporal organization of speech. The monograph merits an expeditious and careful translation into English so as to be more widely accessible to students of the psychology of language use.

Kowal (1987) herself has summarized the archival literature as follows:

> The theoretical generalizations have been thoroughly disproportionate to the empirical findings. The present research has disclosed critical methodological and conceptual deficiencies in the archival research. There has been a deplorable lack of integration with previous research. (p. 29; my trans.)

Kowal chose, however, to present neither a model nor a theory of speech production. She felt that "they would be premature-- unless one is willing to settle for linguistic descriptions that are illegitimately presented as psychological explanations" (p. 30; my trans.).

Sheldon Rosenberg (personal communication, 1980), in a letter addressed to me, once referred to the variability of pause duration as "notorious". Despite the pejorative connotation, pause duration is no more notorious than any other self-respecting response measure. The same is to be said of the various other means that humans use to organize their speech temporally. What the research reviewed in this book has indicated, and above all the research of Kowal, is precisely that speech is temporally organized, i.e., orderly.

Some speaking is indeed so well organized as to well deserve the name performing art.

Part Six

Pulling Things Together

The concluding chapters of a book must say it all, fit everything together nicely. But if it hasn't all been getting said all along, nobody is listening anymore. I would actually prefer that these last three chapters now be considered the first word on something rather than that they be thought of as the last word on anything. We don't have that word, and it is not going to be had -- ever.

My job, as I see it now, is to recapitulate what has been said up to this point regarding the psychology of language use. This is the burden of Chapters 16 and 17.

The first of these is an effort to bring together the argumentation for the importance of temporal organization in language use. Time is the key to understanding the differences between speaking and writing; their temporal organization is not at all the same. The common practice of comparing speaking inappropriately with the written instead of with writing has led to much confusion on this matter in the archival literature.

Most of my research examples have been drawn from investigations of the temporal organization of speech. How does this research fit into the overall picture of the psychology of language use? What should such a psychology be? How should it develop from this point in time? These are the issues to be engaged in Chapter 17.

The final chapter in the book addresses the science of

psychology. What can the psychology of language use tell us about its own home territory, the science of psychology? What does it have to contribute to the basic and comprehensive concepts of the science? [What should psychology contribute to the human family?]

[That last question isn't quite fair! It can't be pulled from the ashes of any of the research mourned in these pages, nor from any of the research that may have survived our critique-- or the reader's. It is not a scientific question. But science is not, in any event, the superordinate concept of human wisdom, is it? In the last analysis, this book was not written by a scientist, but by a human being. That's why he could enjoy questioning so much of what he has read under the category of psychological science.]

The book comes from me, and the question comes from me. Let me put it another way: If human beings do not know what they want to accomplish by means of the science of psychology, they may indeed elaborate it until it is as bloated as a stuffed pig; they will never go anywhere with it because they don't know where they want to go. They will, of course, be led down many paths-- all of them primrose. But psychology itself is fundamentally incapable of telling us where to go. Like all science, it is an arm of society. Somehow human beings must decide what to do with science on antecedent and transcendent grounds, not on intrinsically scientific grounds.]

And so, what should psychology contribute to the human

247

family? <u>For what</u> do we use the tool? Don't ask the American Psychological Association, and don't ask Nobel prize winners, and don't ask the American Academy of Sciences. Even though they are interrogated periodically for their wisdom, they don't know.

You and I are the ones responsible for knowing. Human beings just happen to know things that scientists as such don't know. We have to in order to live, in order to contribute to the human family, in order to use the tools of the trade properly.

Chapter 16

Speaking and Writing: An Essay on Differences and Unfinished Business

At one stage of the preparation of the present book, I circulated what I thought was a final draft of the book to a number of colleagues -- minus the present chapter. Gene Zechmeister (personal communication, June 2, 1987), one of my colleagues at Loyola University of Chicago, after carefully reading the entire manuscript, posed the following question: "Are temporal patterns of speech all that critical to the lessons that you wish the reader to draw?"

Yes!

But I am grateful for the feedback. Obviously the importance of temporal organization needs to be underscored in this final part of the book once again. I have argued that The written language bias in linguistics (Linell, 1982), our tendency to visualize and spatialize, our inappropriate comparisons of speaking and the written, our acceptance of the view that language use (and in particular speech production) is a process of translation, and our emphasis on written research materials and on laboratory approaches to the problems of language use have all conspired to minimize our awareness of the importance of temporal organization in language use.

There has been a tremendous surge of research interest in the questions of orality and literacy in the past decade. Some of this archival literature has incorporated premature generalizations and has persisted in what I have already referred to a number of times as the apples and oranges comparisons between speaking and the written. Perhaps a look at some of this literature will provide just the right setting for underscoring once again the importance of temporal organization in language use and of its careful empirical analysis.

The recent research has been largely anthropological, literary, and sociological. One of the difficulties has been that cross-pollination has languished, despite Goody's (1982) plea:

> Indeed if one is concerned with problems and topics rather
> than boundary-maintaining fields of study, such an inter-
> locking of interests is essential, even if the results fall
> well short of a 'unified social science'. (p. viii)

Since Walter Ong (e.g., 1982) has been one of the scholars who has been concerned with orality and literacy for his entire prolific scholarly career, it is of interest to note that a good deal of the current archival literature (e.g., Ehlich, 1983; Goody, 1982, himself; Ludwig, 1983; and Redeker, 1984) has consistently overlooked Ong's work. Perhaps even more surprising, two recent articles on the subject (Akinnaso, 1982; Redeker, 1984) had exactly the same titles (except for a definite article), but the later one took no account of the earlier one: "On (the) differences between spoken and written language." Obviously, something is missing in the integrative process of science. And indeed, as Ong has warned us, "Study of the contrast between orality and literacy is largely unfinished business" (p. 156).

The Redeker (1984) article can, in fact, serve to bring us back more closely to our concern with temporal organization and the comparison of speaking and the written. An overall description of Redeker's (1984) data read as follows:

> The 16 oral presentations were 3 min to 11 min 15 s long (total 104.5 min) with a minimum of 570 and a maximum of 1,933 words (total number of words spoken: 19,450). The 16 written texts were between 166 and 545 words in length (total: 6,011 words). (p. 47)

Notice that the two sets of data were presented to be compared, but they were not comparable. The description gave the range of time and total time as part of a data base of speaking. The absence of comparable data for the second set of data should have made it clear immediately (but for all the biases we have been considering) that the investigator did not have a comparable set of writing times. The time data for speaking should, of course, not have been mentioned at all because they were not the comparable data that were actually analyzed in the experiment. The recorded "pauses, hesitations, respiratory events, and intonation contours" (p. 47) that were mentioned were also not comparable to anything in the written corpus. Instead, various word counts derived from transcriptions of the speaking were compared with the written corpus.

We have already noted Dell's (1986) conviction that the language-production system is error prone because "the system must be productive" (p. 319). Redeker (1984) localized differences between writing and speaking similarly: "Differences in integratedness within as well as between modalities are a function of the amount of planning" (p. 45). But the reason why planning is differentiating across speaking and writing was once again neglected. The reason, of course, is the availability of time and the manner in which time can be utilized in the two modalities.

Similarly, Akinnaso (1985) was convinced that he could refute "the underlying assumptions that have guided comparative studies of spoken and written discourse" (p. 324). The difficulty with his logic, however, was that, even after all the typical and stereotypical, anecdotal, implicitly or explicitly assumed, and artifactual fallacies have been swept away, there still remain some basic facts. Akinnaso (1985) was able to make his case sound plausible because he considered the two "discourse types" quite abstractly and only in terms of their "lexical, syntactic, and semantic substratum" (p. 350). A clue to his confusion can be found in the following citation, in which speech and writing are treated equivalently to spoken and written discourse:

> Speech and writing, then, should be viewed as a continuum,
> with many overlapping features, rather than a dichotomy with
> discrete boundaries.
>
> The view of spoken and written discourse as a continuum
> is explored in more detail. . . (p. 331).

252

Speech and writing are _not_ a continuum! Such features as "voice quality (tone of voice), tempo (speed/manner of delivery), pausing (including rhythmic regulation of lines), and stylized intonation" (p. 334) had no rightful place in Akinnaso's comparisons simply because he was not comparing the act of speaking with the act of writing, but with the products of these acts. He was not clear, however, about what he wanted to compare. For example, having mentioned "lines" (clearly in the context of speaking) in the passage above, he proclaimed in the very next paragraph that "the basic unit of discourse is the line" (p. 334). He then proceeded to give characteristics of the line, _none_ of which characterize _written_ lines:

(1) extensive patterns of repetition and initial couplings; (2) preponderant use of grammatical parallelism; (3) sequential patterning of action in such a way that each new line builds chronologically on the action reported in the preceding one; (4) the use of a single predicate to indicate one action per line; and (5) prosodic patterns, especially the structuring of pauses and tempo. (p. 334)

It should also be mentioned that the above criteria are not the same as those used by Gee (1986, p. 395) as a unit of oral discourse (see Chapter 6 above). Nor are Akinnaso's "lines" the same as the poetic lines discussed above in Chapter 8. They are certainly not what Ong (1982) has referred to as a "story line" (p. 147).

Ludwig (1983) too has confused the comparisons of writing

and speaking:

> What distinguishes writing from speaking, however, is the
> fact that the writer, as he externalizes his inner state
> in writing, discovers at the same time a definite form for
> it. He objectifies it and thereby, in a certain sense,
> objectifies himself as well. (p. 53; my trans.)

The only hint of a legitimate generalization that I can find in Ludwig's statement is reflected in Ong's (1982) mention of "one characteristic of sound, its evanescence, its relationship to time" (p. 71). Otherwise, Ludwig's logic escapes me.

It is rather embarrassing for an experimental psychologist to have to admit that the best description of the psychology of speaking he has been able to find was written not by a psychologist and not by a social scientist of any description, but by a literary scholar. Ong's (1982) chapter on "Some psychodynamics of orality" (p. 31) has succinctly and accurately described "sound, its evanescence, its relationship to time" (p. 71) as no other scholar's work to date. Ong was quite convinced of "the vast difference between speech and writing" (p. 13) and made the essential concern of his book "undercutting the chirographic and typographic bias" (p. 166).

Before I proceed to sample some of Ong's insights, let me pinpoint once again some of the differences between speaking and writing that have been evident in the research reviewed in these pages, but otherwise neglected in the archival literature or distorted by the apples and oranges comparisons of speaking on

254

the one hand and the written on the other.

It is clear, for example, that the classical hesitation phenomena do not occur in the written; they are edited out in the process of writing. But do analogous phenomena occur in writing? Of course they do! We are just not accustomed to observing the acts of writing of others, and in the case of one's own writing, the preoccupation is still saliently with the final product, the written, not with the process. The VCR data of writing by the subjects in the Van De Water et al. (1987) experiment showed a variety of momentary doodles, gestures, cross outs, write overs, and pauses, all quite parallel to corrections, repeats, filled pauses, and silent pauses. For example, the meditative crossing of a t is quite analagous to a nonphonemic syllabic prolongation. Gesticulating with a writing instrument before beginning a new sentence is rather like a filled pause before speech onset. On the other hand, corrections of pronunciations in speaking cannot be paralleled closely in writing; the nearest analogue would be a correction of spelling. Unlike the standard comparisons to be found in the archival literature on orality and literacy, these are appropriate parallels between production processes in speaking and writing.

Articulation of speech is also motorically faster than articulation of writing. The oral-aural is indeed transient, the manual-visual abiding. Speaking is social in the very basic sense that sound carries; writing is social only in nonstandard situations. Being a "leftie" whose writing is also backhanded, I

255

am very much aware that the manual-visual mode is _not_ necessarily also _visible_ to anyone else. Yes, skywriting is, but it is hardly a typical or common convention of writing. Typically, we write privately. Or as Ong (1982) has commonsensibly posed, if the recipient is present, "why write?" (p. 177). The privacy of writing is also a determinant of how time can be used. In speaking, my "pause" to go off and do more research before I enunciate my wisdom, terminates a conversation or a lecture. In writing, I can pick up my pen or put it down whenever I please; no one is going to walk away, get bored while I reflect, or be insulted.

It should be quite clear that the temporal circumstances associated with the behavior of listeners to or readers of the _products_ of speaking and writing, i.e., the temporal characteristics associated with the use of recordings and books (and analogous devices), are quite different from the temporal characteristics of either speaking or writing. In dealing with the products, one is free to backtrack, anticipate, leave for lunch, review, or replay (reread) however one wishes. Time has been dethroned from its controlling role.

Clear distinctions must be made between speaking, writing, the spoken, and the written, if literary scholars, social scientists, and in particular psychologists of language use are to make valid comparisons. Most of the comparisons in the currently available archival literature yield overgeneralizations that are roughly the equivalents of anecdotal folk wisdom. The apples and oranges epidemic has not as yet been halted.

Just as speaking is the commitment of the word to time, insofar as "sound is an event in time" (Ong, 1982, p. 76), so writing is the "commitment of the word to space" (p. 7).

Indeed, "Study of the contrast between orality and literacy is largely unfinished business" (p. 156).

Chapter 17

"DER SIEG DER WISSENSCHAFT ÜBER DIE ZEIT" (Stern, 1987, February 26, p. 30)

The title is unfair. I apologize. But I simply could not resist using it. It means in translation: THE TRIUMPH OF SCIENCE OVER TIME. How could one possibly find a better title to serve as the banner for a summary chapter on the study of the temporal organization of speech? The irony is that the statement is to be found in an advertisement for a new Christian Dior product for the renewal of milady's aging skin. But even the ironic actuality fits; for time and gerontology are two of those few basic facts of life -- and death -- that science most certainly does not triumph over.

In a similar vein, I want to begin this chapter by recapitulating some of the things we do not know about the temporal organization of speech. Much of our ignorance comes from the fact that we insist on facing in the wrong direction, looking in the wrong place, working from assumptions that are both wrong and, because they are implicit, unrecognized.

Prominent among these ignota is the sentence. The oral sentence is a will-o'-the-wisp. There is in principle no way one can be sure what sets of spoken words of another person constitute his or her individual sentences. The assumption that the sentence had to be the unit of analysis has muddied the waters and muddled our minds to the point that we can no longer see the beautifully nuanced complexity and flexibility of the actual principles of segmentation in speech. Kowal's (1987) recent monograph has indicated what a wealth of orderly data are available in speech. Speakers do segment their speech in an orderly fashion. _That_ is the principle we should have begun with. It is a corollary of the more general principle that is completely indispensable in the science of psychology: Human behavior is orderly. It is left to us to discover that order. I can say without hesitation that, in many instances, orderliness has not been found in the segmentation of human speech because superficial answers were being sought in terms of sentential structure and in terms of dogmatic theorizing.

A close second among the _ignota_ is fluency. We do not know what it is, partly because it has been pursued in terms of naive notions of well-formedness derived from The written language bias in linguistics and from the bias of our otherwise spatially oriented conceptualizations.

Both these lacunae in our knowledge have also persisted partly because of the use of unrealistic, distorted, isolated, noncommunicative experimental speaking situations and response measures dictated largely by a syntactic, written language bias and a laboratory-bound tradition. Beaugrande (1987) has summed up this pathology succinctly:

> The customary experimental approach calls for the observa-
> tion and explanation of concrete events situated in real
> time. The context thus created is specially controlled
> for factors external to the hypothesis being tested. Yet

these same controls can also make the context dissimilar
to ordinary language activity. (p. 4)

Despite all the biases and limitations, we have still
learned a great deal in terms of temporal organization: about
developmental changes in speaking, second language learning,
various speech genre, rhetorical use of language, the various
means and options at a speaker's disposal, the uses of variability, and the nonveridicality of pause reports.

The limitations in all these considerations must also be
acknowledged. The research analyzed in this book has been almost
entirely monologic. It has not as yet been integrated with
studies of intonation, stress, nonverbal context, social interaction, affect, and motivation. For readers who are specifically
looking for the traditional paragraph on "directions for future
research," this was it. Essentially, the direction is optional,
so long as we supplement the laboratory realistically and mind
our logic, our assumptions, and our methods.

Despite the insistence of some editorial reviewers (who
sometimes seem simply to want authors to investigate what they
are interested in), one cannot and need not investigate all these
influences on human speech at the same time. It is not only in
military tactics and strategies that the ancient dictum divide et
impera, divide and conquer, is correct.

I would like to address the organization of speech at a more
comprehensive level at the moment, a level at which all these
various components are relevant. I mentioned earlier that there

is a relationship between rhetoric and eloquence, but not a one
to one relationship, not synonymity. The concept of eloquence
somehow encapsulates the furthest reaches of the human spirit,
our definitive finality. If we define communication as the
sharing of understanding and meaning, then eloquence refers to
the most comprehensive sense of these terms and is accordingly
the antithesis of a primitive notion of information transfer.
Beaugrande (1987) has similarly referred to the primitive notion
of pure denotations:

> An impersonal lexicon of pure denotations (free of personal
> experiences and values) can be but an artificial construct,
> a compilation of those significances primarily used by a
> culture to identify the concepts related to the words or
> standing phrases of the vocabulary. Such a lexicon could
> hardly be the basis of normal communication, nor an ideal
> for the latter to imitate. (p. 19)

Chouinard (1985) too has pinpointed the transcendence of
eloquence over both information exchange and rhetoric:

> Communication is potentially much more than a mere techni-
> cal, or information-exchanging, exercise, or much more than
> a socially strategic device for bringing others' opinions
> into alignment with one's own. For the really sensitive
> writer and conversationalist will express his or her
> viewpoint in such a way as to stimulate further explora-
> tion of the subject-at-hand. In the philosophy of commu-
> nication of such an individual, the "truth" is more impor-

261

tant than being right. (p. 3 f.)

And what he has further said of the writer also applies equally
well to the speaker:

> For the really imaginative writer does not assume
> that one communicates in order to convey that which one
> already knows; rather, he uses the inventions of tech-
> nique and metaphoric novelty as tools of discovery for the
> mutual benefit of author and audience. (p. 5)

Chouinard's notion of "mutual benefit" is very much at the
heart of genuine eloquence. His thesis is that speaking is
characteristically human when it <u>listens</u>. Hence, he referred to
"human consciousness' most primitive yet sophisticated attribute:
the psychological posture of listening, or overhearing" (p. 8).
The listening is part of the setting of human contingency:

> Ultimate judgments may only be rendered ultimately, on the
> other side of death, and not by us as finite creatures.
> The breakthrough to the transcendent is also a break-
> through to a really new relationship with human time as
> well. (p. 55)

But these very limitations are related to the ultimate purpose of
communication:

> We communicate for communion, which is why true com-
> munication inevitably takes us beyond itself, and even be-
> yond its own immediate purposes. If we are listening to
> all we are not saying as we speak or write, then what we
> "say" will alter as it proceeds, "at least" tonally, or at-

titudinally. (p. 60)

To return from the philosophical to the concrete, the concept of eloquence sketched above clearly excludes a multitude of spoken discourse: supercilious, vain, arrogant, superficial, mendacious, seductive, self-seeking, dogmatic, and many other aberrant types. It reduces, for example, the know-it-all braggadocio of an eight-year-old and the arrogance of the university professor to their rightful common base.

And we are light-years away from even beginning to be interested in the investigation of such phenomena -- or from even acknowledging that they exist, that they are important, and that they transcend our capacities of investigation and certainly of comprehension.

This is the juncture at which the psychology of language use really should have something to say to the science of psychology. "Higher Human Processes" was the title of one of my courses during graduate school; we studied "response family hierarchies". And today, under the same or similar rubrics, we study what computers can do when we tell them to do it. Or we epitomize human problem solving with the example of chess playing, while sitting impotently by, watching a society that seems incapable of solving any of the most basic problems of our existence, and listening helplessly to colleagues and loved ones completely disoriented under the burden of daily problem solving. We have not the slightest idea how to deal with prioritization of human values.

263

How does all this relate to the psychology of language use? The psycholinguists have very simply forgotten what real eloquence is. They seem incapable of learning from ordinary humans what the real parameters of human speech are.

Speaking is not only _an_ action or decisive dealing with reality, it is in a very basic sense _the_ characteristically human mode of dealing with reality. If we are unable to engage both the nuances and the higher reaches of speaking, we cannot engage the human condition itself in anything more than a trivial, superficial way. To date, there is precious little evidence that the scientific community in general and psychology in particular are at all capable of such engagement.

In this respect, Blumenthal's (1985) recent historical review is of interest. The only hope for the future he can offer is a "turning away" from wrong-headed paths:

> Perhaps, with the proliferation of linguistic theories and the new discussions about the respective goals of linguists and psychologists, a reverse replay of the scenario of psychologist-linguist relations earlier in this century should not be surprising. We might then expect a turning away, to some degree, of psycholinguists from the current enterprise of writing "grammars" of language performance, or analyzing subjective "lexicons," or from discussions of the "language of thought." (p. 820)

And a turning _to_ what?

Steiner's (1975) advice was much more positive and much more challenging:

> To know more of language and of translation, we must pass
> from the 'deep structures' of transformational grammar to
> the deeper structures of the poet. (p. 108)

One might surely hope that we have come a long way from the conviction that

> One ought to treat the question of, say, the nature of
> language without prejudice and exactly as one would treat
> the question of some physical organ of the body. (Chomsky,
> 1980, p. 73)

The shoe is really on the other foot. It is quite profoundly prejudiced not to recognize the difference in this regard between bodies and corpora.

The future of the psychology of language use is quite open. Perhaps the fact that the present and past have been relatively disastrous can now be seen as advantageous. New beginnings should always be an exciting challenge; it is the dogmatism of the present and past that enslaves.

It is impossible to resist in this context a rather personal paradox regarding my penchant for questioning everything in science. The most important characteristic of my personal and social existence has not as yet been so much as mentioned in these chapters -- the Christian Faith. As a Catholic priest and the member of a religious order (the Society of Jesus), I have for years attended conventions dressed in my clerical black and my Roman collar. A bit odd, perhaps, but graciously accepted by

265

all my colleagues (for which I am very grateful)!

The paradox in all this is the following. My spiritual _Credo_ is quite absolute; my willingness to accept scientific conclusions presented in black and white in the archival literature is close to nil. I find it quite strange that many of my colleagues, who find my Faith mildly amusing or quaint at best, are, frankly, naively credulous when it comes to anything presented under the aegis of science. Enslavement, the stripping away of freedom, comes in many forms.

I say this not arbitrarily or as filler. If the psychology of language use is to become a positive influence in the general stream of psychological science instead of a muddied little creek, we must have the courage to turn our backs on the experts. It is a form of prostitution to accept the status quo just because the big guys think it's wonderful stuff. It isn't and they aren't. They have not covered themselves with glory in willingness to listen to criticism, to study opposition, or in general to do more than multiply entities and taxonomies. This was supposedly the prerogative of a decadent late scholasticism, but the pinheads have been preempted for other than angelic choreography.

Greenwald, Leippe, Pratkanis, and Baumgardner (1986) did not have psycholinguistics in mind as their primary example in writing their article on the conditions under which theory obstructs research progress. But if the shoe fits, wear it:

Theory obstructs research progress when testing theory

is taken as the central goal of research, if (as often happens) the researcher has more faith in the correctness of the theory than in the suitability of the procedures that were used to test it. In other words, theory obstructs research progress when the researcher is an ego-involved advocate of the theory. (p. 227)

The shoe fits!

At the other extreme, research on the temporal organization of speech has long had a reputation for "theoretical sterility" (O'Connell & Kowal, 1983, p. 274). Such was surely the case until recently. Chapter 4 of the present volume has been intended to comfortably localize the research on temporal organization of speech within an appropriate theoretical framework. I find the framework described there, with its contributions from Bühler, Derwing, Hörmann, Linell, Rommetveit, and others quite adequate in this regard. It should be noted that our research was not undertaken by my colleagues and myself in order to confirm such a theoretical framework; quite the contrary, our findings led us off in search of an appropriate theory. The communicative, social, and dynamic components of the speaking situation can be appropriately emphasized in such a theoretical framework; and above all, a theory of meaning and understanding adopted from Hörmann serves as the lever to extricate our research from the theoretical traditions of mainstream psycholinguistics, where "the fundamental assumptions incorporated into the theory tend to remain invisible and immune from attack"

(Beaugrande, 1987, p. 1).

Such a version of the psychology of language use is definitely not interested in détente with psycholinguistics. The two approaches are not mutually compatible. Something has to give! And something will give eventually, though not without a good deal of midwifery.

Part of my personal epistemology has long been the firm conviction that scientific and intellectual rectification does occur -- not suddenly and not easily, but eventually and as the result of painstaking, meticulous critique. Perhaps by now the intended purpose of my own critical approach will appear less offensive and less negative than at the outset.

What O'Connell and Kowal (1983) said a few years ago about research on the temporal organization of speech, can well be said about both the psycholinguistics we would like to bury and the psychology of language use we would like to christen: "A moderately unimpressive past and a promising future" (p. 276).

Chapter 18

"Tools of Discovery for the Mutual Benefit of Author and Audience" (Chouinard, 1985, p. 5)

The quotation from Chouinard used above as title for the chapter has been seen already in the previous chapter. Chouinard was speaking primarily about writing, and I applied his words there to speaking as well. I'd like to apply them now to the science of psychology.

As a reasonable undertaking on the part of intelligent beings, psychology must have a purpose. Like speaking, psychology too is a tool of discovery; like speaking, it should be used for the mutual benefit of psychologist and society. For over a century now, modern psychology has been defended as a way of understanding and improving the human condition. Somehow the second part of this purpose has come loose from the first part in recent years. A recent report of the Committee on Employment and Human Resources of the American Psychological Association (Howard, Pion, Gottfredson, Flattau, Oskamp, Pfafflin, Bray, & Burstein, 1986) has summarized the situation:

> Psychology is increasingly becoming focused on health service provision, and APA appears to be appealing more to members in those fields than to members in other fields. . . . decline in the traditional academic/research areas may be cause for alarm, as may the proliferation of practitioner programs, which has eroded psychology's overall ranking in the national scientific community as a produ-

cer of scientists from high-quality programs. (p. 1326)

Perhaps one might pose the problem as follows: Is there some connection between understanding human beings and providing health service? Stated thus, it appears to be a silly question; of course, there's a connection. But let's pursue the logic.

Let's presume for the moment the traditional view. There is an intimate connection between understanding human beings and provision of health service, and the understanding is primarily communicated in graduate training in the academic/research areas. Then the low rankings due to practitioner programs and the alienation of the academic/research areas from APA are both alarmingly diagnostic and prognostic of pathology within the science of psychology.

But, on the other hand, perhaps the understanding of human beings that the academic/research areas pursue is really disparate, unrelated to health service provision. In that case, the APA should give up its snobbery about rankings; in fact, the APA should in that event also give up its inveterate insistence upon training of psychological health service providers by the academic/research areas. Whether the practitioner programs should then be pursued energetically still remains questionable, however, until it becomes sufficiently clear that they provide the understanding of human beings really needed for health service provision.

But we can also look at the other side of the same coin. If the academic/research areas are really irrelevant to health service provision, for what are they relevant? What can they really be telling us about human beings that is not trivial, if it does not contribute to health service provision in some substantive way?

The authors of the report were very careful not to overinterpret and not to speculate, but the possibilities are ominous. It is quite conceivable that we have painted ourselves into an isolated corner with our fancy theories and magnificently controlled laboratory research, to the point that our findings are no longer relevant to anything or anybody other than ourselves. Indeed, if they are not relevant even <u>within</u> the professional community of psychology, who on earth <u>outside</u> the professional community could imaginably make use of them? We can even inquire further: Do we ourselves, within the academic/research areas, make use of these scientific generalizations in any way other than to further multiply theories and models, write articles, and get promotion and tenure? If so, what on earth <u>are</u> their possible applications? Tell me that they are in artificial intelligence and computer technology, and I will tell you that neither is psychology. We can literally learn all there is to know about artificial intelligence and computer technology, and still be left with a scientific psychology that attains only a primitive, distorted understanding of human beings.

One of the facts that lends credence to the above speculation about the academic/research areas is the incidence of what I will call the "hit and run" research project. We have seen a number of instances in the foregoing chapters of archival literature in which the related literature has not been reviewed at all or has been reviewed only superficially. Then in turn the "new" research is accepted as the gospel truth, without any interest in replication, without careful reading or critique, and without any effort on the part of the next generation to do the catch-up work on the background literature. It becomes a self-perpetuating cycle that has the net effect of granting to modern psychological truths a half-life of approximately two decades. After that, someone else will invent a new taxonomy, ask the question differently, fail to go back to the old research, and do a nicely packaged little study. Then the cycle begins again. Relating findings to findings has not been a strong point of modern psychology, to say the least.

Another of the facts that lends credence to the notion that the academic/research areas have become irrelevant is the incidence of fads. Fads and hit-and-run research are not unrelated, but the important consideration regarding fads is that burning issues are frequently not solved but shelved. One suspects after a while that we are dealing with one tempest in a teapot after another.

The competence-performance discussions in psycholinguistics are an excellent example. The dichotomy was nonsense from the very beginning, but it provided recreation for decades. Then it was simply dropped. One can still find a sprinkling of nonsense about this nonsense in textbooks, but no one seems to care a great deal. It was fun while it lasted.

The _reason_ why the competence-performance discussions were nonsense is also important. The integrity of linguistic theory became more important than the psychological reality of the dichotomy. It is an excellent example of the obstruction of research progress by theory (Greenwald, Leippe, Pratkanis, & Baumgardner, 1986) or of "determination in seeking to preserve the elegance of their theory at the expense of its goals" (Hörmann, 1981, p. 107).

Related to both the "hit and run" syndrome and the pathology of fads is the fanaticism in modern psychology to be up to date. "Old" research doesn't count; it's automatically out of date. We look for the date of publication and formulate our evaluation accordingly. Most of what we know of the history of psychology is from secondary sources and is fraught with naive stereotypes.

All this criticism converges on one radical conclusion. The specific, concrete research problems dissected in these chapters are _not_ peculiar to psycholinguistics (to revert deliberately to the traditional term) nor to cognitive psychology, but to the science of psychology itself. Time was when we were all securely enwombed within positivism, and everything was clear and distinct. The paradox is that information technology has now made everything else clear and distinct, while psychology has become muddier and muddier.

There is no particular reason to believe that people will listen to the present writer, when they have failed to listen to the voices of Sarason (1981) and many others like him who have called for radical change. Nonetheless, I must say it: Psychology cannot survive, except through use of terminal life support systems (which the APA, with its bureaucracy and its political meddling, are coming to resemble more every year), without immediate, revolutionary change.

When one speaks of revolutionary change, a political revolution is almost always implied. That's the last thing in the world psychology needs. One of the major problems of the APA has already become its unabashed pursuit of liberal American politics under the guise of professionalism. The APA should learn to mind its own business. The problem is that it doesn't really know what its rightful business is. The organization reflects the very scientific wallowing we have been talking about throughout this book. The APA has become the gadfly gossip of the national neighborhood, because, like most gadfly gossips, the APA doesn't know what to do at home.

No, we don't need politics; we don't need public relations; we don't need a better image; we don't even need to have the answers to all the burning problems of the modern world (though, to listen to the triumphalism of many psychologists, one might be led to believe that psychology _has_ the answers). We've tried all that silliness and have come away empty handed. Empire building, lobbying, public relations, hype we have. Mutual benefit? I'm afraid that evidence of substantial service to the human family on the part of the science of psychology is hard to come by.

Is it, then, because of the very nature of science that psychology cannot pursue substantial service to the human family as a goal? Such a philosophy of science for its own sake is the works and pomps of the ivory tower at its stereotypic worst. Quite to the contrary, ⌈if there are characteristic ways of dealing with reality that are appropriate for human beings-- socially, personally, ethically, psychologically -- , then even the most abstract and meticulously dedicated academic/research areas of the science of psychology ought to be able to discover them and say something intelligent and mutually beneficial for all about them. Our almost total inability to address the real problems of the human family has nothing to do with a proper concept of science, but rather has much to do with our wrong-headed notions of science.

What is needed is a radical change in perspective. We are essentially in the same situation as Ronald Reagan on March 4, 1987. Modern psychology has approached the understanding of the human condition in all the wrong ways. No one will ever demand an apology or humble admission of error from us, because our only real accountability is to be found in our own integrity. But we are quite capable of recognizing the lessons of history. And history has caught up with us: We do not understand the human condition, and we have not served society well. God knows, we have worked hard at both; that has not been the problem. Psychology has been passionately dedicated to the principle of service. In fact, that has long been one source of the tension between the academic/research areas and the health service providers. The latter have become impatient with the former and have forged ahead on their own.

What have caught up with us are a false epistemology and an inadequate philosophy of science. We have been so busy fighting devils such as introspectionism, phrenology, graphology, surplus meaning, homunculi, that we cannot find the beam in our own eye. Positivism is dead; behaviorism is dead; neobehaviorism is dead; operationalism is dead; cognitivism is dead; psycholinguistics is dead. And we are still talking triumphalistically. But we are not at the same time engaging the really important domains of human life: suffering, meaning, love, the commonweal, purpose, consciousness, family, joy, anger, virtue, sadness, religion, solitude, aesthetics, human agency, motivation. Don't argue with me about it; just pick up the programs of any of the national and regional conventions and read for yourself what psychology is up to today.

Nor is the argument cogent that such patterns only reflect the research of second-rate or at best up-and-coming psychologists. The patterns have been set by the leaders of the field for years, and they are precisely the ones who have failed to engage the real issues of the human condition at any depth.

In this respect, I cannot but think back with embarrassment on the September morning in 1961 when I was commuting on the Long Island Railroad with a number of New York businessmen. The morning New York Times carried a front page story on the address

276

by Neal Miller about his obesity research. For my edification, one of the businessmen read aloud the conclusion of the expensive, careful, in depth research: In general, people who eat more become obese. There was a roar of laughter, followed by jovial teasing and even some philosophizing, while I smiled and played the good sport.

I'm quite sure the <u>New York Times</u> did <u>not</u> understand all the implications of the research. I'm sure too that Miller's research was well planned and executed. But then, none of these is the point. Obesity is marvelous (as a research topic); but in the ultimate order of things, it's way down the ladder in importance. We have neglected all those other things either because we don't believe in any "ultimate order of things" or because we think <u>they</u> are way down the ladder in importance.

Let's look, for example, at one of those neglected research topics. Consciousness has been almost a taboo topic, and for many reasons. It has been associated with introspectionism, phrenology, mentalism, spiritualism, subjectivism, phenomenology, philosophy, and a host of negative connotations.

And yet, any realistic psychology of language use must assume consciousness before even beginning the scientific enterprise. In fact, it is difficult to imagine any realistic approach to human psychology that does not actually begin with consciousness. It is, therefore, a key concept for us to examine among neglected topics.

The fact is that "consciousness as a data-base problem is a

huge historical red herring" (O'Connell, 1986, p. 32). Concepts, just like people, sometimes acquire bad reputations. This is what has happened to consciousness. There has never been any question as to whether psychologists use the concept of consciousness; they always have. The only question is whether they are willing to reflect enough to realize what they have been doing all along. It's a question, then, of acknowledging the use of the concept. The whole Watsonian/Skinnerian nonsense succeeds simply in dancing around the obvious. The terrible thing about anything that is obvious is that one can indeed ignore it. Proving consciousness is impossible -- as with myriads of other things in life that are obvious. None of them will go away just because we turn the other way. That's why I have never taken Skinner's philosophy seriously. Subversive and seductive as it may be, it remains a daydream, in which everything is excessively orderly precisely because it is a daydream.

A closely related, and similarly neglected, concept is that of human agency. There are probably more homunculi concepts wandering about within cognitive psychology today than ever before in the history of psychology, and largely because the integrative concept of human agency is untouchable. Chouinard (1985) touches perceptively on the relationship of consciousness and human agency in the following:

In Western tradition, we have believed that to the degree to which our thinking apparently achieves "logical objectivity" (as opposed to psychological subjectivity?), then to that proportionate degree we have successfully transcended the limits of our personal perspective. Of course, this is not true. Instead, . . . to the degree that our thinking is analytically self-corrective, it becomes more than personal, implying not only an expansion beyond person but also -- and coordinately -- an expansion of person. . . .

In other words, our awareness of what we are and are not doing when we are thinking is grounded in our thinking about the originator of that thinking, namely, our own self. Therefore, unless we recognize our limits as a person, we are unlikely to recognize the limits of our thoughts. Minus this recognition, thinking tends toward totalitarian certainty. Consequently, we are only objective to the degree that we recognize as precisely and as comprehensively as possible the grounding of such objectivity in subjectivity. (p. 220 f.)

There has been an extraordinary amount of "totalitarian certainty" within the science of psychology, partly because of the unhinging of our thinking from our thinking.

Our human agency and the human agency we find all around us (definitely not beyond human freedom and dignity) are just as well known to us as is consciousness. We cannot and do not proceed in everyday life nor in the science of psychology without assuming them, although, just as with consciousness, we are quite capable of not acknowledging our assumptions.

No one should find my claim of unacknowledged and unrecognized assumptions at all surprising. Anyone who has read even a handful of empirical articles or manuscripts knows that researchers are astoundingly capable of making assumptions without either acknowledging or recognizing them. The science of psychology is fraught with them. We must get over the idea once and for all that making assumptions is something unscientific; it is quite scientific, and in fact, ineluctable. But if we are to understand our own logic, our implicit assumptions must be made explicit.

That does not mean that every empirical study must begin with a complete listing of all assumptions. Such a tactic is completely absurd. For example, every one of my own publications is firmly based on my personal and philosophical conviction of human freedom. It was not crucial to the intrinsic logic of each of my studies to list that and many other assumptions. But it is equally important to recognize the other side of the coin: The assumption of human freedom does not in any way interfere with scientific logic in psychological research.

The arguments against human freedom in the psychological literature have been enormities illogically addressed at a philosophically naive strawman caricature of human freedom. Human freedom is not disprovable anymore than it is provable. Again, one cannot prove or disprove the obvious; one can only play arrogant little games with words.

I tried to summarize my convictions about human psychology

in a recent publication:

> Human higher processes transcend biological, mechanistic,
> materialistic, informational, and reductionistic efforts
> to explain them. Human thought is sui generis; it is not
> explicable in terms of any lower systems. Nor can we ever
> encompass or comprehend our own thought. (O'Connell, 1986,
> p. 33)

Or, as Henle (1983) has put it: "Our understanding of consciousness is a primary one. . . and cannot be explicated in any other
or more basic terms" (p. 7). Ong (1982) too was quite clear
about the uniqueness of human consciousness:

> There is no adequate model in the physical universe for
> this operation of consciousness, which is distinctively
> human and which signals the capacity of human beings to
> form true communities wherein person shares with person
> interiorly, intersubjectively. (p. 177)

One of his chapters was entitled "Writing restructures consciousness" (p. 78).

The efforts to simplify human psychology have been monumental and in vain. I like to use the anecdote I have given elsewhere from the good old days at the Harvard Center for Cognitive
Studies:

> The undergraduates from Harvard College were (a) paid for
> participation, (b) usually had as their personal motivation
> to "crack" the experiment, and (c) my assistant was dis-
> tractingly pretty. But (d) there were definite socially

281

acceptable limits of fair play, contractual obligation,
and gentlemanly conduct controlling the experimental
situation. (O'Connell, 1986, p. 33)

Dynamic and dyadic sources of variance are never irrelevant to an
experiment:

> Cognitive psychology and psycholinguistics dare not continue
> to isolate themselves from dynamic (telic, conative, emo-
> tional, volitional) and dyadic (dialogic, social, contrac-
> tual) aspects of human higher processes. (O'Connell, 1986,
> p. 33)

The venerable concept of the _finis operantis_ (the goal the agent
has in mind) is quite relevant here. For me, the experiment with
Harvard College subjects had as its purpose the study of integrative visual perception. For them, the goal was quite different;
it was a game they were to win. This was not what they were
instructed by me to do, nor what they were being paid to do; it
was what they were self-instructed to do and chose to do. How
often do experimenters think their subjects are performing the
instructed task, when the subjects are doing something quite
different?

It is not the business of psychology to predict and control,
but to understand the human condition. As Kolers and Smythe
(1984) have well said, "Psychological experience and performance
are intrinsically dense and autographic and so are not properly
described in computational terms" (p. 293). The human condition
is not that simply understood.

But we need not face the future with dismay, only with honesty. As scientists our task is to pursue the truth steadfastly and with complete integrity. Wilhelm von Humboldt (1827-1829/1963) summed up the task a century and a half ago:

> The subjectivity of all mankind is once again something objective in itself. The original agreement between the world and man, on which the possibility of any cognition of truth is based, is acquired by following the footsteps of the phenomenon, step by step, gradually. (cited in Innis, 1982, p. 37)

Yes, human subjectivity is objective. Karl Bühler's trinity of human behavior, human experience, and the products of human endeavor is extraordinarily convoluted, devious, cryptic -- and intelligible. Essential as it is, honesty turns out not to be enough; a patient, humble encounter with that intelligibility is also necessary for the science of psychology. It is not amiss to note that honesty, humility, and patience are moral virtues.

The steadfast pursuit of truth requires -- auf die Dauer, in the long haul -- a great deal of virtue. The very worst published psychological research I ever encountered had been carried out by the same researcher who also exhibited the most extreme arrogance and disdain for his colleagues. The correlation is not unexpected! On the other hand, as the career-long assistant of one Nobel prize winner once said to me: "Anyone can win a Nobel prize, if he's selfish enough." Selfishness is still not a virtue.

We must come to realize somehow that our scientific work, as my German colleagues might say, steckt in den Kinderschuhen (literally: is still wearing its baby shoes). And if and when the science of psychology finally does grow up, we must then come to realize further that the wisdom of this world is, even at its Nobel-prize-winning best (or worst), as Paul of Tarsus knew so well (1 Cor. 3: 20), foolishness before God. For the Lord knows our thoughts: They are nothing but a breath (Ps. 94: 11).

The science of psychology has at its disposal all the tools of meaning and understanding that it needs to do its job well-- "tools of discovery for the mutual benefit of author and audience".

But don't hold your breath. The progress of science may indeed not be linear, but it is certainly gradual (allmählich), just as is the "working-out of one's thoughts in the process of speaking" (Kleist, c. 1806/undated, p. 975; my trans.).

Hubris, on the contrary, is impatient in its claims of control and prediction. It is to be earnestly hoped that we come to "recognize our limits as a person" and thus to "recognize the limits of our thoughts" (Chouinard, 1985, p. 228 f.). Ultimately, that is the only cure for "totalitarian certainty"; but, although a cure for scientists, it is an essentially human cure, not a scientific one.

Epilogue

The Final Word

There is none. In a book that began with cynicism and the loss of all my academic books in a foreign land and ended with the breath of life as a symbol of the extreme fragility and tentativeness of human thought, there can be no final word. I have claimed, in any event, that it is in keeping with the very finality of the human dealings that we call communication, that there be no final word this side of the grave.

If it is indeed part of the finality of human communication to transcend the present state of our knowledge, then it should also be part of the finality of the psychology of language use and of modern psychology in general, to transcend their present fragile forms. There is nothing particularly scientific about being _laudatores temporis acti_ -- ambassadors of the good old days. There is too much to be learned for us to remain enmeshed in any forms and structures, models and theories, or in respect for any institutions or persons or dogmatisms that threaten to stifle -- in any kind of unfreedom -- our ability to work out our thoughts in our speaking and in all our uses of language.

I spoke earlier of wonder and awe. Anyone who is incapable of approaching human speech -- indeed, human dealings of any kind -- with awe, approaches instead to prod beauty, as cummings (1954) expressed it so well in his "O Sweet Spontaneous," with "the naughty thumb of science". Without the experience of awe, all "the influential assertions of this century" and all "the

285

secular certainties so many of us find appealing" (Coles, 1986, p. 18) are straw.

My last, unfinal word must, then, be spoken in awe: I am grateful for the gift of speech -- your words, my words, the Word -- and for the gift of time in which to speak. The true finality of Bühlers Organon model of speech is to be found in the free and responsible use of this magnificent means for worthy ends-- discovery in the service of one another.

Apart from the Lord Himself and my family, there have been two exemplars in my life whom I have genuinely hero worshiped. Both were fellow priests and Jesuits; neither were brilliant intellectuals. Father Joe Boland taught me the courage to travel my own road (and hence may be partly to blame for this book); Father Al Jacobsmeyer taught me the dedication and caring needed to teach the young. He may also have the very last word in this book; for he used to say to us: "Si tacuisses, philosophus mansisses." It was indeed an excellent example of the past contrary to fact condition, but it was often true of his students, this one not excluded: "If you had been silent, you would have remained a philosopher."

References

Adams, C. (1979). English speech rhythms and the foreign learner. The Hague: Mouton.

Ades, T. (1981). Time for a purge. Cognition, 10, 7-15.

Aitchison, J. (1976). The articulate mammal: An introduction to psycholinguistics. London: Hutchinson.

Aitchison, J. (1982). Der Mensch -- das sprechende Wesen: Eine Einführung in die Psycholinguistik. Tübingen: Gunter Narr Verlag.

Aitchison, J. (1983). The articulate mammal: An introduction to psycholinguistics (2nd ed.). New York: Universe Books.

Akinnaso, F. N. (1982). On the differences between spoken and written language. Language and Speech, 25, 97-125.

Akinnaso, F. N. (1985). On the similarities between spoken and written language. Language and Speech, 28, 323-359.

Aleksandrova, O. V., & Shishkina, T. N. (1982). Frazirovka kak sintaktikostilisticheskaya problema. Voprosy yazykoznaniya, 31, 21-27.

American Psychological Association. (1985). Awards for distinguished scientific contributions: 1984. American Psychologist, 40, 285-300.

American Psychological Association. (1986). Statement on the curriculum for the high school psychology course. Washington, DC: American Psychological Association.

Anderson, J. (1980). Cognitive psychology and its implications. San Francisco: Freeman.

Anderson, J. (1985). Cognitive psychology and its implications (rev. ed.). New York: Freeman.

Appel, G., Dechert, H.-W., & Raupach, M. (1980). A selected bibliography on temporal variables in speech. Tübingen: Gunter Narr Verlag.

Aquinas, T. (c. 1265/1978). In Ständige Kommission für die Herausgabe der gemeinsamen liturgischen Bücher im deutschen Sprachgebiet (Ed.), Lektionar zum Stundenbuch, I/4. Einsiedeln, Switzerland: Benziger.

Baars, B. J. (1986). (Ed.). The cognitive revolution in psychology. New York: Guilford.

Barik, H. C. (1973). Simultaneous interpretation: Temporal and quantitative data. Language and Speech, 16, 237-270.

Barik, H. C. (1975). Simultaneous interpretation: Qualitative and linguistic data. Language and Speech, 18, 272-297.

Barik, H. C. (1977). Cross-linguistic study of temporal characteristics of different types of speech materials. Language and Speech, 20, 116-126.

Battista, J. R. (1978). The science of consciousness. In K. S. Pope & J. L. Singer (Eds.), The stream of consciousness: Scientific investigations into the flow of human experience (pp. 55-87). Chichester: Wiley.

Beattie, G. (1983). Talk: An analysis of speech and non-verbal behaviour in conversation. Milton Keynes, England: Open University Press.

Beattie, G. (1984). Are there cognitive rhythms in speech? -- A reply to Power (1983). <u>Language and Speech</u>, <u>27</u>, 193-195 (Letter).

Beattie, G. W., & Bradbury, R. J. (1979). An experimental investigation of the modifiability of the temporal structure of spontaneous speech. <u>Journal of Psycholinguistic Research</u>, <u>8</u>, 225-248.

Beaugrande, R. de. (1980). <u>Text, discourse, and process: Toward a multidisciplinary science of texts</u>. Norwood, NJ: Ablex.

Beaugrande, R. de. (1987). Writing and meaning: Contexts of research. In A. Matsuhashi (Ed.), <u>Writing in real time</u>: <u>Modelling production processes</u> (pp. 1-33). Norwood, NJ: Ablex.

Bereiter, C., & Scardamalia, M. (1987). <u>The psychology of written composition</u>. Hillsdale, NJ: Erlbaum.

Berman, J. S., & Norton, N. C. (1985). Does professional training make a therapist more effective? <u>Psychological Bulletin</u>, <u>98</u>, 401-407.

Bever, T. G. (1970). The cognitive bases for linguistic structures. In J. R. Hayes (Ed.), <u>Cognition and the development of language</u> (pp. 279-362). New York: Wiley.

Bever, T. G., Carroll, J. M., & Miller, L. A. (Eds.). (1984). <u>Talking minds: The study of language in the cognitive sciences</u>. Cambridge, MA: The MIT Press.

Birdwhistell, R. L. (1971). <u>Kinesics and context</u>. London: Allan Lane.

Bloch, B. (1946). Studies in colloquial Japanese. II: Syntax. Language, 22, 200-248.

Bloomfield, L. (1933). Language. New York: Holt, Rinehart, & Winston.

Blumenthal, A. L. (1970). Language and psychology: Historical aspects of psycholinguistics. New York: Wiley.

Blumenthal, A. L. (1985). Psychology and linguistics: The first half-century. In S. Koch & D. E. Leary (Eds.), A century of psychology as science (pp. 804-824). New York: McGraw Hill.

Böll, H. (1958). Doktor Murkes gesammeltes Schweigen. Köln: Kiepenheuer und Witsch.

Boomer, D. S. (1965). Hesitation and grammatical coding. Language and Speech, 8, 148-158.

Boomer, D. S., & Dittmann, A. T. (1962). Hesitation pauses and juncture pauses in speech. Language and Speech, 5/6, 215-220.

Botha, R. P. (1979). Methodological bases of a progressive mentalism. Stellenbosch Papers in Linguistics, 3; reprinted in Synthese, 1980, 44, 1-112.

Braehler, E., & Zenz, H. (1975). Artifacts in the registration and interpretation of speech-process variables. Language and Speech, 18, 166-179.

Brentano, F. (1874/1960). The distinction between mental and physical phenomena. In R. M. Chisolm (Ed.), Realism and the background of phenomenology (pp. 39-61). Glencoe, IL: Free

Press.

Brotherton, P. (1979). Speaking and not speaking: Processes
for translating ideas into speech. In A. W. Siegman & S.
Feldstein (Eds.), Of speech and time. Temporal speech
patterns in interpersonal contexts (pp. 179-209). Hillsdale,
NJ: Erlbaum.

Brown, E., & Miron, M. S. (1971). Lexical and syntactic predictors of the distribution of pause time in reading. Journal of Verbal Learning and Verbal Behavior, 10, 658-667.

Brown, R. (1987, February). Social psychology at secondary
level II. Paper presented at the Fachtagung der Sektion
Ausbildung des Berufsverbandes Deutscher Psychologen, König-
stein/Taunus, West Germany.

Bruner, J. S. (1957). Going beyond the information given.
In J. S. Bruner, E. Brunswick, L. Festinger, F. Heider, K. F.
Muenzinger, C. E. Osgood, & D. Rapport (Eds.), Contemporary
approaches to cognition: A symposium held at the University of
Colorado (pp. 41-69). Cambridge, MA: Harvard University
Press.

Bühler, K. (1908). Tatsachen und Probleme zu einer Psychologie
der Denkvorgänge. II. Über Gedankenzusammenhänge. Archiv für
die gesamte Psychologie, 12, 1-23.

Bühler, K. (1927). Die Krise der Psychologie. Jena: Gustav
Fischer.

Bühler, K. (1934). Sprachtheorie: Die Darstellungsfunktion der
Sprache. Stuttgart: Gustav Fischer.

Butcher, A. (1981). Aspects of the speech pause: Phonemic cor-
relates and communicative functions. Kiel, West Germany: In-
stitut für Phonetik der Universität Kiel.

Butterworth, B. (1973). The science of silence. New Society,
26, 771-773.

Butterworth, B. L. (1975). Hesitation and semantic planning in
speech. Journal of Psycholinguistic Research, 4, 75-87.

Butterworth, B. L. (1980). Evidence from pauses in speech. In
B. Butterworth (Ed.), Language production (Vol. 1, Speech and
talk; pp. 155-176). London: Academic Press.

Cahalan, J. C. (1985). Causal realism: An essay on philosophical
method and the foundations of knowledge. Lanham, MD:
University Press of America.

Carpenter, S., & O'Connell, D. C. (in press). More than meets
the ear: Some variables affecting pause reports. Language and
Communication.

Carroll, D. W. (1986). Psychology of language. Monterey, CA:
Brooks/Cole.

Carroll, J. B. (1964). Language and thought. Englewood Cliffs,
Prentice-Hall.

Carroll, J. B. (1985). Psychology and linguistics: Detachment
and affiliation in the second half-century. In S. Koch & D.
E. Leary (Eds.), A century of psychology as science (pp. 825-
854). New York: McGraw Hill.

Cattell, J. McK. (1886). The time it takes to see and name

objects. _Mind_, _11_, 63-65.

Chafe, W. L. (1977). Creativity in verbalization and its implications for the nature of stored knowledge. In R. O. Freedle (Ed.), _Discourse production and comprehension_ (pp. 41-55). Norwood, NJ: Ablex.

Chafe, W. L. (1980a). The deployment of consciousness in the production of a narrative. In W. L. Chafe (Ed.), _The pear stories: Cognitive, cultural, and linguistic aspects of narrative production_ (pp. 9-50). Norwood, NJ: Ablex.

Chafe, W. L. (1980b). Some reasons for hesitating. In H. W. Dechert & M. Raupach (Eds.), _Temporal variables in speech. Studies in honour of Frieda Goldman-Eisler_ (pp. 169-180). The Hague: Mouton.

Chafe, W. L. (1982). Integration and involvement in speaking, writing, and oral literature. In D. Tannen (Ed.), _Oral and written discourse_ (pp. 35-53). Norwood, NJ: Ablex.

Chakoian, L., & O'Connell, D. C. (1981). Evaluations of poetry readings of English and drama professors. _Bulletin of the Psychonomic Society_, _18_, 173-175.

Chiappetta, J., Monti, L. A., & O'Connell, D. C. (1987). Pause perception: Some cross-linguistic comparisons. _Bulletin of the Psychonomic Society_, _25_, 103-105.

Chomsky, N. (1957). _Syntactic structures_. The Hague: Mouton.

Chomsky, N. (1959). Review of _Verbal behavior_ by B. F. Skinner. _Language_, _35_, 26-58.

Chomsky, N. (1965). _Aspects of the theory of syntax_. Cambridge,

MA: The MIT Press.

Chomsky, N. (1968). Language and mind. New York: Harcourt
Brace & World.

Chomsky, N. (1980). Discussion. In M. Piatteli-Palminari
(Ed.), Language and learning: The debate between Jean Piaget
and Noam Chomsky (pp. 73-75). Cambridge, MA: Harvard
University Press.

Chouinard, T. (1985). T. S. Eliot: A philosophy of communication for literature and speech. Unpublished doctoral dissertation, St. Louis University.

Clark, H. H., & Clark, E. V. (1977). Psychology and language:
An introduction to psycholinguistics. New York: Harcourt
Brace Jovanovich.

Clemmer, E. J., & Carrocci, N. M. (1984). Effects of experience
on radio language performance. Communication Monographs, 51,
116-139.

Clemmer, E. J., O'Connell, D. C., & Loui, W. (1979). Rhetorical
pauses in oral reading. Language and Speech, 22, 397-405.

Coles, R. (1986). Harvard diary. New Oxford Review, 53, No. 4,
17-18.

Cowan, J. M., & Bloch, B. (1948). An experimental study of
pauses in English grammar. American Speech, 23, 89-99.

Cranach, M. von. (1986). Der Molch im Gewande oder Denken wir
uns eigentlich wirklich nichts bevor wir sprechen? Sprache
und Kognition, 3, 163-166.

Cummings, E. E. (1954). Poems 1923-1954. New York: Harcourt

Brace.

Dechert, H. W., & Raupach, M. (Eds.). (1980). <u>Temporal variables in speech. Studies in honour of Frieda Goldman-Eisler</u>.
The Hague: Mouton.

Deese, J. (1970). <u>Psycholinguistics</u>. Boston: Allyn and Bacon.

Deese, J. (1978). Thought into speech. <u>American Scientist</u>, <u>66</u>,
314-321.

Deese, J. (1980). Pauses, prosody, and the demands of production in language. In H. W. Dechert & M. Raupach (Eds.),
<u>Temporal variables in speech: Studies in honour of Frieda
Goldman-Eisler</u> (pp. 69-84). The Hague: Mouton.

Deese, J. (1984). <u>Thought into speech: The psychology of a
language</u>. Englewood Cliffs, NJ: Prentice-Hall.

Dell, G. S. (1986). A spreading-activation theory of retrieval
in sentence production. <u>Psychological Review</u>, <u>93</u>, 283-321.

Denes, P., & Pinson, E. (1963). <u>The speech chain</u>. Baltimore,
MD: Bell Telephone Laboratories.

Derwing, B. (1973). <u>Transformational grammar as a theory of
language acquisition</u>. Cambridge: Cambridge University Press.

Derwing, B. L. (1979). Against autonomous linguistics. In T.
A. Perry (Ed.), <u>Evidence and argumentation in linguistics</u>
(pp. 163-189). Berlin: de Gruyter.

Derwing, B. L., & Baker, W. J. (1978). On the re-integration of
linguistics and psychology. In R. N. Campbell & P. T. Smith
(Eds.), <u>Recent advances in the psychology of language</u>. New

York: Plenum Press.

Dillon, G. L. (1976). Clause, pause, and punctuation in poetry. Linguistics, 169, 5-20.

Dreyfus, H. L., & Dreyfus, S. E. (1986). Mind over machine. New York: The Free Press.

Duez, D. (1985). Perception of silent pauses in continuous speech. Language and Speech, 28, 377-389.

Dulany, D. E., & O'Connell, D. C. (1963). Does partial reinforcement dissociate verbal rules and the behavior they might be presumed to control? Journal of Verbal Learning and Verbal Behavior, 2, 361-372.

Ehlich, K. (1983). Text und sprachliches Handeln. Die Entstehung von Texten aus dem Bedürfnis nach Überlieferung. In A. Assmann, J. Assmann, & C. Hardmeier (Eds.), Schrift und Gedächtnis: Beiträge zur Archäologie der literarischen Kommunikation (pp. 24-43). München: Fink.

Ellis, A., & Beattie, G. (1986). The psychology of language and communication. New York: The Guilford Press.

Engelkamp, J. (1974). Psycholinguistik. München: Wilhelm Fink Verlag.

Ericsson, K. A., & Simon, H. A. (1980). Verbal reports as data. Psychological Review, 87, 215-251.

Ericsson, K. A., & Simon, H. A. (1984). Protocol analysis: Verbal reports as data. Cambridge, MA: The MIT Press.

Esser, U. (1977). Untersuchungen zum Pausenverhalten in der

spontanen und experimentell-provozierten Sprachproduktion.
Unpublished doctoral dissertation, University of Leipzig.

Fillmore, C. J. (1972). Subjects, speakers, and roles. In D.
Davidson & G. Harman (Eds.), <u>Semantics of natural language</u>
(pp. 1-24). Dordrecht: Reidel.

Fliess, R. (1949). Silence and verbalization: A supplement to
the theory of the "analytic rule." <u>International Journal of
Psychoanalysis</u>, <u>30</u>, 21-30.

Flower, L., & Hayes, J. R. (1980). The dynamics of composing:
Making plans and juggling constraints. In L. Gregg & E.
Steinberg (Eds.), <u>Cognitive processes in writing: An inter-
disciplinary approach</u> (pp. 31-50). Hillsdale, NJ: Erlbaum.

Flower, L., & Hayes, J. R. (1981). Plans that guide the composing process. In C. H. Frederiksen & J. F. Dominic (Eds.),
<u>Writing: The nature, development, and teaching of written
communication</u> (Vol. 2; pp. 39-58). Hillsdale, NJ: Lawrence
Erlbaum.

Fodor, J. A. (1981). <u>Representations: Philosophical essays on
the foundations of cognitive science</u>. Montgomery, VT:
Bradford Books.

Fodor, J. A. (1987). <u>Psychosemantics</u>. Cambridge, MA: The MIT
Press.

Fodor, J. A., Bever, T. G., & Garrett, M. F. (1974). <u>The psychology of language: An introduction to psycholinguistics and
generative grammar</u>. New York: McGraw Hill.

Foppa, K. (1984). Redeabsicht und Verständigung. Manuskripte, 23, 73-74.

Ford, M., & Holmes, V. M. (1978). Planning units and syntax in sentence production. Cognition, 6, 35-53.

Foss, D. J., & Hakes, D. T. (1978). Psycholinguistics: An introduction to the psychology of language. Englewood Cliffs, NJ: Prentice-Hall.

Fromkin, V. A. (1971). The non-anomalous nature of anomalous utterances. Language, 47, 27-52.

Fromkin, V. A. (1973). Speech errors as linguistic evidence. The Hague: Mouton.

Frost, R. (1964). To Sidney Cox. In L. Thompson (Ed.), Selected letters of Robert Frost (pp. 107-108). New York: Holt, Rinehart, & Winston.

Fucks, W. (1955). Mathematische Analyse von Sprachelementen, Sprachstil und Sprachen. Köln: Westdeutscher Verlag.

Fulwiler, T. (1984). How well does writing across the curriculum work? College English, 46, 113-125.

Funkhouser, L. (1978). Acoustical rhythm in performances of three twentieth century American poems. Unpublished doctoral dissertation, St. Louis University.

Funkhouser, L. (1979a). Acoustical rhythms in cummings' "Buffalo Bill's." Journal of Modern Literature, 7, 219-242.

Funkhouser, L. (1979b). Acoustical rhythms in Randall Jarrell's The Death of the Ball Turret Gunner. Poetics, 8, 381-403.

Funkhouser, L. (1982). Acoustic rhythm in Frost's "Dust of

Snow." Language and Style, 14, 287-303.

Funkhouser, L., & O'Connell, D. C. (1978). Temporal aspects of
poetry readings by authors and adults. Bulletin of the
Psychonomic Society, 12, 390-392.

Funkhouser, L., & O'Connell, D. C. (1984). cummings reads
cummings. Linguistics in Literature, 9, 91-126.

Funkhouser, L., & O'Connell, D. C. (1985). "Measure" in
William Carlos William's poetry: Evidence from his readings.
Journal of Modern Literature, 12, 26-42.

Gardner, H. (1985). The Minds New Science: A History of the
Cognitive Revolution. New York: Basic Books, Inc.

Garnham, A. (1985). Psycholinguistics: Central topics.
London: Methuen.

Garrett, M. F. (1982). Production of speech: Observations from
normal and pathological language use. In A. W. Ellis (Ed.),
Normality and pathology in cognitive functions (pp. 19-76).
London: Academic Press.

Gauger, H.-M. (1980). Psycholinguistik. In H. P. Althaus, H.
Henne, & H. E. Wiegand (Eds.), Lexikon der Germanistischen
Linguistik, Studienausgabe II (2nd ed.; pp. 421-428).
Tübingen: Max Niemeyer Verlag.

Gee, J. P. (1986). Units in the production of narrative discourse. Discourse Processes, 9, 391-422.

Gee, J., & Grosjean, F. (1983). Performance structures: A psycholinguistic and linguistic appraisal. Cognitive Psycho-

logy, 15, 411-458.

Gibbs, R. (1979). Contextual effects in understanding indirect requests. Discourse Processes, 2, 1-10.

Glukhov, A. A. (1975). Statistical analysis of speech pauses
for Romance and Germanic languages. Soviet Physics. Acous-
tics, 21, 71-72.

Goldman-Eisler, F. (1951). The measurement of time sequences
in conversational behaviour. British Journal of Psychology,
42, 355-362.

Goldman-Eisler, F. (1954). On the variability of the speed of
talking and on its relation to the length of utterance in
conversation. British Journal of Psychology, 45, 94-107.

Goldman-Eisler, F. (1961). Hesitation and information in
speech. In C. Cherry (Ed.), Information theory (pp. 162-174).
London: Butterworth.

Goldman-Eisler, F. (1964). Hesitation, information and levels
of speech production. In A. V. S. De Reuck & M. O'Connor
(Eds.), Disorders of language (pp. 96-111). London: J. & A.
Churchill.

Goldman-Eisler, F. (1968). Psycholinguistics: Experiments in
spontaneous speech. London: Academic Press.

Goldman-Eisler, F. (1972). Pauses, clauses, sentences. Language and Speech, 15, 103-113.

Goody, J. (1986). The logic of writing and the organization of
society. Cambridge: Cambridge University Press.

Graumann, C. F. (Ed.). (1969). I. Psycholinguistisches Sym-

<u>posium</u>. Heidelberg: Psychologisches Institut der Universität Heidelberg.

Graumann, C. F. (1984). Wundt -- Mead -- Bühler. In C. F. Graumann & T. Herrmann (Eds.), <u>Karl Bühlers Axiomatik</u> (pp. 217-247). Frankfurt am Main: Vittorio Klostermann.

Greenwald, A. G., Leippe, M. R., Pratkanis, A. R., & Baumgardner, M. H. (1986). Under what conditions does theory obstruct research progress? <u>Psychological Review</u>, <u>93</u>, 216-229.

Grimm, H., & Engelkamp, J. (1981). <u>Sprachpsychologie: Handbuch und Lexikon der Psycholinguistik</u>. Berlin: Erich Schmidt Verlag.

Grosjean, F., & Collins, M. (1979). Breathing, pausing, and reading. <u>Phonetica</u>, <u>36</u>, 98-114.

Grosjean, F., & Deschamps, A. (1975). Analyse contrastive des variables temporelles de l'anglais et du francais: Vitesse de parole et variables composantes, phénomènes d'hésitation. <u>Phonetica</u>, <u>31</u>, 144-184.

Grosjean, F., Grosjean, L., & Lane, H. (1979). The patterns of silence: Performance structures in sentence production. <u>Cognitive Psychology</u>, <u>11</u>, 58-81.

Gülich, E. (1970). <u>Makrosyntax der Gliederungssignale im gesprochenen Französisch</u>. München: Fink Verlag.

Gumperz, J. J. (1977). Sociocultural knowledge in conversational inference. In M. Saville-Troike (Ed.), <u>Georgetown University Round Table</u> (pp. 191-211). Washington, D.C: Georgetown University Press.

301

Hahn, E. (1949). An analysis of the delivery of the speech of first grade children. Quarterly Journal of Speech, 35, 338-343.

Halliday, M. A. K. (1973). Explorations in the functions of language. London: Edward Arnold.

Hänni, R. (1972). Auswirkungen der Störung von Sprechpausen. Bericht über den 28. Kongress der Deutschen Gesellschaft für Psychologie (pp. 169-177). Göttingen: Hogrefe.

Harris, M., & Coltheart, M. (1986). Language processing in children and adults: An introduction. London: Routledge & Kegan Paul.

Hartman, C. O. (1980). Free verse: An essay on prosody. Princeton, NJ: Princeton University Press.

Hayes, J. R., & Flower, L. (1980). Identifying the organization of writing processes. In L. Gregg & E. Steinberg (Eds.), Cognitive processes in writing: An interdisciplinary approach (pp. 3-30). Hillsdale, NJ: Erlbaum.

Henle, R. J. (1983). Theory of knowledge: A textbook and substantive theory of epistemology. Chicago: Loyola University Press.

Henze, R. (1953). Experimentelle Untersuchungen zur Phänomenologie der Sprechgeschwindigkeit. Zeitschrift für experimentelle und angewandte Psychologie, 1, 214-243.

Herriot, P. (1970). An introduction to the psychology of language. London: Methuen.

302

Herrmann, T. (1985). <u>Allgemeine Sprachpsychologie: Grundlagen</u>
<u>und Probleme</u>. München: Urban & Schwarzenberg.

Hieke, A. E. (1981). A content-processing view of hesitation
phenomena. <u>Language and Speech</u>, <u>24</u>, 147-160.

Hieke, A. E. (1984). Linking as a marker of fluent speech.
<u>Language and Speech</u>, <u>27</u>, 343-354.

Hieke, A. E. (1985). A componential approach to oral fluency
evaluation. <u>The Modern Language Journal</u>, <u>69</u>, 135-142.

Hieke, A.E., Kowal, S., & O'Connell, D. C. (1983). The trouble
with "articulatory" pauses. <u>Language and Speech</u>, <u>26</u>, 203-214.

Hilgard, E. R., Atkinson, R. L., & Atkinson, R. C. (1979).
<u>Introduction to psychology</u> (7th ed.). New York: Harcourt
Brace Jovanovich.

Hörmann, H. (1967). <u>Psychologie der Sprache</u>. Berlin: Springer-
Verlag.

Hörmann, H. (1971). <u>Psycholinguistics: An introduction to re-</u>
<u>search and theory</u> (H. H. Stern, Trans.). New York:
Springer.

Hörmann, H. (1976). <u>Meinen und Verstehen: Grundzüge einer psy-</u>
<u>chologischen Semantik</u>. Frankfurt am Main: Suhrkamp Verlag.

Hörmann, H. (1977). <u>Psychologie der Sprache</u> (2nd ed.). Berlin:
Springer.

Hörmann, H. (1979). <u>Psycholinguistics: An introduction to</u>
<u>research and theory</u> (H. H. Stern & P. Leppman, Trans.).
New York: Springer.

Hörmann, H. (1981a). <u>Einführung in die Psycholinguistik</u>.

Darmstadt: Wissenschaftliche Buchgesellschaft.

Hörmann, H. (1981b). <u>To mean -- to understand. Problems of</u>
<u>psychological semantics</u> (D. A. Jankowski, Trans.). Berlin:
Springer-Verlag.

Hörmann, H. (1986). <u>Meaning and context. An introduction to</u>
<u>the psychology of language</u>, Ed. & Intro. by R. E. Innis.
New York: Plenum.

Howard, A., Pion, G. M., Gottfredson, G. D., Flattau, P. E.,
Oskamp, S., Pfafflin, S. M., Bray, D. W., & Burstein, A. G.
(1986). The changing face of American psychology: A report
from the Committee on Employment and Human Resources.
<u>American Psychologist</u>, <u>41</u>, 1311-1327.

Howard, G. S., & Conway, C. G. (1986). Can there be an empirical science of volitional action? <u>American Psychologist</u>, <u>41</u>,
1241-1251.

Humboldt, W. von. (1827-1829/1963). <u>Über die Verschiedenheit</u>
<u>des menschlichen Sprachbaues</u>. Darmstadt: Wissenschaftliche
Buchgesellschaft.

Hunt, E., & Lansman, M. (1986). Unified model of attention and
problem solving. <u>Psychological Review</u>, <u>98</u>, 446-461.

Hunt, M. (1982). How the mind works. <u>New York Times Magazine</u>,
January 24, pp. 30-33; 47-52; 64-68.

Innis, R. E. (1982). <u>Karl Bühler: Semiotic foundations of</u>
<u>language theory</u>. New York: Plenum.

Jakobovits, L. A., & Miron, M. S. (Eds.). (1967). Readings in the psychology of language. Englewood Cliffs, NJ: Prentice-Hall.

Jarvella, R., & Klein, W. (Eds.). (1981). Speech, place and action: Studies in deixis and related topics. Chichester: Wiley.

Johnson-Laird, P. N. (1981). Cognition, computers, and mental models. Cognition, 10, 139-143.

Johnson-Laird, P. N. (1983). Mental models: Towards a cognitive science of language. Cambridge, MA: Harvard University Press.

Johnson, M. L. (1986). Applying the breaks: A review of the poetic line. Unpublished manuscript, University of Kansas, Department of English, Lawrence, KS.

Johnson, T. H. de, O'Connell, D. C., & Sabin, E. J. (1979). Temporal analysis of English and Spanish narratives. Bulletin of the Psychonomic Society, 13, 347-350.

Kainz, F. (1969). Psychologie der Sprache (Vol. 5, Part 2). Stuttgart: Enke.

Katz, J. J., & Fodor, J. A. (1963). The structure of a semantic theory. Language, 39, 170-210.

Keilson, H. (1984). Wohin die Sprache nicht reicht. Psyche, 38, 915-926.

Kilpatrick, W. K. (1983). Psychological seduction. Nashville, TN: Thomas Nelson.

Kilpatrick, W. K. (1985). The emperor's new clothes. Westchester, IL: Crossway Books.

Kleist, Heinrich von. (c. 1806/undated). Über die allmähliche Verfertigung der Gedanken beim Reden, an R[ühle] v[on] L[ilienstern]. In K. F. Reinking (Ed.), <u>Heinrich von Kleist, Sämtliche Werke</u> (pp. 975-980). Wiesbaden: R. Löwit.

Knobloch, C. (1984). <u>Sprachpsychologie</u>. Tübingen: Max Niemeyer.

Kolers, P. A., & Smythe, W. E. (1984). Symbol manipulation: Alternatives to the computational view of mind. <u>Journal of Verbal Learning and Verbal Behavior</u>, <u>23</u>, 289-314.

Kowal, S. (1983a). Zeitverläufe in persuasiver Rede: Ansätze zu einer empirischen Rhetorik. <u>Kodikas/Code, Ars Semeiotica</u>, <u>6</u>, 71-84.

Kowal, S. (1983b). Zur Funktion von Füllauten in spontaner Textproduktion: Zum Beispiel Helmut Schmidt. In E. W. B. Hess-Lüttich (Ed.), <u>Angewandte Linguistik</u>. (Vol 3) <u>Textproduktion und Textrezeption</u> (pp. 63-71). Tübingen: Narr.

Kowal, S. (1987). <u>Über die allmähliche Verfertigung der Gedanken beim Reden: Die Fortsetzung</u>. Bericht an die Deutsche Forschungsgemeinschaft.

Kowal, S., Bassett, M. R., & O'Connell, D. C. (1985). The spontaneity of media interviews. <u>Journal of Psycholinguistic Research</u>, <u>14</u>, 1-18.

Kowal, S., & O'Connell, D. C. (1983). Practice makes fluent -- but how? <u>Rassegna Italiana di Linguistica Applicata</u>, <u>15</u>, 161-168.

Kowal, S., & O'Connell, D. C. (1985). Cognitive rhythms reluctantly revisited. Language and Speech, 28, 93-96 (Letter).

Kowal, S., & O'Connell, D. C. (1987a). Some temporal aspects of stories told while or after watching a film. Bulletin of the Psychonomic Society, 25, 364-366.

Kowal, S., & O'Connell, D. C. (1987b). Writing as language behavior: Myths, models, methods. In A. Matsuhashi (Ed.), Writing in real time: Modelling production processes (pp. 108-132). Norwood, NJ: Ablex.

Kowal, S. H., O'Connell, D. C., O'Brien, E. A., & Bryant, E. T. (1975). Temporal aspects of reading and speaking: Three experiments. American Journal of Psychology, 81, 549-569.

Kowal, S., O'Connell, D. C., & Sabin, E. J. (1975). Development of temporal patterning and vocal hesitations in spontaneous narratives. Journal of Psycholinguistic Research, 4, 195-207.

Kowal, S., Wiese, R., & O'Connell, D. C. (1983). The use of time in storytelling. Language and Speech, 26, 377-392.

Kozhevnikov, V. A., & Chistovich, L. A. (1965). Speech, articulation, and perception. Washington, DC: U. S. Department of Commerce, Joint Publication Service (JPRS #30, 543).

Kroll, B. (1977). Ways communicators encode propositions in spoken and written English: A look at subordination and coordination. In E. O. Keenan & T. Bennett (Eds.), Discourse across time and space. Southern California Occasional Papers in Linguistics, 5, 69-108.

Lehiste, I. (1984, June). Rhythm in spoken sentences and read poetry. Paper presented at the International Phonology Meeting, Eisenstadt, Austria.

Levelt, W. J. M. (1981a). Déjà vu? Cognition, 10, 187-192.

Levelt, W. J. M. (1981b). The speaker's linearization problem. Philosophical Transactions of the Royal Society, London, B295, 305-315.

Levelt, W. J. M. (1983a). Monitoring and self-repair in speech. Cognition, 14, 41-104.

Levelt, W. J. M. (1983b). The speaker's organization of discourse. In S. Hattori & K. Inoue (Eds.), Proceedings of the XIIIth International Congress of Linguists (pp. 278-290). Tokyo: CIPL.

Linell, P. (1979a). On the similarity between Skinner and Chomsky. In T. A. Perry (Ed.), Evidence and argumentation in linguistics (pp. 190-199). Berlin: de Gruyter.

Linell, P. (1979b). Psychological reality in phonology. A theoretical study. Cambridge: Cambridge University Press.

Linell, P. (1982). The written language bias in linguistics. Linköping, Sweden: University of Linköping.

List, G. (1972). Psycholinguistik: Eine Einführung. Stuttgart: Verlag W. Kohlhammer.

List, G. (1981). Sprachpsychologie. Stuttgart: Verlag W. Kohlhammer.

Lounsbury, F. G. (1954). Transitional probability, linguistic

structure, and systems of habit-family hierarchies. <u>Journal</u>
<u>of Abnormal and Social Psychology</u>, <u>49</u>, supplement, C. E.
Osgood & T. A. Sebeok (Eds.), 93-101.

Ludwig, O. (1983). Einige Gedanken zu einer Theorie des Schrei-
bens. In S. Grosse (Ed.), <u>Schriftsprachlichkeit</u> (pp. 37-73).
Düsseldorf: Schwann.

Maclay, H., & Osgood, C. E. (1959). Hesitation phenomena in
spontaneous English speech. <u>Word</u>, <u>15</u>, 19-44.

Mahl, G. F. (1958). On the use of "ah" in spontaneous speech:
Quantitative, developmental, characterological, situational,
and linguistic aspects. <u>American Psychologist</u>, <u>13</u>, 349
(abstract).

Mandler, G. (1985). <u>Cognitive psychology</u>. Hillsdale, NJ:
Lawrence Erlbaum.

Martin, J. G. (1970). On judging pauses in spontaneous speech.
<u>Journal of Verbal Learning and Verbal Behavior</u>, <u>9</u>, 75-78.

Martinet, A. (1962). <u>A functional view of language</u>. Oxford:
Clarendon Press.

McCarthy, D. (1954). Language development in children. In
L. Carmichael (Ed.), <u>Manual of child psychology</u> (pp. 492-630).
New York: Wiley.

McLuhan, M. (1964). <u>Understanding media: The extensions of man</u>.
London: Routledge & Kegan Paul.

McMahon, L. E. (1963). <u>Grammatical analysis as part of under-</u>
<u>standing a sentence</u>. Unpublished doctoral dissertation,

Harvard University.

McNeill, D. (1985). So you think gestures are nonverbal? _Psychological Review, 92,_ 350-371.

McNeill, D. (1987). _Psycholinguistics: A new approach._ New York: Harper & Row.

Meinhold, G. (1967). Quantität und Häufigkeit von Pausen in gelesenen deutschen Texten in Zusammenhang mit dem Sprechtempo. _Wissenschaftliche Zeitschrift der Friedrich-Schiller-Univerität Jena, 1,_ 107-111.

Miller, G. A. (1965). Some preliminaries to psycholinguistics. _American Psychologist, 20,_ 15-20.

Miller, G. A. (1974). Toward a third metaphor for psycholinguistics. In W. Weimer & D. Palermo (Eds.), _Cognition and the symbolic processes_ (pp. 397-413). Hillsdale, NJ: Lawrence Erlbaum.

Miller, G. A. (1981). _Language and speech._ San Francisco: Freeman.

Miller, G. A., Galanter, E., & Pribram, K. H. (1960). _Plans and the structure of behavior._ New York: Holt, Rinehart, & Winston.

Miller, G. A., Galanter, E., & Pribram, K. H. (1973). _Strategien des Handelns: Pläne und Strukturen des Verhaltens._ Stuttgart: Ernst Klett Verlag.

Miller, G. A., & McNeill, D. (1969). Psycholinguistics. In G. Lindzey & E. Aronson (Eds.), _Handbook of social psychology_ (Vol. 3; pp. 666-794). New York: Academic Press.

Miller, H. (1970). Sexus (K. Wagenseil, Trans.). Hamburg: Rowohlt.

Moore, T. V. (1939). Cognitive psychology. Chicago: Lippin-cott.

Mowrer, O. H. (1954). The psychologist looks at language. American Psychologist, 9, 660-694.

Neisser, U. (1967). Cognitive psychology. New York: Appleton-Century-Crofts.

Neisser, U. (1975). Self-knowledge and psychological knowledge: Teaching psychology from the cognitive point of view. Educational Psychologist, 11, 158-170.

Neisser, U. (1976). Cognition and reality. Principles and implications of cognitive psychology. San Francisco: Freeman.

Neisser, U. (1979). Kognition und Wirklichkeit. Prinzipien und Implikationen der kognitiven Psychologie. Stuttgart: Klett-Cotta.

Neisser, U. (1985). Toward an Ecological Oriented Cognitive Science. In T. M. Slechter & M. P. Toglia (Eds.), New Directions in Cognitive Science (pp. 17-32). Norwood, NJ: Ablex Publishing Corporation.

Neumann, O. (1985). Informationsverarbeitung, künstliche Intelligenz und die Perspektiven der Kognitionspsychologie. In O. Neumann (Ed.), Perspektiven der Kognitionspsychologie (pp. 3-37). Berlin: Springer.

Newman, S., & Mather, V. G. (1938). Analysis of spoken language of patients with affective disorders. <u>American Journal of Psychiatry</u>, <u>94</u>, 913-942.

Norman, D. A., & Rumelhart, D. E. (1975). <u>Explorations in cognition</u>. San Francisco: Freeman.

Norrick, N. R. (1981). <u>Semiotic principles in semantic theory</u>. Amsterdam: Benjamins.

O'Connell, D. C. (1958). Idiographic knowledge. <u>Journal of General Psychology</u>, <u>59</u>, 21-33.

O'Connell, D. C. (1961). Is mental illness the result of sin? <u>Lumen Vitae</u>, <u>2</u>, 55-64.

O'Connell, D. C. (1962). The black box revisited: A critique of Osgood's general theory of behavior. <u>Methodos</u>, <u>14</u>, 153-196.

O'Connell, D. C. (1965). Concept learning and verbal control under partial reinforcement and subsequent reversal or non-reversal shift. <u>Journal of Experimental Psychology</u>, <u>69</u>, 144-151.

O'Connell, D. C. (1977). One of many units: The sentence. In S. Rosenberg (Ed.), <u>Sentence production: Developments in research and theory</u> (pp. 307-313). Hillsdale, NJ: Lawrence Erlbaum.

O'Connell, D. C. (1980a). Cross-linguistic investigation of some temporal dimensions of speech. In H. W. Dechert & M. Raupach (Eds.), <u>Toward a cross-linguistic assessment of speech production</u> (pp. 23-28). Frankfurt am Main: Peter Lang.

O'Connell, D. C. (1980b). Toward an empirical rhetoric: Some

comparisons of expressiveness in poetry readings by authors,
English professors, and drama professors. Archiv für Psychologie, 133, 117-128.

O'Connell, D. C. (1982a). Performance characteristics of poetry: Some cross-linguistic comparisons. Psychological Research, 44, 381-392.

O'Connell, D. C. (1982b). Review of H. Hörmann's To mean --
to understand. Journal of Psycholinguistic Research, 11,
408-416.

O'Connell, D. C. (1984a). Review of J. S. Bruner's In search of
mind. America, January 14, p. 20.

O'Connell, D. C. (1984b, April). Will the real poem please
stand up? Paper presented at the Conference on Linguistics in
the Humanities and Sciences, Birmingham, AL.

O'Connell, D. C. (1985). Performance characteristics of oral
readings: Analyses of Italian poetry. In C. Cornoldi (Ed.),
Aspects of reading and dyslexia (pp. 257-265). Padua, Italy:
Cleup.

O'Connell, D. C. (1986). Consciousness: Stepchild of modern
psychology. In R. Brungs (Ed.), Workshop: Brain research/
human consciousness (pp. 25-39). St. Louis, MO: The Institute
for Theological Encounter with Science and Technology.

O'Connell, D. C. (1987). Review of D. McNeill's Psycholinguistics: A new approach. Manuscript submitted for publication.

O'Connell, D. C., & Kowal, S. (1983). Pausology. In W. Sedelow
& S. Sedelow (Eds.), Computers in language research (Vol. 2;

pp. 221-301). Berlin: de Gruyter.

O'Connell, D. C., & Kowal, S. (1984). Comparisons of native and foreign language poetry readings: Fluency, expressiveness, and their evaluation. Psychological Research, 46, 301-313.

O'Connell, D. C., & Kowal, S. (1986). Use of punctuation for pausing: Oral readings by German radio homilists. Psychological Research, 48, 93-98.

O'Connell, D. C., Kowal, S., & Hörmann, H. (1969). Semantic determinants of pauses. Psychologische Forschung, 33, 50-67.

O'Connell, D. C., & Slaymaker, F. (1984). Evidence for the phonemic clause as an encoding unit. Language and Communication, 4, 273-283.

O'Connell, D. C., & Wiese, R. (1987). The state of the art: The fate of the start. In H. W. Dechert & M. Raupach (Eds.), Psycholinguistic models of production (pp. 3-16). Norwood, NJ: Ablex.

O'Connor, M. P. (1982). "Unanswerable the knack of tongues": The linguistic study of verse. In L. Obler & L. Menn (Eds.), Exceptional language and linguistics (pp. 143-168). New York: Academic Press.

Ohem, K. (1987, June 30). Der Mensch spricht siebenmal schneller als er schreibt. Frankfurter Allgemeine Zeitung, p. 18.

Ong, W. J. (1969). World as view and world as event. American Anthropologist, 71, 634-647.

Ong, W. J. (1982). Orality and literacy. London: Methuen.

Osgood, C. E. (1963). On understanding and creating sentences.

American Psychologist, _18_, 735-751.

Osgood, C. E., & Sebeok, T. A. (Eds.). (1954). Psycholinguistics. A survey of theory and research problems. _Journal of
Abnormal and Social Psychology_, _49_, Supplement.

Osgood, C. E., & Sebeok, T. A. (Eds.). (1965). _Psycholin-
guistics. A survey of theory and research problems_. Reprinted with _A survey of psycholinguistic research 1954-1964_,
by A. R. Diebold. Bloomington, IN: Indiana University Press.

Paivio, A., & Begg, I. (1981). _Psychology of language_.
Englewood Cliffs, NJ: Prentice-Hall.

Palermo, D. S. (1978). _Psychology of language_. Glenview, IL:
Scott Foresman.

Perkell, J. S., & Klatt, D. H. (Eds.). (1986). _Invariance and
variability in speech processes_. Hillsdale, NJ: Erlbaum.

Pöppel, E. (1985). _Grenzen des Bewu tseins: Über Wirklichkeit
und Welterfahrung_. Stuttgart: Deutsche Verlags-Anstalt.

Power, M. J. (1983). Are there cognitive rhythms in speech?
Language and Speech, _26_, 253-261.

Pribram, K. H. (1985). 'Holism' could close cognition era.
APA Monitor, _16_, No. 9, 5-6.

Reddy, M. (1979). The conduit metaphor. A case of frame con-
flict in our language about language. In A. Ortony (Ed.),
Metaphor and thought (pp. 284-324). Cambridge: Cambridge
University Press.

Redeker, G. (1984). On the differences between spoken and
     written language. Discourse Processes, 7, 43-55.

Richards, I. A. (1929). Practical criticism. New York: Har-
     court, Brace, & World.

Rochester, S. R. (1973). The significance of pauses in spon-
     taneous speech. Journal of Psycholinguistic Research, 2,
     51-81.

Rochester, S. R. (1975/76). Defining the silent pause in
     speech. Journal of the Ontario Speech and Hearing Associa-
     tion, 8, 1-4.

Rochester, S. R., Thurston, S., & Rupp, J. (1977). Hesitations
     as clues to failures in coherence: A study of the thought-
     disordered speaker. In S. Rosenberg (Ed.), Sentence produc-
     tion: Developments in research and theory (pp. 65-87).
     Hillsdale, NJ: Erlbaum.

Rommetveit, R. (1972). Deep structure of sentences versus
     message structure. Some critical remarks on current para-
     digms, and suggestions for an alternative approach. Nor-
     wegian Journal of Linguistics, 26, 3-22.

Rommetveit, R. (1974). On message structure. A framework for
     the study of language and communication. London: Wiley.

Rommetveit, R. (1979). Deep structure of sentences versus
     message structure: Some critical remarks on current para-
     digms, and suggestions for an alternative approach. In R.
     Rommetveit & R. M. Blakar (Eds.), Studies of language,
     thought and verbal communication (pp. 17-34). London:

Academic Press.

Rubenstein, H., & Aborn, M. (1960). Psycholinguistics. <u>Annual Review of Psychology</u>, <u>11</u>, 291-322.

Rumelhart, D. E., McClelland, J. L., & the PDP Research Group (1986). <u>Parallel Distributed Processing: Explorations in the Microstructure of Cognition</u>. Cambridge: MIT Press.

Rychlak, J. R. (1978). The stream of consciousness: Implications for a humanistic psychological theory. In K. S. Pope & J. L. Singer (Eds.), <u>The stream of consciousness: Scientific investigations into the flow of human experience</u> (pp. 91-116). Chichester: Wiley.

Sabin, E. J., Clemmer, E. J., O'Connell, D. C., & Kowal, S. (1979). A pausological approach to speech development. In A. Siegman & S. Feldstein (Eds.), <u>Of speech and time: Temporal speech patterns in interpersonal contexts</u> (pp. 35-55). Hillsdale, NJ: Erlbaum.

Sachs, J. S. (1967). Recognition memory for syntactic and semantic aspects of connected discourse. <u>Perception and Psychophysics</u>, <u>2</u>, 437-442.

Sampson, E. E. (1981). Cognitive psychology as ideology. <u>American Psychologist</u>, <u>36</u>, 730-743.

Sarason, S. B. (1981). <u>Psychology misdirected</u>. New York: Free Press.

Schank, R., & Birnbaum, L. (1984). Memory, meaning, and syntax. In T. G. Bever, J. M. Carroll, & L. A. Miller (Eds.), <u>Talking</u>

317

minds: The study of language in the cognitive sciences (pp. 209-251). Cambridge, MA: The MIT Press.

Scheerer, E. (1985). Edmund Husserls Phänomenologie und ihre Perspektiven für die Kognitionspsychologie. In O. Neumann (Ed.), Perspektiven der Kognitionspsychologie (pp. 231-267). Berlin: Springer.

Shallice, T. (1978). The dominant action system: An information-processing approach to consciousness. In K. S. Pope & J. L. Singer (Eds.), The stream of consciousness: Scientific investigations into the flow of human experience (pp. 117-157). Chichester: Wiley.

Siegman, A. W. (1979). Cognition and hesitation in speech. In A. W. Siegman & S. Feldstein (Eds.), Of speech and time: Temporal speech patterns in interpersonal contexts (pp. 151-178). Hillsdale, NJ: Erlbaum.

Skinner, B. F. (1957). Verbal behavior. New York: Appleton-Century-Crofts.

Slobin, D. I. (1971). Psycholinguistics. Glenview, IL: Scott Foresman.

Slobin, D: I. (1974). Einführung in die Psycholinguistik (A. Becker, Trans.). Kronberg/Taunus, West Germany: Scriptor Verlag.

Slobin, D. I. (1979). Psycholinguistics (2nd ed.). Glenview, IL: Scott Foresman.

Smith, F. (1982). Writing and the writer. New York: Holt, Rinehart, & Winston.

Snell, A. L. F. (1918). Pause: A study of its nature and its rhythmical function in verse, especially blank verse. In F. N. Scott (Ed.), Contributions to rhetorical theory, Vol. 8. Ann Arbor, MI: The Ann Arbor Press.

Spittle, K. B., & Matsuhashi, A. (1981). Semantic aspects of real time written discourse production. In M. Hairston & C. Selfe (Eds.), Selected papers from the 1981 Texas writing research conference (pp. 137-164). Austin, TX: Department of English, University of Texas at Austin.

Starkweather, C. W. (1980). Speech fluency and its development in normal children. In N. J. Lass (Ed.), Speech and language. Advances in basic research and practice (Vol. 4; pp. 143-200). New York: Academic Press.

Steiner, G. (1975). After Babel: Aspects of language and translation. London: Oxford University Press.

Stemberger, J. P. (1985). An interactive activation model of language production. In A. P. Ellis (Ed.), Progress in the psychology of language (Vol. 1; pp. 143-186). London: Lawrence Erlbaum.

Stuckenberg, A., & O'Connell, D. C. (in press). The long and the short of it: Reports of pause occurrence and duration in speech. Journal of Psycholinguistic Research.

Szawara, J., & O'Connell, D. C. (1977). Temporal reflections of spontaneity in homilies. Bulletin of the Psychonomic Society, 9, 360-362.

Trager, G. L., & Smith, H. L., Jr. (1951). An outline of English structure (Studies in linguistics, occasional papers, 3). Norman, OK: Battenberg Press.

Turner, F., & Pöppel, E. (1983). The neural lyre: Poetic meter, the brain, and time. Poetry, 142, 273-309.

Van De Water, D. A., Monti, L. A., Kirchner, P. B., & O'Connell, D. C. (1987). Speaking and writing: Comparisons of two psycholinguistic siblings. Bulletin of the Psychonomic Society, 25, 99-102.

Van De Water, D. A., & O'Connell, D. C. (1985). In and about the poetic line. Bulletin of the Psychonomic Society, 23, 397-400.

Van De Water, D. A., & O'Connell, D. C. (1986). From page to program: Some typographical and temporal variables in radio homilies. Journal of Psycholinguistic Research, 15, 525-538.

Verplanck, W. S. (1962). Unaware of where's awareness: Some verbal operants -- notates, monents and notants. In C. W. Ericksen (Ed.), Behavior and awareness -- A symposium of research and interpretation (pp. -). Durham, NC: Duke University Press.

Vygotsky, L. L. (1934/1962). Thought and language (G. Vakar & E. Hanfmann, Trans.). Cambridge, MA: The MIT Press.

Waller, R. H. W. (1980). Graphic aspects of complex texts: Typography as macro-punctuation. In P. A. Kolers & M. E.

Wrolstad (Eds.), <u>Processing of visible language</u> (Vol. 2; pp.
241-253). New York: Plenum Press.

Wallin, J. E. W. (1901). Researches in the rhythm of speech.
<u>Studies from the Yale Psychological Laboratory</u>, <u>9</u>, 1-142.

<u>Webster's ninth new collegiate dictionary</u>. (1983). Springfield,
MA: G & C Merriam.

Weinert, F. E. (1987). Zur Lage der Psychologie. <u>Psycho-
logische Rundschau</u>, <u>38</u>, 1-13.

Wells, R. (1951). Predicting slips of the tongue. <u>Yale
Scientific Magazine</u>, <u>26</u>, 3-12.

Wiese, R. (1983). <u>Psycholinguistische Aspekte der Sprach-
produktion</u>. Hamburg: Helmut Buske Verlag.

Wilkes, A. L., & Kennedy, R. A. (1969). Relationship between
pausing and retrieval latency in sentences of varying grammatical form. <u>Journal of Experimental psychology</u>, <u>79</u>, 241-
245.

Wimsatt, W. K., & Beardsley, M. C. (1959). The concept of
meter: An exercise in abstraction. <u>Publication of the
Modern Language Association</u>, <u>74</u>, 585-598.

Wittgenstein, L. (1958). <u>Philosophical investigations</u> (G. E.
M. Anscombe, Trans.). Oxford: Basil Blackwell.

Yngve, V. H. (1985, April). <u>Grammar or science: The choice
facing linguistics</u>. Paper presented at Loyola University of
Chicago, Chicago, IL.

Yngve, V. H. (1986). <u>Linguistics as a science</u>. Bloomington,
   IN: Indiana University Press.

Name Index

323

331

339

345